SEARCH, PONDER, AND PRAY

ILLINOIS

GUIDE FOR TRAVEL AND STUDY

Explore more Church History Sites in the Search, Ponder, Pray Series:

New England Guide for Travel and Study

Historic Kirtland Guide for Travel and Study

Missouri Guide for Travel and Study

CASEY PAUL GRIFFITHS, MARY JANE WOODGER,
& BRYAN READY

SEARCH, PONDER, AND PRAY

ILLINOIS

GUIDE FOR TRAVEL AND STUDY

ISBN 13: 978-1-4621-4369-6

Published by CFI, an imprint of Cedar Fort, Inc.
2373 W. 700 S., Suite 100, Springville, UT 84663
Distributed by Cedar Fort, Inc., www.cedarfort.com

Cover design by Courtney Proby

Printed in Colombia

10 9 8 7 6 5 4 3 2 1

Printed on acid-free paper

For Brent Top, Craig Ostler, and Richard Bennett,
wise mentors and my first guides to
the sacred places of the Restoration.
–Casey

To my children,
Bryan, Carrie, Caleb, Matthew, Kaylee and Rebekah
who share my love for Nauvoo.
–Bryan

Contents

Acknowledgments

This series is the result of years of visits and study at the sacred sites of the Restoration. Over the years, dozens of missionaries assisted us in gaining access to the sites, sharing their insight, and their expertise they have gained from their service. First and foremost, we offer our gratitude to all of the missionaries of all ages and stages of life who have so graciously hosted us at the Church History Sites and allowed us to produce these guides. We offer our sincere thanks to Gary L. Boatright, who has acted as a liaison between us and the Church History Sites as we were doing our research.

A number of colleagues at Brigham Young University have also played a key role in helping us gain insights into the Church History Sites as well. Craig Manscil and Craig Ostler directed the BYU Travel Study program for several years, and the insights gained from extensive time at the sites with them and the wonderful students of the programs was invaluable in producing this book. Richard Bennett, Alex Baugh, and JB Haws also played a key role in funding site visits and contributing their expertise. Brent L. Top, Daniel K. Judd, and Scott C. Esplin all encouraged our research during their respective terms as the Deans of the College of Religious Education, and we appreciate their contributions and encouragement. We also wish to acknowledge the fund of the Religious Studies Center at BYU whose support made this volume possible. Finally, the wonderful editors at the BYU Faculty Publishing Service were a great help in preparing the final manuscripts.

We also appreciate the support and help of the wonderful contributors to Doctrine and Covenants Central, who generously allowed us to share materials written for their site in this volume. Scott Woodward played a key role in developing the site, and we appreciate John Welch and Kirk Magleby for reaching out to us to create such a wonderful resource to study Church History. Several staff members from Scripture Central, the parent site to Doctrine and Covenants Central, accompanied us on trips to the sites and greatly assisted our work. These include Zander and Angel Sturgill, Benjamin Griffin, Taylor and Alexis Riley, Avery Kirk, Daniel Smith, and Brenden Fulmer.

We are especially grateful for several student assistants who have been involved in varying degrees in the large task of selecting, transcribing, writing, and editing the material included in this manuscript. Afton Beard, and Christian Ames are surely some of the most cheerful, capable, dependable, and intelligent of assistants.

We also want to express our deep gratitude to Valerie Loveless of Cedar Fort Publishing & Media for her conception, vision, encouragement, expertise, and editing of our manuscript; she was indispensable in the creation of this series.

In writing this book we also wish to extend our sincere appreciate to Lachlan and Christin Mackay, directors of the Joseph Smith Historic site, for all of their insights in helping us write about a place that we deeply love.

Finally, we express our gratitude to our families for all of their patience with the travel and research involved in producing this book. One of the great joys of our lives is taking our loved ones to these sacred places, and they are among our most cherished traveling companions. We hope that our work allows our readers to have special experiences at all of the sites, just as we have had!

Introduction

A Cornerstone of Zion

The Nauvoo Temple at sunset. Photo by Casey Paul Griffiths.

In 1839, the Latter-day Saints arrived in Illinois as exhausted, impoverished refugees, fleeing a literal order for their extermination in the state of Missouri. Citizens of Quincy, Illinois treated the Saints with kindness, offering them shelter and refuge from the harsh winter of 1838-39. Within a few weeks the Saints set their sights on a new home. Lacking nearly any resources, the Saints purchased land at Commerce, Illinois, a swampy peninsula jutting out in the Mississippi River next to some dangerous rapids. Though the land was infested with mosquitoes carrying malaria and other deadly diseases, the Saints still pressed ahead with faith to make the wilderness blossom as the rose. Within a few years, they managed to build one of the largest cities in Illinois which they named "Nauvoo," a Hebrew word meaning "beautiful place or situation."

With Nauvoo, Joseph Smith and the early Church members carried out their vision of Saintly city. Working on a virtual blank canvas, they managed to develop a city with a stately temple at its center and a diverse community of converts from around the world. Many Saints in Nauvoo were converts from European nations who immigrated to America seeking a new home to live their faith in peace. They would find a welcoming community in Nauvoo, but not necessarily peace.

Some of the most significant doctrinal teachings of the Restoration took place in Nauvoo. The Relief Society was organized and women were given a greater and more active role in the work of the Church. Missionaries were sent to Great Britain, Palestine, and widespread locations around the globe. Both men and women were inducted into the sacred priesthood rites of the temple, and the great work to redeem the dead commenced. Some of the most important and controversial teachings of the Restoration were also revealed in Nauvoo, including eternal marriage and plural marriage. The foundations of the Restoration were established, and as a witness to their sincerity, Joseph and Hyrum Smith laid down their lives as testators to the work (Doctrine and Covenants 135:5).

After the martyrdom of their beloved Prophet and Patriarch, the Saints completed the temple and ensuring that all who wished to make the sacred covenants of that holy house were able to. However, even before the temple was dedicated, the Saints began preparations to leave their city behind and embark on a journey into the wilderness. Their epic journey, an exodus paralleling the departure of the Children of Israel from Egypt, became a remarkable story in its own right, as they crossed a continent to find a new home. Looking backward at the temple as they crossed the river in the cold winter of 1846, the Saints bade farewell to their city, knowing it was the final resting place of the Prophet Joseph Smith and many of their loved ones.

In the last several decades, the city of Nauvoo has begun to be restored to its appearance when it was home to the Saints. As old hostilities have faded it has become another sacred site of pilgrimage for Latter-day Saints around the world. Visitors to Nauvoo can see the place where the Saints arrived in poverty and built a mighty city. They can visit the jail where a Prophet sealed his testimony with his blood and visit the grave of that Prophet, his brother who fell with him, and his beloved wife, Emma Hale Smith. Finally, they can stand on the banks of the Mississippi River and gaze back at the majestic temple, now rebuilt, and reflect on the sacrifices the Saints made as they left their city behind to travel to an unknown destination in the West.

Why We Wrote This Book

This book is part of a series of guides designed to enhance your visit to Church History sites. This book focuses on the sacred sites found in Illinois, primarily around the city of Nauvoo. Joseph Smith lived in Nauvoo from 1839 to his death in 1844 where he placed the final foundation stones of the Restoration. There are sites of joy, controversy, and deep meaning found throughout the city of Nauvoo and the surrounding area.

However, any site can become just another stop on a road without a knowledge of the history that took place there. Many sites have visitor centers staffed by helpful missionaries who can assist you in knowing the story that makes the place sacred. Many pilgrims enlist the help of a guide during the travels through the lands of the early Restoration. On occasion, during our visits to the sites we have often seen families pull up to a site, wander a few moments, and then return to their car without fully knowing what makes the place they visited so special.

In the past, there were many site books available that were mostly concerned with direction to find the site. With the advent of new technology, finding most Church history sites has become relatively simple. This has rapidly increased the number of people who seek out the sites on their own. Because of this, directions to the sites have been placed in this book only when they are absolutely necessary. Instead, these books are designed to provide you with the background stories behind the sites. Whenever possible we have drawn from first-hand accounts produced by those who lived on these properties and played their vital roles in the work of the Restoration. The intent behind these books is to enhance your visits to the sites by putting primary sources into your grasp, arranged site by site.

Another notable departure in these volumes is the scope we have chosen. Many guidebooks have chosen to list every site possible within a given area. This can be very useful, but this usually limits each site narrative to just a few paragraphs because of the need to cover so many locations. Where other authors have chosen breadth over depth, we have chosen instead to focus on the primary sites in each region and provide a thorough account of the events that took place there from primary sources. This means that there might be other places worth visiting not in the book. For instance, about an hour from Nauvoo stands the traditional site Yelrome, where Isaac Morley and his family lived during the Nauvoo period. This site is difficult to find but well worth visiting, and you might want to consult with the local missionaries if you are interested in more out of the way sites like this one. For our purposes here, we have chosen to focus on the primary sites in each region instead. We were assisted in this book by Bryan Ready, a native of Illinois and an excellent historian, who provided many valuable insights into the significance and history of these sites.

How to Use This Book

This book is arranged to give you the stories that took place at each of the sites, with special emphasis on the relationship of each location to the scriptures, particularly the Doctrine and Covenants. Chapters are arranged roughly chronologically, beginning in Nauvoo with the places where Joseph Smith lived and then moving to the homes of other important leaders. Later chapters cover sites linked to the development of temple doctrines, or monuments to early Saints found in the cemeteries of Nauvoo. In contrast to other Church history sites, there are dozens of historic buildings clustered together in Nauvoo, and it can be difficult to fit them all into one trip. Other books in the series will cover the Church history sites and their stories in New England, Ohio, Missouri, and other locations.

Each chapter begins with a few bullet points which overview the most significant events at each site, and the revelations received at these locations. The story behind each site is organized around these events, with emphasis given to the times and places where revelations were received that became part of the scriptural canon. Many Illinois sites, such as the Brigham Young Home or Carthage Jail, are staffed by missionaries who can help guide you through the sites. These books are not intended to take the place of the missionaries, whose testimonies and teachings are an important part of each site visit. The missionaries at the sites will help you find the key locations and briefly share the stories with you. These books are designed to enhance the experience with the missionaries by providing you with the primary sources and cutting edge scholarship for each location.

At other sites, such as the Old Pioneer Burial Grounds or the homes of early Church members, missionaries are unavailable. These sites can be more difficult to find. Information at these sites can be difficult to locate, so we have included photographs and more specific directions to find these sites. At these locations the information in this book will help you to act as your own tour guide, or serve as a guide to others. Sites without visitor centers or missionaries are often overlooked but can provide an array of edifying experiences if visitors are provided with the right information.

In each chapter, a series of mini-devotionals are embedded into the text to deepen your experience at each of the sites, using questions provided to guide your reflection on the site you visit or can be used to teach your friends and loved ones visiting the sites with you. At most locations you will visit, areas are provided where visitors can take a few moments for reflection. The devotionals provided point out some of the most important principles learned by the early Saints at this location. Taking a little time to reflect and review the events and personalities associated with each site will bring deeper meaning to your time spent in these special places.

Finally, we would remind you that reverence invites revelation. We would invite you to spend a few moments during your travels reading the revelations given by the Lord to the early Saints as they struggled to accomplish their work. As you do so, we feel you will become a part of the stories you are learning about. One of the great blessings of living in our time is that there is no end to the story of the Restoration for only those who pick up the sacred commandments and teachings given to the early Saints and make them a part of their own story. As you search, ponder, and pray in these holy places, we hope that your love for the Savior will increase, and your testimony of His work in the latter-days will continue to grow.

Casey Paul Griffiths
Bryan Ready
Mary Jane Woodger

Significant events at this location:

- Main Street was the center of civic life in the city of Nauvoo during the time the Saints spent here (1839-1846).
- The Saints in Nauvoo enjoyed a rich cultural life, with frequent musical recitals, plays, and other cultural events.
- A Masonic lodge was established on Main Street in Nauvoo. It eventually became a hub where many cultural events took place.
- Nauvoo was known for publishing several active newspapers. Many important items concerning Church history and doctrine were first published in these papers.

Nauvoo Main Street

Historic Main Street in Nauvoo. Photo by Casey Paul Griffiths.

Many of the most significant Nauvoo sites are found on Main Street. The businesses that the Saints established on Main Street have been reconstructed so visitors can experience the everyday life of the Saints and see how they made their living. Visitors can learn even more about life in Nauvoo in the Pioneer Trades building, located just behind Main Street. Talking a walk up and down Main Street sends visitors back in time as they experience the joy of daily life in Nauvoo.

History of Main Street

Several of the businesses located on Main Street. Photo by Casey Paul Griffiths.

At the southwest corner of Water and Main Streets, a pyramid-shaped "survey stone" peaks up from the ground. It was from this point in 1839 that Church leaders laid out the plan for the city of Nauvoo. In the original plans, Main Street ran true north, began and ended in the Mississippi River, and was eighty-two feet wide, the widest street in the city (the average street in Nauvoo was roughly fifty feet wide). Church leaders added the extra width to Main Street in hopes of running a canal down its middle.

Nauvoo sat on a limestone peninsula that jutted out into the river.[1] The limestone created a series of rapids in the Mississippi River known as the Des Moines Rapids. When the river level was low, steamboats and other river traffic could not travel over the rapids fully loaded. The passengers and freight had to be unloaded at one end of Main Street and carted down to the other end so the watercraft could make it over the rapids safely. Church leaders thought that

1 This limestone is also one of the reasons why the land in Nauvoo was so swampy. Water would run of the bluffs and seep into the soil. Once the soil was saturated the limestone prevented it from draining any further and the swampland was formed.

by building a canal right through Main Street, the boats could avoid the rapids altogether.

Excavation for the canal began on the north side of town, but the same limestone that created the rapids prevented workers from digging out the canal. They would have had to blast a path all the way down Main Street. That was cost prohibitive and counterproductive. The canal project was abandoned, but the initial excavation would go on to become the site of one of the quarries for the Nauvoo Temple.

The original survey of Nauvoo placed businesses and homes right next to each other. There was no zoning. In those days, most business owners lived in or next to their businesses, so this plan made a lot of sense. You would pass by homes, businesses, gardens, and livestock pens with milk cows and horses just on Main Street alone. Farms and larger herds of cattle would have been managed outside of the city. The Prophet Joseph Smith wanted everyone to live within the city limits of Nauvoo. He wanted everyone to have the opportunity to take advantage of the cultural, educational, and religious activities that would be found in the city. Even those who cared for farms would have lived within the city limits.

It may be hard to believe, but Nauvoo once had scores of businesses scattered all over the city. In his book *In Old Nauvoo: Everyday Life in the City of Joseph,* George Givens wrote that Nauvoo had more than thirty-five general stores, five drug stores, eight tailors, nine dressmaking shops, eleven grist mills, a half-dozen brickyards, five livery stables, and three lumberyards as well as a watchmaking shop, daguerreotype shops, potteries, several silversmiths, a comb factory, a match factory, a foundry, and many other assorted shops and businesses. Givens described these stores as follows: "They [the stores] were usually quite small and unimposing, unpainted buildings with narrow doors and small paned windows [glass was expensive] . . . . The dim interiors were further darkened by the heavy traffic, smoke from the fireplaces and stoves, and natural wood stained from endless sprinklings and sweepings. There was always a distinctive odor of a mixture of spices, grains, leather, textiles, wood, molasses, cheese and so on. Goods were hung wherever a hook could be driven, and overflowing shelves and barrels and kegs filled any available floor space." [2]

Laborers often worked twelve to fourteen hours a day, six days a week. The average wage for a laborer was less than four dollars a week. A skilled craftsman might earn as much as six dollars a week.[3]

---

2 George W. Givens, *In Old Nauvoo: Everyday Life in the City of Joseph* (Salt Lake City: Deseret Book, 1990),79–80.

3 Givens, *In Old Nauvoo*, 92.

Diagonally across from the survey stone is the Mansion House as well as the home of Sidney Rigdon.[4] As you cross Sidney Street, you will see the remaining wing of an old hotel known as the "City Hotel" or the "Mills Hotel." This building is not open for tours. While we do not know much about the hotel, we do know of a humorous incident that took place on the street in front of it. The Prophet Joseph Smith once came across a couple of boys fighting in the street. The Prophet broke up the fight and lectured the boys saying, "Nobody is allowed to fight in Nauvoo but me!"[5]

As you journey down Main Street today, you may notice many wide-open spaces between buildings. Back in 1840, these open spaces would have been filled with log cabins and brick homes, gardens, corrals, craftsmen, and other trade shops. There would not have been a lot of open space on Main Street since it was generally bustling with people, wagons, and livestock.

As you cross Parley Street, you come to the heart of Main Street, which features the following shops: Riser Boot and Shoe Shop, The Print Shop and Post Office, Jonathan Browning's Home and Workshop, Stoddard Tin Shop, Scovil Bakery, and the Cultural Hall.

Riser Cheap Boot and Shoe Manufactory

George Riser and his wife, Christiana, built their home on Main Street in 1843[6]. They lived on the upper floor, and George operated his shop on the main floor. The Riser Boot Shop was one of fourteen businesses that sold boots and shoes in Nauvoo. Prices for local footwear ranged from $1.00 for a pair of slippers to $5.50 for a pair of fine boots.[7] The adjective *cheap* did not refer to the quality of the craftsmanship but rather the lower prices, which were sure to be attractive to consumers who were struggling to make ends meet in Nauvoo.

George Riser was born in Germany in 1818. He emigrated to the United States in 1831. George married his wife in Ohio in 1841. After hearing about the restored gospel from an associate, the Risers traveled to Nauvoo, arriving in October 1842. George was baptized by Elder Albert Brown in the frozen Mississippi River on December 12, 1842. Remembering his baptism, George

4 For more information on these buildings, see the chapter on the Joseph Smith Historic Site.

5 Joseph Smith History, vol. D-1, 1473, accessed July 9, 2022, https://www.josephsmithpapers.org/paper-summary/history-1838-1856-volume-d-1-1-august-1842-1-july-1843/116.

6 The current building was reconstructed by the Church in 1989.

7 Givens, *In Old Nauvoo*, 97.

wrote: "The weather was extremely cold. The river was so frozen that a hole had to be cut in the ice to baptize us in. . . . We were confirmed the same day at our residence by the same Elder."[8]

Like most families living in Nauvoo, George and Christiana Riser and their children had struggles with sickness and death. Around the same time as the couple was baptized, their infant son became seriously ill. George wrote, "My little child; John, was sick nigh to death. I was led to send for Joseph the Prophet to lay hands on him. Elder Orson Hyde accompanied him. Joseph advised us to keep the child in a room that was not so hot and predicted that he would recover, which he instantly did as soon as they took their hands from him."[9] Sometimes it seemed that the battle with sickness was never ending in Nauvoo. A few months later, the Riser's child was ill again. This time, there would be no miraculous healing. George wrote: "The following spring my little boy, John was again taken very ill. I had him administered to by a number of Elders, among whom were two of the Apostles. . . . Brother Joseph called. . . . I again asked him to administer to the child, but for some cause he was not led to make the same promise of life as before. He died on the 6th of May at the age of fourteen months and was buried the next day."[10]

George and Christiana Riser and their family stayed in Nauvoo until 1846 when they left with the Saints heading west. George and Christiana eventually settled in Salt Lake City, Utah and lived there until their deaths.

Mini-Devotional—When God Says "No"

We have all heard stories of the great miracles that God performed in both ancient and modern days. We may have even experienced a miracle ourselves. But what happens when the miracle does not come? George and Christiana Riser lost a young child to death while they lived in Nauvoo. He had been healed once before, but why did God not heal him again? We will not find the answer to that question on this side of the veil. In both instances, the Risers had faith that the baby could be healed. In both instances, a prophet of God performed a priesthood blessing of healing. Yet God's responded differently.

- How did the Risers respond in faith when Heavenly Father said "no"?

8 Richard N. Holzapfel and T. Jeffery Cottle, *Old Mormon Nauvoo and Southeastern Iowa,* (Santa Ana, CA: Fieldbrook Productions Inc, 1990), 123.

9 George Riser, Journal, University of Utah, Salt Lake City, as cited in Holzapfel and Cottle, *Old Mormon Nauvoo,* 122–24.

10 George Riser, Journal.

- How can you respond in faith when Heavenly Father says "no" to your prayer?
- Have you ever experienced a miracle? What happened? How did it make you feel? What did the miracle say about Heavenly Father's love for you?

Remember that Heavenly Father always loves you, even (especially) when he says "no."

Print Shop and Post Office

The Print Shop and Post Office on Nauvoo Main Street. Photo by Casey Paul Griffiths.

James Ivins, a convert from New Jersey, purchased a parcel of land in Nauvoo from the Prophet Joseph Smith on April 27, 1842. James constructed three buildings on this lot, two of which still stand. He used one of them as his home and the other as a store. (The buildings labeled "Printing Office" and "John Taylor Home" are original, while the one labeled "Post Office" was reconstructed.) Bricks in these buildings bear the imprint of one of the many brickyards in Nauvoo. James sold the property to the Church in May 1845, and the printing office, which had been at the corner of Bain and Water Streets since 1840, moved to this location. Apostle John Taylor, who was editor of *Times and Seasons* and *Nauvoo Neighbor*, moved into the house shortly thereafter. The printing office consisted of a stereotype foundry, typesetting department, pressroom, book bindery, and a book and stationary store.

The printing office was originally established by Ebenezer Robinson in partnership with the Prophet's brother Don Carlos Smith. The office printed books, including editions of the Book of Mormon and Doctrine and Covenants (though none were printed at its second location), and two newspapers: *Times and Seasons*, an official publication of the Church (the equivalent of *Church News* or the Church Newsroom website today), and *The Wasp*, a "public journal" that published non-Church-related news. *Times and Seasons* was sixteen pages in length. Ebenezer and Don Carlos were the editors of *Times and Seasons*. It was published monthly and then semimonthly as Nauvoo and the Church began to grow. William Smith, also one of the Prophet's brothers, was the editor of *The Wasp*. According to George Givens, "William Smith, brother of the Prophet, founded the *Wasp* to aid his own Candidacy for the state House of Representatives and to counter the violently anti-Mormon *Warsaw Signal*."[11] *Warsaw Signal* was a newspaper published in nearby Warsaw, Illinois. Its editor, Thomas Sharp, was an ambitious twenty-two-year-old who developed a hatred for the Church in general and Joseph Smith in particular.

William Smith and Thomas Sharp would print frequent diatribes against each other, often ending in vicious personal attacks. Church leaders realized that William's rhetoric was doing them more harm than good, so when John Taylor took over editorship of *Times and Seasons* in 1842, they decided before long that he should take over editing duties of *The Wasp* as well. John renamed the paper *Nauvoo Neighbor* and toned down the rhetoric.

Nauvoo Neighbor was a weekly paper. It was four pages long with each page having six columns. The first edition of the *Neighbor* was published on May 3, 1843. Rates to advertise in the *Neighbor* were one dollar per square (a column wide and of equal length).[12] An annual subscription for the *Neighbor* was two dollars.[13]

Like most frontier publications, *Nauvoo Neighbor* got much of its news from other newspapers, and news traveled slowly. News from a neighboring state could take three to four months to arrive. News from other countries took even longer. Missionaries returning to Nauvoo also brought the news from other parts of the country and world.

11 Givens, *In Old Nauvoo*, 265.

12 Givens, *In Old Nauvoo*, 271.

13 Givens, *In Old Nauvoo*, 267.

By 1845, it was obvious that the Saints would be leaving Nauvoo. *Nauvoo Neighbor* published its last issue on October 29, 1845. The last issue of *Times and Seasons* was published on February 15, 1846. In his final editorial for *Nauvoo Neighbor*, John Taylor summed up the experience of Nauvoo: "The power that made Nauvoo; that gathered thousands from various climes and kingdoms; that reared the Temple; and that whispers to us now, 'Peace be still and see the salvation of God,' can guide us to bring forth a better city, a hundred fold of gathering, and five times as good a temple."[14]

The Nauvoo post office was established on April 21, 1840. George W. Robinson was appointed postmaster. George was succeeded by his father-in-law, Sidney Rigdon, on February 24, 1841. During Sidney's tenure as postmaster, he maintained the post office in his home. After Sidney left the Church, Elias Smith was appointed postmaster. Elias maintained the post office in the printing office, since he was a supervisor there, until the printing office moved to this location on Main Street.

During this time, the postal service was slow and somewhat unreliable. "The usual means of carrying mail from town to town in Illinois was the four-horse post-coaches or two-horse states. Where the roads were more primitive, mail was carried on horseback or in sulkies (light, uncovered rigs). Between the river towns, of course it was carried by steamboat."[15] By 1844, mobs would frequently intercept mail going in and out of Nauvoo. They would read and destroy the letters they expropriated. Important Church documents had to be sent by armed courier.

There were no envelopes during this time. Letters were written on folded sheets of paper. Since postage was calculated based on the number of sheets in the letter, people wrote horizontally, vertically, and sometimes diagonally across the same sheet of paper. This method saved the sender money on postage but made some letters very hard to decipher. In general, mailing a letter was not cheap. According to George Givens, "throughout most of the Nauvoo period, postage rates varied considerably, from six cents for mail traveling up to thirty miles to 25 cents for mail traveling more than four hundred miles. Two pages doubled the postage rate and three pages tripled it, regardless of the size of the paper." He expounded, "Mailing a letter to Great Britain cost the person between a quarter and a third of a day's wages."[16]

Sometimes the sender would pay the postage, but most of the time, they would send the letter postage due. People were so desperate to hear from

14 Givens, *In Old Nauvoo*, 273.

15 Givens, *In Old Nauvoo*, 76.

16 Givens, *In Old Nauvoo*, 74.

friends and family, most would try to save up enough money to pay for the postage, but not everyone could. Every year, thousands of letters would be left unclaimed. Post offices would put ads in local newspapers listing those who had unclaimed letters. After all, if a postage-due letter was never claimed, the post office did not make any money. Unclaimed letters were eventually sent to the dead letter office in Washington, DC.

The fact that you could send a letter postage due was especially a problem for Joseph Smith. People would write hateful letters to the Prophet and mail them postage due. At first, Joseph paid for the postage on all the letters he received because he did not know whether they were coming from friend or foe. But eventually the hate mail became so burdensome that Joseph put an ad in the paper announcing that he could no longer accept postage-due letters. If you wanted him to read your letter, you had to pay the postage.

After the exodus began in 1846, Almon W. Babbitt moved into this complex owned by the Church. He was one of the five trustees appointed to manage and sell the properties left behind by the Saints. This complex was transferred to these trustees, Babbitt was appointed postmaster, and he maintained the post office at this property until 1848. Like many of the buildings in Nauvoo, over time these three fell into disrepair. The post office building was razed in 1913, but it was later reconstructed by the Church.

Mini-Devotional—The Challenge of Communication

Imagine having to wait months for the most recent news or for a letter from home. In the 1840s, if a person emigrated from Europe, or even to another part of the United States, it was unlikely that they would ever see their family and friends again. When a letter came, they were desperate for news and to see the handwriting of a loved one. Imagine being so poor, that you had to write horizontally and vertically on the same paper just so you could save money on postage. Imagine trying to read a letter written like that!

- How has modern technology made it easier for friends and families to stay in touch? How has it made it harder?
- Imagine living in a time when the only means of long-distance communication was letter writing. Now say that you lived thousands of miles away from your family. What would you say to them in your letter?

Jonathan Browning

The Browning Gun Shop and Home on Nauvoo Main Street. Photo by Casey Paul Griffiths.

Jonathan Browning was born on October 22, 1804, at Brushy Fork, Sumner County, Tennessee. As a young teenager, Jonathan noticed a neighbor's broken flintlock rifle. He worked to pay for the rifle, took it home, repaired it, and then sold it back to the neighbor. At age nineteen, Jonathan moved to Nashville to become an apprentice under a gunsmith named Samuel Parker. He picked up the skill quickly and moved back home to set up his own shop. He married Elizabeth Stalcup in 1826.

Sometime around 1834, Jonathan Browning's cousin Orville Browning wrote to him about the business opportunities in Quincy, Illinois. By then most of Jonathan's family had moved away, so he packed up shop and moved to Quincy with his wife and children. Once established, Orville convinced Jonathan to get involved in politics, and before long, Jonathan was elected justice of the peace. Jonathan's connections with his cousin Orville, who had become a prominent lawyer in Quincy, helped him make the acquaintance of another young lawyer named Abraham Lincoln. Abraham stayed with the

Browning family during a few of his visits to Quincy.[17] Jonathan and his family saw first-hand the plight of the Saints as the survivors arrived as refugees from Missouri persecutions in 1838-1839.

In 1840, Jonathan and Elizabeth Browning took a steamboat up the Mississippi River to Nauvoo, Illinois. Jonathan wanted to investigate some of the stories he had been hearing about the new city. There he met the Prophet Joseph Smith. Within a few months, Jonathan and Elizabeth were baptized and confirmed members of The Church of Jesus Christ of Latter-day Saints. Three years later, in the summer of 1843, the Brownings moved to Nauvoo and purchased a parcel of land on the east side of Main Street. Jonathan built a log cabin and then later a brick home and shop.[18]

Though he trained as a gunsmith, Jonathan Browning worked as a blacksmith in Nauvoo. He was known to have shod Joseph and Emma Smith's horses from time to time.[19] But guns were his major interest. While living in Illinois, Jonathan invented several different types of repeating firearms, including a "slide gun" which consisted of a steel block which passed horizontally through the rifle. Slide guns ranged from five to twenty-five shots.[20] Some of Jonathan's more ornate guns had an engraved plate on the stock that read "Holiness to the Lord—Our Preservation." In October 1845, Jonathan was ordained a Seventy and appointed one of the presidents of his quorum.

Jonathan and Elizabeth Browning and their family left Nauvoo with the Saints in 1846. They settled just south of Kanesville, Iowa. Brigham Young asked Jonathan to remain in Kanesville to construct guns and make gun repairs for the Saints heading west.[21] Jonathan was released from his assignment in 1852 and made the journey to Utah with his wife and (at that time) twelve children. The Browning family settled in Ogden, Utah, and Jonathan continued gunsmithing. He passed on his skills to his children. Two of his sons, John Moses Browning and Matthew Browning, would found the Browning Arms Company. John Moses became one of the most successful gunsmiths in American history. He would eventually hold more than 120 firearm patents.[22]

17 "Life Sketches of Jonathan Browning and Elizabeth Stalcup," 128, FamilySearch, accessed July 11, 2022, https://ancestors.familysearch.org/en/K2W3-743/jonathan-browning-1805-1879.

18 The current brick home is original. The shop was reconstructed by the Church around 1969. Descendants of Jonathan and Elizabeth Browning helped fund the restoration of the home and the reconstruction of the shop.

19 "Life Sketches," 129.

20 *The Jonathan Browning Houses and Workshops* (Nauvoo, IL: Nauvoo Restoration Inc, 1980).

21 *Jonathan Browning Houses and Workshops.*

22 *Jonathan Browning Houses and Workshops.*

Mini-Devotional—Holiness to the Lord

The phrase "holiness to the Lord" is inscribed above the entrance to every temple built by the Church. Why do you think Jonathan Browning engraved the phrase "Holiness to the Lord—Our Preservation" on his gunstocks?

Was it a reminder that, when it came to providing food or protecting one's family, a person should trust the Lord and not themselves or a weapon?

Maybe it was a reminder that every aspect of our life is supposed to reflect "holiness to the Lord." President Brigham Young taught, "Every moment of [our lives] must be holiness to the Lord, . . . which is the only course by which [we] can preserve the Spirit of the Almighty to [ourselves]."[23]

- Would things be different if the words "holiness to the Lord" were inscribed above the front door to your house?
- Imagine having the phrase "holiness to the Lord" inscribed above your heart or on your forehead. Would that change the way you live your life?

23 *Deseret News*, April 2, 1862, 313.

Stoddard Tin Shop

The Stoddard Tin Shop on Nauvoo Main Street. Photo by Casey Paul Griffiths.

Sylvester B. Stoddard was born in 1801 in Perrysburg, New York. He married a young widow, Charity Cole Nutter, in 1833, and the couple joined The Church of Jesus Christ of Latter-day Saints a few months later. Sylvester served missions for the Church in Maine, Ohio and Michigan. By 1836, the Stoddard family was living in Kirtland. In 1839, they moved to Missouri and later to Quincy, Illinois. By October 1841, they had made their way to Nauvoo.

While living in Nauvoo, Sylvester Stoddard served on the Nauvoo high council and as a captain in the Nauvoo Legion. He was also a member of the Nauvoo Masonic Lodge. His wife, Charity, died of consumption (tuberculosis) in Nauvoo on October 19, 1844. She is buried at the Old Nauvoo Burial Grounds east of town. Sylvester married Almira Knight a month later.

While in Nauvoo, Sylvester Stoddard worked as a tinsmith. A tinsmith made all manner of things using tin or one of its alloys. Tin was desirable because it was somewhat affordable and was resistant to rust. You could make just about anything out of tin—coffee pots, pans, plates, cups, candle safes, and lanterns. The lanterns had small decorative patterns punched into them. The pattern would be punched into the tin before the lantern was assembled with the hole punches protruding from the outside. This technique provided the candle some protection from the wind and allowed it to keep shining. Some families had custom-designed patterns punched into their lanterns. There were no streetlights in Nauvoo, and if the moon was not shining bright, it could get very dark in the city at night. It was said that oftentimes you could tell who was walking down the street by the pattern of their lantern. Stoddard also sold nails, buckets, stoves, scales, axes, sheets of tin, hand irons, and stove pipes.[24]

Sylvester Stoddard did not remain a member of the Church. After the Prophet's death in 1844, many men emerged claiming to be the rightful leader of the Church. Although the majority of Church members voted to follow Brigham Young, other challengers still managed to gain followers. In 1846, Sylvester and his wife joined one of these schismatic groups led by James J. Strang. The Stoddard Tin Shop building on Main Street is original. It was restored by the Church in 1989.

Mini-Devotional—Endure to the End

When the author of this chapter joined the Church, the ward mission leader was Lynn Ennis. Lynn's favorite phrase was "endure to the end." He would frequently remind the new converts that it did not matter what they had done, it did not matter what covenants they had made, if they did not endure to the end. The life of Sylvester Stoddard serves as warning to Church members—we should always be striving to endure to the end. Sylvester served multiple missions. He served on the high council and in the Nauvoo Legion. He lived only a few blocks away from the Prophet, yet he did not endure to the end.

People leave the Church for various reasons. It is not up to us to judge them. Rather, we need to focus on our own faith in Christ. The Apostle Paul wrote, "Work out your own salvation with fear and trembling" (Philippians 2:12).

- What do you think Paul meant by "work out your own salvation"?
- What does "with fear and trembling" mean?
- What steps can you take to ensure that you endure to the end?

---

24 LaMar C. Berrett, ed., *Sacred Places: A Comprehensive Guide to Early LDS Historical Sites*, vol. 3, *Ohio and Illinois*, ed. Keith W. Perkins and Donald Q. Cannon (Salt Lake City: Deseret Book, 2002), 154.

Scovil Bakery

Lucius Scovil was born in Connecticut in 1806. In 1828, he married Lury[25] Snow (cousin to Eliza R. Snow). They moved to Kirtland, Ohio, in 1835. There they accepted the gospel and were baptized by the Prophet Joseph Smith. They moved to Missouri sometime in 1838 and settled in Adam-ondi-Ahman.

According to family history, Lucius Scovil would often ride guard duty while living in Missouri. One time he was spotted and chased by a mob who opened fire upon him. He escaped the mob, but a bullet grazed his ear and damaged his hearing.[26] The Scovil family left Missouri in 1839 and settled in different locations in Illinois and Iowa. By 1841, they were living in Nauvoo.

Lucius Scovil served on the committee to build the cultural hall next door to his home, and he donated the land for its construction. By 1843, he had built a bakery just south of the hall. The following advertisement appeared in the January 10, 1844 publication of *Nauvoo Neighbor*: "The subscriber wishes to inform the citizens of Nauvoo and the adjacent towns, that he has established a Bakery and Confectionary, in this city, on main Street, first door South of the new Masonic Hall, where he intends to manufacture everything connected with that kind of business—Breads, Crackers, Cakes, Jellys and Candies of all description which he will sell at St. Louis Prices wholesale or retail. L.N. SCOVIL. N.B. Marriage cakes made to order on the shortest notice from one to twenty-five dollars each. L.N.S. NAUVOO DEC. 27, 1843." Based on the average laborer's wage of four dollars a day, twenty-five dollars was two months' pay! The bakery likely made most of its income by catering to events at the cultural hall next door. Most families of the day baked their own bread and considered cakes, sweets, and candies as a luxury. Many parents felt that candy was not healthy for children.[27]

In addition to being on the building committee for the cultural hall, Lucius Scovil served as a captain in the Nauvoo Legion. He was also a member of the Masonic Lodge.

On January 14, 1846, Lury gave birth to twins—Martha and Mary. The twins would only live for thirteen days. They passed away on January 27, 1846. Lury passed away soon after. In the early 1800s, between one and two percent of woman died during childbirth. That number was likely higher in Nauvoo.

25 Also spelled *Lucy* in some publications.

26 June Barton Bartholomew, "Life Story of Lucius Nelson Scovil," FamilySearch, accessed July 9, 2022 https://ancestors.familysearch.org/en/KWJR-L2D/lury-snow-1807-1846.

27 Givens, *In Old Nauvoo*, 200.

Some scholars estimate that the mortality rate for children in Nauvoo was as high as sixty-four percent.[28] Lury, the twins, and another Scovil child are buried in the Old Nauvoo Burial Grounds just east of town.

Lucius Scovil and his family left with the Saints in 1846. While staying in Garden Grove, Iowa, Brigham Young called Lucius on a mission to England. Lucius had married another woman, Alice Hearst, and he left her and his five children in the care of friends in Garden Grove and set out on his mission. Lucius wrote of this difficult time, "This seemed like a painful duty for me to perform, to leave my family to go into the wilderness and I to turn and go the other way. It cost all that I had on this earth . . . [but] I thought it was best to round up my shoulders like a bold soldier of the crop . . . and assist in rolling forth the Kingdom of God."[29]

While passing through Nauvoo, he saw the shining temple on the hill and felt impressed that he should do something to preserve its likeness. While in Sheffield, England, he contracted a potter by the name of J. Twigg to make 1,800 plates with an image of the Nauvoo Temple. The plates have a sketch of the temple in the center surrounded by the names of the Twelve Apostles. Two original plates can still be seen in Nauvoo—one in the Scovil Bakery and the other in the Heber C. Kimball Home. Because so few images of the original Nauvoo Temple exist, the temple plate has become a valuable reminder of the beauty of the original temple.

After his mission, Lucius Scovil returned to the United States, where he served the Church in New Orleans, Louisiana, and in Winter Quarters, Nebraska. He finally arrived in Utah in 1850 and died in Springville, Utah, in 1889.

The Scovil Bakery was reconstructed on the original foundation in 1982.

Mini-Devotional—Counting the Cost

One can feel the anguish in Lucius Scovil's words as he described leaving on his mission for England.

- When Lucius wrote, "It cost all that I had on this earth," do you think he was talking about money? What other "costs" could he be talking about?

28 Givens, *In Old Nauvoo*, 113. Givens attributes this percentage to the prevalence of malaria and to the Saints' weakened condition after the Missouri persecutions.

29 Margie Brown, *Nauvoo Restored* (Ogden, UT: The Living Scriptures, 2002), 132.

- How would you respond if God called you to leave your family and go on a mission?
- How can you prepare yourself to serve faithfully in your callings?

Cultural Hall/Masonic Hall

The Cultural Hall on Nauvoo Main Street. Photo by Casey Paul Griffiths.

In 1841, eighteen Church brethren, including Hyrum Smith and Heber C. Kimball, petitioned to form a Masonic[30] Lodge in Nauvoo. These brethren had previously joined the Masons and thought forming a Lodge in Nauvoo would be beneficial to the Saints.

On March 15, 1842, in the upper room of Joseph Smith's Red Brick Store, a "dispensation" was granted by the Illinois Grandmaster Mason for the organization of the Lodge and the installation of officers. Joseph Smith and Sidney Rigdon were initiated into the Masonic order at this time.

Membership in the Lodge grew rapidly, and in time, the organization needed a building of its own. Lucius Scovil donated land for the hall, and construction on the Lodge began in 1843. The Masonic Hall was dedicated by Hyrum Smith on April 5, 1844, with five hundred people present.

30 The Masons are a fraternal organization that trace their heritage back to the era of Solomon's temple. Much has been written about the connection between the Masons and early Church members. For a brief discussion, visit https://www.churchofjesuschrist.org/study/history/topics/masonry?lang=eng.

Interior of the upstairs floor of the Nauvoo Cultural Hall. Photo by Casey Paul Griffiths.

The hall was one of the few three-story buildings in Nauvoo and was used for Masonic as well as other meetings. The Masons met primarily on the third floor. The second floor was used for public meetings and Church and political meetings and housed offices for the Nauvoo Legion and city police. The main floor was used for theatrical and musical productions.[31]

In the 1840s, people would go to concerts or lyceums or the theater, all of which could be had in Nauvoo. William Pitt's Nauvoo Brass Band gave concerts in the hall. The members wore white trousers and were proficient on trumpets, French horns, piccolos, clarinets, coronets, bugles, trombone, and bass drum. [32]

The Nauvoo Lyceum was formed for the purpose of encouraging debate. The first topic discussed is one that is still debated today: "Ought Capital Punishment to be Abolished."[33] At a time when many Americans believed the theater was a tool of the devil, Church leaders encouraged participation. Brigham Young even took a small role of an Incan priest when the traveling production of *Pizzaro* made a stop in Nauvoo.[34] So many non-Masonic

31 Berrett, *Sacred Places*, 155.

32 Givens, *In Old Nauvoo*, 177.

33 Givens, *In Old Nauvoo*, 170.

34 Givens, *In Old Nauvoo*, 173.

events were held in the "Masonic" hall that it eventually became known as the "Cultural Hall."

One citizen of Nauvoo who was so enamored with the quality of a concert held at the hall wrote the following, "Where are we to go for music if we do not find it in Nauvoo? I will boldly assert no where. Witness the concert the over evening at the Masonic Hall; got up for the most laudable and praiseworthy purpose. The music in its selection was of the most varied character; and the electrifying feeling that was manifest, proved to a demonstration, that Nauvoo can furnish us with ladies and gentlemen whose instrumental and vocal powers are of no unpolished order."[35]

One of the most poignant moments in Church history took place in front of the hall. On June 24, 1844, as the Prophet was leaving to go to Carthage for the last time, he stopped in front of the hall and said: "Boys, if I don't come back, take care of yourselves; I am going like a lamb to the slaughter."[36]

As the Saints made preparations to leave Nauvoo, the benches were removed from the main floor of the hall, and it became a workshop where wagon boxes were built. It was sold at an auction for approximately $4.50.[37] The third floor was eventually removed.

The Church purchased the building in 1967 and restored it to three stories.

Mini-Devotional—"Praise the Lord with Singing, with Music, with Dancing" (Doctrine and Covenants 136:28)

In the early nineteenth century, many Christians believed dancing and the theater were taboo, but members of The Church of Jesus Christ of Latter-day Saints embraced them both. Both Joseph Smith and Brigham Young believed that the arts were important to the well-being of people. The Church embraces all of the arts and encourages members to use their artistic talents to express themselves and their faith.

- What artistic talents do you have or enjoy?
- How do the arts strengthen your faith?
- How can you use the arts to share your faith?

---

35 Holzapfel and Cottle, *Old Mormon Nauvoo*, 109.

36 Berrett, *Sacred Places*, 156.

37 "Cultural & Masonic Hall, Nauvoo, Illinois," Ensign Peak Foundation, accessed 9 July 2022, https://ensignpeakfoundation.org/cultural-masonic-hall/.

It must have been disheartening for the business owners in Nauvoo to leave their businesses behind and head west. Perhaps the words of George Givens aptly sum up this chapter and the feelings of those pioneers:

> Empty houses are distressing to view, but sadder still is the sight of vacant businesses. . . . A vacant business means miscarried plans and broken dreams. Anyone can take over a vacant house, but vacant businesses must await another dreamer, who may never come. And in Nauvoo the wait was eternal: the shops were shuttered, the wharves began their slow rotting away, the warehouses never again housed more than scurrying mice or barn swallows. The merchants might plan greater enterprises in the west and build more imposing businesses, but these would never quite compensate for the lost city that had offered such great promise—a city planned by a prophet of God, settled by a people of faith, and given life by merchants with dreams.[38]

38 Givens, *In Old Nauvoo*, 88.

The Joseph Smith Historic Site

The Mansion House at the Joseph Smith Historic Site in Nauvoo. Photo by Casey Paul Griffiths.

The historic sites in Nauvoo are shared between The Church of Jesus Christ of Latter-day Saints and Community of Christ. Located on the southern end of Nauvoo near the banks of the Mississippi River, the Joseph Smith Historic Site features several important locations in telling the story of the Saints in Nauvoo. Two notable sites are the homes where Joseph and Emma Smith lived during their time in Nauvoo—the Joseph Smith Homestead and the Mansion House. Another important site is the Nauvoo House, a boarding house that the Lord commanded the Saints to build "that the weary traveler may find health and safety" (Doctrine and Covenants 124:23). Visitors can also tour a recreation of Joseph Smith's Red Brick Store,[39] where the Relief Society was organized and the first endowments were given, and reverently spend time in

39 The Red Brick Store is discussed on its own in a separate chapter.

the Smith Family Cemetery, where the graves of Joseph, Emma, and Hyrum Smith are found. In these several locations, the Saints began transforming the swampy land of Nauvoo into what the Lord has called a "cornerstone I have appointed for Zion" (Doctrine and Covenants 124:23).

Coming to Nauvoo

Forced to leave Missouri in the winter of 1838–39, most of the Saints turned back east to Illinois. These religious refugees were welcomed by the locals who lived in Quincy, Illinois, and in other nearby communities. But they also knew that they must find a new gathering place. Destitute and struggling to find resources, the Saints needed a place to regroup and rebuild the Church. While still in Liberty Jail, the Prophet Joseph Smith had instructed local Church leaders to find a suitable location for the Saints to establish a permanent settlement. In the spring of 1839, Joseph and the other Church leaders, who were still imprisoned, were granted a change of venue to Boone County, Illinois. While on their way to Boone County, the prisoners were allowed to escape. Joseph arrived in Quincy on April 22, 1839.

After a tear-filled reunion with his wife, Emma Smith, and with his family, Joseph met with Church leaders and learned that they were in touch with a land speculator name Isaac Galland. Isaac had acquired several hundred acres along the Mississippi River in Iowa and Illinois, and he was willing to sell to the Saints. After a few days, Joseph journeyed north to see the property, which included a small paper town called Commerce. Joseph described the property in his journal:

> When I made the purchase of White and Galland, there were one stone house, three frame houses, and two block houses, which constituted the whole city of Commerce. Between Commerce and Mr. Davidson Hibbard's, there was one stone house and three log houses, including the one that I live in, and these were all the houses in this vicinity, and the place was literally a wilderness. The land was mostly covered with trees and bushes, and much of it so wet that it was with the utmost difficulty a footman could get through, and totally impossible for teams. Commerce was so unhealthful, very few could live there; but believing that it might become a healthful place by the blessing of heaven to the Saints, and no

> more eligible place presenting itself, I considered it wisdom to make an attempt to build up a city. [40]

By the end of the 1839, the Church purchased land around a horseshoe bend of the Mississippi River: six hundred acres on the Illinois side and twenty thousand acres on the Iowa side. The six hundred acres of land in Illinois would eventually become a new gathering place for the Saints. Despite the rough frontier conditions found in this swampy, malarial swamp, Joseph named the city Nauvoo, after a Hebrew word meaning "beautiful."[41]

The Joseph and Emma Smith Homestead

The Homestead at the Joseph Smith Historic Site. Joseph and Emma lived in the older part of the home for most of their time in Nauvoo. Photo by Casey Paul Griffiths.

---

40 Joseph Smith, *History of the Church* (Salt Lake City: Deseret Book Co., 1980), 3:375.

41 Alex D. Smith, "Organizing the Church in Nauvoo," in *Revelations in Context: The Stories Behind the Sections of the Doctrine and Covenants*, ed. Matthew McBride and James Goldberg (Salt Lake City: The Church of Jesus Christ of Latter-day Saints, 2016), 264.

Significant events at this location:

- On May 9–10, 1839, Joseph and Emma Smith moved to Commerce, Illinois.
- The Homestead served as Church headquarters until the Red Brick Store was built in 1842.
- On July 22, 1839, later called a "Day of God's Power," Joseph Smith healed dozens of Saints who laid ill on the banks of the Mississippi River.
- Doctrine and Covenants 124, 125, and 126 were received while Joseph Smith lived in the Homestead.

In 1839, Commerce consisted of a small collection of buildings. When Joseph and Emma Smith arrived in May, they moved into one of these buildings, a humble log cabin now known as the Homestead. The cabin was originally built sometime around 1824 by Captain James White, one of the earliest White settlers in the area. The Homestead's west and north wings were added later.

Originally from Ohio, Captain White was a trader and keel boat captain. He arrived in the area in the early 1820s and purchased the land from the federal government, who gained ownership of land from the local Fox and Sac tribe through the Treaty of 1804.[42] He went on to serve as the Indian agent for the area, and the cabin he built was the site of the Indian Agency. Joseph purchased the cabin from Hugh White, Captain White's son.[43]

In the months that followed the Smith family's move to Commerce (later renamed to Nauvoo), refugees from Missouri poured into the area. Weakened by the privations experienced in Missouri, many of the Saints succumbed to

---

42 Lisa Knopp, "Nauvoo, The Beautiful Place," Southeast Missouri State Missouri University Press, accessed October 29, 2022, http://www.semopress.com/nauvoo-the-beautiful-place/.

43 Lamar C. Berrett, Keith W. Perkins, and Donald Q. Cannon. *Sacred Places*, vol. 3, *Ohio and Illinois: A Comprehensive Guide to Early LDS Historical Sites* (Salt Lake City: Deseret Book, 2002), 100.

malaria (they called it the "ague"), which was spread by the mosquitoes that thrived in the area's swampland.[44]

By July, hundreds were sick with the disease, including Joseph himself. With very few shelters in the area, the Homestead quickly became a hospital, and the front yard was filled the tents and pallets of the sick. Joseph himself gave up his bed to someone sicker than he and camped out in a tent in his front yard. Emma and those who could still function tended to the sick, bringing them water and blankets as the waves of chills and fever racked their bodies. In this moment of great suffering, God worked a great miracle through his prophet. Wilford Woodruff described what happened:

> On the morning of the 22nd of July 1839, he [Joseph Smith] arose, reflecting upon the situation of the Saints of God in their persecutions and afflictions, and he called upon the Lord in prayer, and the power of God rested upon him mightily, and as Jesus healed all the sick around Him in His day, so Joseph, the Prophet of God, healed all around on this occasion. He healed all in his house and door-yard, then, in company with Sidney Rigdon and several of the Twelve, he went through among the sick lying on the bank of the river, and he commanded them in a loud voice, in the name of Jesus Christ, to come up and be made whole, and they were all healed. When he healed all that were sick on the east side of the river, they crossed the Mississippi river in a ferry-boat to the west side, to Montrose, where we were. The first house they went into was President Brigham Young's. He was sick on his bed at the time. The Prophet went into his house and healed him, and they all came out together. As they were passing by my door, Brother Joseph said: "Brother Woodruff, follow me." These were the only words spoken by any of the company from the time they left Brother Brigham's house till we crossed the public square and entered Brother Fordham's house. Brother Fordham had been dying for an hour, and we expected each minute would be his last.
>
> I felt the power of God that was overwhelming His Prophet.
>
> When we entered the house, Brother Joseph walked up to Brother Fordham, and took him by the right hand; in his left hand he held his hat.

44 The Saints soon realized that the swampland was not a result of water coming in from the river but rather runoff from the bluffs. Limestone lies beneath Nauvoo's soil. The water would run off the bluffs and settle in the flatland. The limestone prevented it from draining any further. Eventually, the Prophet called for a series of ditches to be dug at the base of the bluffs. These ditches would catch the runoff and drain it into the river. One of these drainage ditches can still be seen along the east side of Durphy Street in front of Nauvoo State Park.

He saw that Brother Fordham's eyes were glazed, and that he was speechless and unconscious.

After taking hold of his hand, he looked down into the dying man's face and said: "Brother Fordham, do you not know me?" At first, he made no reply; but we could all see the effect of the Spirit of God resting upon him.

He again said: "Elijah, do you not know me?"

With a low whisper, Brother Fordham answered, "Yes!"

The Prophet then said, "Have you not faith to be healed?"

The answer, which was a little plainer than before, was: "I am afraid it is too late. If you had come sooner, I think I might have been." . . .

Joseph then said: "Do you believe that Jesus is the Christ?"

"I do, Brother Joseph," was the response.

Then the Prophet of God spoke with a loud voice, as in the majesty of the Godhead: "Elijah, I command you, in the name of Jesus of Nazareth, to arise and be made whole!"

The words of the Prophet were not like the words of man, but like the voice of God. It seemed to me that the house shook from its foundation.

Elijah Fordham leaped from his bed like a man raised from the dead. A healthy color came to his face, and life was manifested in every act.

His feet were done up in Indian meal poultices. He kicked them off his feet, scattered the contents, and then called for his clothes and put them on. He asked for a bowl of bread and milk and ate it; then put on his hat and followed us into the street, to visit others who were sick. . . .

As soon as we left Brother Fordham's house, we went into the house of Joseph B. Noble, who was very low and dangerously sick.

When we entered the house, Brother Joseph took him by the hand, and commanded him, in the name of Jesus Christ, to arise and be made whole. He did arise and was immediately healed. . . .

When we left Brother Noble, the Prophet Joseph went, with those who accompanied him from the other side, to the banks of the river, to return home.

While waiting for the ferry-boat, a man of the world, knowing of the miracles which had been performed, came to him and asked him if he would not go and heal two twin children of his, about five months old, who were both lying sick nigh unto death.

They were some two miles from Montrose.

The Prophet said he could not go; but, after pausing some time, he said he would send some one to heal them; and he turned to me and said: "You go with the man and heal his children."

> He took a red silk handkerchief out of his pocket and gave it to me, and told me to wipe their faces with the handkerchief when I administered to them, and they should be healed. He also said unto me: "As long as you will keep that handkerchief, it shall remain a league between you and me."
>
> I went with the man, and did as the Prophet commanded me, and the children were healed.
>
> I have possession of the handkerchief unto this day.[45]

As the Saints' settlement grew, the Homestead grew as well. Joseph added the north wing in 1840 (the west wing was added by Joseph Smith III in 1858). Another small cabin was built just behind the Homestead and served as the home of Joseph Smith Sr. and Lucy Mack Smith. Eventually, a larger cabin was built for Joseph and Lucy, and the cabin behind the Homestead functioned as a summer kitchen.

By 1840, Joseph Smith Jr.'s "escape" from Missouri had become an embarrassment to some of the state's political leaders. They convinced the governor of Missouri to seek Joseph's extradition back to Missouri. Initially, the governor of Illinois agreed to the extradition order. When Joseph learned of this extradition attempt, he went into hiding. According to Joseph Smith III, when Joseph built the north wing of the homestead, he included a secret room by the cellar.

> As for hiding places, there was, in this addition to the old building . . . a small hidden retreat . . . a little way down the stairway to the cellar the bearers of the steps were cut in two and the upper portion of the stairs furnished with hinges to allow that part to be lifted forward. This provided an entrance into the small retreat mentioned. It was a vaulted place, with a dry floor of brick and bricked walls, and was large enough for a couple of people to occupy, either sitting or lying down. . . . This small room was occupied a few times by Father when hunted, and was never, so far as I know, discovered by any of those who sought him, though members of the family knew of its existence.[46]

By 1841, the warrant for Joseph's extradition would be discharged as faulty by an Illinois judge. But Joseph's legal troubles in Missouri were far from over.

45 Wilford Woodruff, *Leaves from My Journal* (Salt Lake City: Juvenile Instructor Office, 1882), Mormon Texts Project, accessed August 6, 2022, https://www.gutenberg.org/files/46028/46028-h/46028-h.htm#CHAPTERXIV.

46 Berrett, Perkins, and Cannon, *Sacred Places*, 3:158.

When Joseph was home, visitors were constantly calling. It did not take much time for the Homestead to be overwhelmed. Joseph Smith III recalled: "Father's home in Nauvoo was generally overrun with visitors. There was scarcely a Sunday in ordinary weather that the house and yard were not crowded—the yard with teams and the house with callers. This made a great deal of bustle and confusion and also a heavy burden of added toil for Mother and an unnecessary expense for Father."[47] The Prophet and his family needed a larger home, and Nauvoo desperately needed more hotel space. Since the construction of the Nauvoo House was taking longer than expected, it was decided that another building would be constructed to provide much needed space for the Prophet and his family. Joseph and Emma moved their family into the Mansion House on August 31, 1843. Joseph would live in this house for only ten months.

Mini-Devotional—Selfless Service

Look at the front yard of the Homestead as it slopes down to the Mississippi River. Imagine it is filled with the tents and blankets of people who are sick with malaria. In one of those tents is the Prophet Joseph Smith. Emma Smith and other sisters move about and tend to the needs of the sick.

- Imagine you are sick with a fever. Would you be willing to not only give up your bed but also move out of your house and sleep in a tent outside so that those in worse condition than you can sleep in your bed?
- How do the actions of Joseph and Emma Smith inspire you to serve others selflessly?
- Can you think of someone you know who is sick or suffering in some way? How can you minister to them? How can you demonstrate selfless service to those around you?
- The Prophet Joseph Smith was able to use priesthood power to heal many. How does selflessness enable bearers of the priesthood to heal and bless others?

---

47 Lane K. Newberry, *Nauvoo, "Beautiful Place," Welcomes You* (Nauvoo, IL: Nauvoo Area Foundation, 1963), 13.

The Mansion House

Joseph and Emma Smith rented rooms in the Mansion House during the last year of his life. Photo by Casey Paul Griffiths.

Significant events at this location:

- On August 31, 1843, Joseph and Emma Smith move into the Mansion House,.
- On June 18, 1844, Joseph Smith gave his last public discourse across the street from the Mansion House at the corner of Water and Main Streets.
- On June 24, 1844, Joseph and Hyrum Smith departed for Carthage, Illinois.
- On June 29, 1844, a public viewing of Joseph and Hyrum Smith's bodies was held in the dining room of the Mansion House.

The Mansion House was first built to serve as a residence for the Smith family, but during its construction, Joseph Smith decided to add a hotel wing to accommodate his many visitors to Nauvoo. When finished, the Smith's beautiful new home would have twenty-two rooms, including a large dining room. Emma Smith traveled to St. Louis, Missouri, to purchase furnishings for the new home and hotel. The Smith family moved into their new home on August 31, 1843.[48] It quickly became known as the Mansion House. Joseph and Emma soon realized that they did not have the time to be hotel keepers, so in January 1844, Joseph leased the hotel to Ebenezer Robinson for one thousand dollars per year. Joseph retained use of a few rooms for his family's personal use. Joseph lived there during the last few months of his life.

The Mansion House hosted several social events for the Saints in Nauvoo. On Tuesday, October 3, 1843, an open house was held at the Mansion House. Around one hundred couples attended. The event culminated in the wedding of two of the guests.[49] On December 25, 1843, Joseph and Emma hosted a Christmas supper when a surprise visitor appeared. Joseph wrote in his journal, "A large party supped at my house & spent the evening in Music Dancing &c. in a most cheerful & friendly manner. During the festivities a man apparently drunk, with his hair long & falling over his shoulders came in and acted like a Missourian I commanded the captain of the police to put him out of doors. In the scuffle, I looked him full in the face and to my great surprise and joy untold, I discovered it was Orrin Porter Rockwell, just arrived from a year's imprisonment in Missouri."[50]

The Prophet and his family likely had many happy memories during the ten months they lived together in the Mansion House. Things would change forever when Joseph and Hyrum Smith left for Carthage on the morning of June 24, 1844. Joseph's family would not see him alive again.

The martyrs' bodies were brought back to the Mansion House on June 28, 1844. After the bodies were cleaned and dressed, a private viewing was held for the family. Emma was inconsolable. Lucy Mack Smith, their mother, related,

> I was swallowed up in the depths of my afflictions; and though my soul was filled with horror past imagination, yet I was dumb, until I arose again to contemplate the spectacle before me. Oh! at that moment how my mind flew through every scene of sorrow and distress which we had passed together, in which they had shown the innocence and sympathy which filled their guileless hearts. As I looked upon their peaceful smiling countenances., I seemed almost to hear them say—"Mother, weep not for

48 Richard Neitzel Holzapfel and T. Jeffery Cottle, *Old Mormon Nauvoo and Southeastern Iowa* (Santa Ana, CA: Fieldbrook Productions, Inc., 1991), 162.

49 Holzapfel and Cottle, *Old Mormon Nauvoo*, 162.

50 Joseph Smith, Journal, December 25, 1843, pp. [211–12], JSP.

> us, we have overcome the world by love; we carried to them the Gospel, that their souls might be saved; they slew us for our testimony, and thus placed us beyond their power; their ascendancy is for a moment, ours is an eternal triumph."[51]

On June 29, 1844, Joseph and Hyrum's bodies were placed in the large dining room so that the citizens of Nauvoo could pay their respects. It is estimated that some twenty thousand people came through the Mansion House that day.[52]

After the martyrdom, Emma and the children continued to live in the Mansion House until September 1846. With the Battle of Nauvoo imminent, Emma decided to move in with relatives near Fulton, Illinois. She leased the mansion house to a local businessman. In time, Emma learned that he was making plans to sell off the hotel's furnishings, so she returned to Nauvoo, confronted the businessman, and resumed residence in the Mansion House. She declared, "I have no friend but God, and no place to go but home."[53]

Emma continued to live in the Mansion House and operate it as a hotel until she moved into the Nauvoo House in 1871. Without occupants, the hotel wing fell into disrepair and was demolished in 1893. By 1918, the Homestead and Mansion House had been acquired by the Reorganized Church of Jesus Christ of Latter Day Saints (RLDS; now known as Community of Christ), and they started offering tours of the historic buildings.

---

51 James Linforth, ed., *Route from Liverpool to Great Salt Lake Valley* (Liverpool, 1855), 71.

52 Holzapfel and Cottle, *Old Mormon Nauvoo*, 164.

53 Scott C. Esplin, *Return to the City of Joseph* (Urbana, IL: University of Illinois Press, 2018), 33.

Mini-Devotional—The Footsteps of the Prophet

Regarding the significance of the intersection of Water and Main Streets, Donald Q. Cannon wrote: "Perhaps no street corner in Nauvoo was more honored with the footprints of Joseph Smith than the corner of Main and Water Streets. Here, between the Prophet's two houses, you walk where Joseph walked and learn where Joseph taught."[54] When you walk across the floors of the Homestead and the Mansion House, you walk where the Prophet walked. When you touch the handrail in the Mansion House, you touch the same railing that Joseph and Emma Smith touched. When you gaze into the mirror of the dresser upstairs, you see your reflection in the same mirror that Joseph and Emma saw theirs.

- Is walking where Joseph and Emma walked meaningful to you? Why or why not?
- How can physically touching history, or being in the places where history occurred, make it come alive to you?
- What can we learn from being in the places where Joseph Smith taught?

54 Berrett, Perkins, and Cannon, *Sacred Places*, 3:197.

The Nauvoo House

The Nauvoo House at the Joseph Smith Historic Site. Photo by Casey Paul Griffiths.

Significant events at this location:

- On January 19, 1841, Joseph Smith received a revelation in which the Saints were commanded to build the Nauvoo House and the Nauvoo Temple (see Doctrine and Covenants 124).
- On October 2, 1841, the cornerstones of the Nauvoo House were laid.
- During the cornerstone ceremony, Joseph Smith placed the original manuscript of the Book of Mormon into one of the cornerstones.
- On June 29, 1844, Joseph and Hyrum Smith's bodies were secretly buried in the unfinished basement.
- On April 30, 1879, Emma Smith passed away in her bedroom.

On January 19, 1841, the Prophet Joseph Smith received a revelation that called for the construction of two new houses (see Doctrine and Covenants 124). The first was to be "a house that strangers may come from afar to lodge therein" (verse 23)—the Nauvoo House. The second was to be "a house unto me [the Lord]" (verse 31)—the Nauvoo Temple. On February 23, 1841, the Nauvoo House Association was formed to provide financing and to oversee the construction of the building. It was estimated that it would cost $150,000 dollars to build.[55] Stock in the building was sold for $50 a share. Lucian Woodworth was the architect. The house was to be built in an "L" shape, with a 120-foot wing facing the riverfront and a 120-foot wing facing Main Street. The building was to be three stories high. One story was to be constructed of rock and the other two of brick.[56] Joseph Smith donated land for the building, and in return, he and his descendants were to receive rooms in the structure in perpetuity.[57]

On October 2, 1841, a cornerstone ceremony was held for the Nauvoo House. Joseph placed the original manuscript of the Book of Mormon, along with a small Bible, a copy of the Doctrine and Covenants, copies of the *Times and Seasons*, and some coins, in one of the cornerstones.[58] The lid to the cornerstone was sealed with lead, and construction continued on the house. In 1882, Lewis Bidamon, whom Emma Smith married after Joseph was martyred, found the old cornerstone and opened it. Water had seeped into the cornerstone through the years and destroyed most of its contents. Several pages of the *Book of Mormon* manuscript survived, and Lewis gave them away to visitors as souvenirs. Of the roughly 500 pages of the original manuscript, only portions of 232 pages remained, constituting about 28 percent of the original text. The Church now owns a significant portion of this manuscript.[59]

Construction on the Nauvoo House progressed slowly and was halted altogether when Church leaders decided to focus all their efforts on completing the temple. By the time of the Saints' exodus in 1846, the house walls had only reached the top of the first story.

After Joseph and Hyrum Smith were killed, a faux burial of coffins filled with sand was held for the public. Emma was deeply concerned that someone would try to steal Joseph's body to claim a bounty offered by the state of Missouri. She decided to secretly bury the bodies of Joseph and Hyrum in

55 Holzapfel, and Cottle, *Old Mormon Nauvoo*, 151.

56 Berrett, Perkins, and Cannon, *Sacred Places*, 3:130.

57 Holzapfel and Cottle, *Old Mormon Nauvoo*, 151.

58 Berrett, Perkins, and Cannon, *Sacred Places*, 3:130.

59 Trent Toone, "'Tremendous Achievement': Church Publishes Photographic Record of Original Book of Mormon Manuscript," *Deseret News*, January 25, 2022.

the unfinished basement of the Nauvoo House. A thunderstorm swept across Nauvoo that night, completely obliterating any sign that the ground had been disrupted.[60] Sometime in the fall and winter of 1844–45, Emma had the bodies reinterred in the basement of a small outbuilding about forty feet southwest of the Homestead.

After the exodus, the Nauvoo House stood empty until 1869 when Lewis began tearing it down. In its place, he constructed the building that stands there today, which Lewis called the Riverside Mansion. When it was finished, Emma and Lewis moved into the house and ran it as a small hotel until Emma passed away on April 30, 1879. Emma's bedroom was on the southeast corner of the second floor (the ground floor being the first floor). Upon Emma's death, the Homestead, Mansion House, and Red Brick Store were deeded to her surviving sons. The Riverside Mansion was given to Lewis, who died in 1891. Community of Christ purchased the building from Lewis's son a few years after Lewis's death.

Though the Nauvoo House never fulfilled its purpose as a hotel, the riverboat landing built next to the house (at the foot of Main Street) bustled with activity. It was one of the four main riverboat landings in Nauvoo[61] and functioned as the principal landing for the Church-owned riverboat, *Maid of Iowa*. Captained by Welshman Dan Jones, the *Maid of Iowa* was a sternwheeler steamboat. It weighed 60 tons and measured 115 feet in length. The steamboat frequently made trips to St. Louis, Missouri and New Orleans, Louisiana to pick up immigrants headed to Nauvoo. The Prophet could see their arrival from his living room window in the Homestead, and he would frequently come down to greet the new arrivals personally.

The Nauvoo House Landing was also frequently used for baptisms of new converts. On March 20, 1842, Joseph baptized eighty people at this location following a nearby preaching service.[62] Some of the earliest baptisms for the dead also took place at the Nauvoo House Landing. The first documented baptism for the dead took place on September 12, 1840. On that occasion, Jane Neyman asked Harvey Olmstead to baptize her by proxy for her deceased son Cyrus Livingston Neyman. The witness for the baptism was Vienna Jaques,

60 Barbara Hands Bernauer, *Still Side by Side* (Kansas City, MO: Barbara J. Bernauer, 1994), 2. This booklet is a fascinating account of the search for the bodies of Joseph and Hyrum Smith. It is highly recommended if the reader wants more information on this subject.

61 The other three landings were the Parley Street Landing (also known as the Lower Stone House Landing), the Kimball Warf (also known as Kimball Landing), and the Upper Stone House Landing.

62 Berrett, Perkins, and Cannon, *Sacred Places*, 3:134.

who rode her horse into the Mississippi River to observe the ceremony. Shortly after the baptism, Joseph gave his approval of the ceremony, upon hearing the words Harvey used to perform the ordinance. The place where the Nauvoo House met the Mississippi River was among the most popular of the sites used to perform baptisms for the dead. Other locations included the Upper Stone House Landing, the Kimball Wharf, and the Lower Stone House Landing.[63] Later, the Lord commanded that baptisms for the dead only take place in temples (see Doctrine and Covenants 124:29–36).

Mini-Devotional—Remembering Emma

Emma Hale was born on July 10, 1804. She married Joseph Smith on January 18, 1827. Emma gave birth to nine children and adopted two. Of those eleven children, only five survived to adulthood. Emma was a remarkable woman. She compiled the Church's first hymnal. She also cofounded and served as the first president of the Relief Society. But for most of her marriage to Joseph, she never had a home of her own. She lived with her parents, Joseph's parents, and other Church members. Only briefly in Kirtland and Missouri did she have her own home. It is no wonder that the roots she put down in Nauvoo meant so much to her. In Nauvoo, she did have her own house, but she was constantly entertaining guests.

Church history has not always been kind to Emma. She did not get along with Brigham Young, she did not follow the Saints west, and she really struggled with the revelation on plural marriage. Yet she never denied her belief in the Book of Mormon or her husband's prophetic calling. Emma was not perfect and she often struggled, but she maintained her faith. One can only imagine what the scrutiny must have been like being the wife of the Prophet. Yet she handled this pressure and scrutiny with incredible grace.

- In Doctrine and Covenants 25, the Lord calls Emma Smith "an elect lady." Why do you think he called her this? In what ways do you think Emma demonstrated that she was an "elect lady"?
- How does Emma Smith's example of holding fast to her testimony despite all of her trials and struggles inspire you to do the same? What can we learn from Emma's example?

---

63 Alexander L. Baugh, "For This Ordinance Belongeth to My House": The Practice of Baptism for the Dead Outside the Nauvoo Temple," *Mormon Historical Studies* 3, no. 1 (2002): 48–49.

Smith Family Cemetery

The grave of Joseph, Emma, and Hyrum Smith. Photo by Casey Paul Griffiths.

Significant events at this location:

- In the winter of 1844–45, Joseph and Hyrum Smith's bodies were reburied in the cemetery at Emma Smith's request.
- In January 1928, Joseph, Hyrum, and Emma Smith's remains were located and reinterred.
- On August 4, 1991, the Smith Family Cemetery was dedicated by Wallace B. Smith and M. Russell Ballard.

The sacred use of the ground of the Smith Family Cemetery predates the Smith family by two thousand years. Archaeological discoveries indicate that this land was likely used as a burial place for Native Americans during the

Hopewell era (roughly 200 BC to AD 500).[64] During Joseph Smith's lifetime, most of the Smith family members were buried in Nauvoo's first cemetery located near the near the southeast corner of White and Durphy Streets.[65] After Emma had Joseph and Hyrum Smith reinterred near the Homestead, members of the Smith family decided to move the bodies of those buried in the cemetery on Durphy Street closer to Joseph and Hyrum's. Joseph Smith Sr., Robert B. Thompson (Hyrum's brother-in-law), and Don Carlos Smith (Joseph and Hyrum's brother) were moved to "Emma's Garden" sometime in 1846.[66] Don Carlos Smith (Joseph and Emma's son) and another stillborn son were also reinterred near their father.

The grave markers of Joseph Smith Sr. and Lucy Mack Smith. Photo by Casey Paul Griffiths.

64 Rosemary G. Palmer, "Laid to Rest in Nauvoo," *Meridian Magazine*, July 17, 2014. When the Saints arrived in Nauvoo, there were burial mounds scattered all around the area. There are a few that can still be seen about two miles north of Nauvoo on Sycamore Haven Drive. Please be aware that this is private property. The current owners allow visitors, but please be respectful of the owner's privacy and property.

65 This cemetery is no longer extant. Most of the bodies were reinterred into the Old Nauvoo Burial grounds, east of town on Parley Street, in 1842.

66 Lachlan Mackay, "A Brief History of the Smith Family Nauvoo Cemetery," *Mormon Historical Studies* 3, no. 1 (2002): 242.

Over the next fifty years, many Smith family members and friends were buried in what would become known as the Smith Family Cemetery. These included Samuel H. Smith (Joseph and Hyrum's brother), Lucy Mack Smith, Emma, and Joseph Smith III's first wife and two of his children. The last person to be buried in this cemetery was Lewis C. Bidamon, Emma's second husband. He died on February 11, 1891. By Emma's death in 1879, all traces of the outbuilding under which Joseph and Hyrum were buried had vanished. Joseph Smith III died in 1914, and with him went the memory of where Joseph and Hyrum were buried.

In 1913, a dam was built at Keokuk, Iowa, and the rising waters of the Mississippi River formed Lake Cooper. As the water continued to rise, concern grew over the possibility that the graves of Joseph and Hyrum could soon be underwater. In 1927, Frederick M. Smith, President of the RLDS Church, commissioned engineer W. O. Hand of Independence, Missouri, to find and move the remains of Joseph and Hyrum to a safer location. The brothers' remains were located on January 16, 1928. Joseph, Hyrum, and Emma's remains were reinterred in their present location on January 20, 1928.[67] Their remains were arranged in silk-lined wooden boxes and buried under a slab of concrete ten feet square and three-and-a-half-feet deep.[68]

In 1990, members of the Joseph and Hyrum Smith Family Foundation joined with the RLDS Church to improve and beautify the cemetery. New walkways and lighting were installed, and new trees and flowers were planted. A new headstone on Joseph, Hyrum, and Emma's granite grave marker was also erected. Known by some family members as "God's Acre,"[69] the Smith Family Cemetery was formally dedicated by Wallace B. Smith, then president of the RLDS Church and great-grandson of Joseph Smith Jr., and M. Russell Ballard of the Quorum of the Twelve Apostles of The Church of Jesus Christ of Latter-day Saints and great-great-grandson of Hyrum Smith.[70]

67 Bernauer, *Still Side by Side*, 1.

68 Berrett, Perkins, and Cannon, *Sacred Places*, 3:140.

69 Mackay, "A Brief History," 243.

70 Mackay, "A Brief History," 245.

Mini-Devotional—In the Twinkling of an Eye

The Apostle Paul wrote, "Behold, I shew you a mystery; We shall not all sleep, but we shall all be changed, in a moment, in the twinkling of an eye, at the last trump: for the trumpet shall sound, and the dead shall be raised incorruptible, and we shall be changed" (1 Corinthians 15:51–52). Cemeteries can be sad and scary places, but for those of us that believe in Jesus Christ, they can also give us hope. Because of Jesus's Atonement in Gethsemane, his death on the cross, and his Resurrection from the grave, we know that death is not the end.

You may have experienced the death of a loved one, perhaps recently. Or maybe you know someone that lost someone close to them. The accompanying pain and grief can sometimes be unbearable, but because of the Atonement of Jesus Christ, you can know that they are not gone forever. One day you will see them again. If we place our faith and trust in Jesus Christ and endure to the end, we know that one day we will be raised from the dead, as Jesus was, and live forever with our families.

- How does the Atonement and Resurrection of Jesus Christ bring you hope?
- In what ways can the knowledge of Jesus Christ's Resurrection help you as you grieve the loss of a family member or close friend? Or how can this knowledge help you support someone else who is grieving?
- One day, every person in the Smith Family Cemetery will be raised with glorified bodies. What would you like to say to Joseph, to Hyrum, to Emma (or perhaps to another Smith family member) on that day?

Sidney Rigdon Home

The Sidney Rigdon home in Nauvoo. Photo by Casey Paul Griffiths.

Though the Sidney Rigdon Home is not open for public tours, the authors thought that, given the important role that Sidney Rigdon played in the establishment of the Church, his home should be included in this chapter. Sidney served as the First Counselor in the First Presidency during the entirety of Joseph Smith's time as President of the Church. He remained an important influential leader during the Saints' time in Nauvoo, though he was not as active in leading as in earlier times because of his health.

Sidney was born in Pennsylvania on February 19, 1793. He married Phebe Brooks in June 1820. He was licensed to preach as a Baptist minister in 1819. He met Alexander Campbell in 1821 and soon joined his restoration movement called the Disciples of Christ.[71] From 1824 to 1826, Sidney served as a traveling preacher for Campbell's group. In 1826, Sidney became the pastor of the Baptist church in Mentor, Ohio.

In 1830, Parley Pratt, an associate of Sidney came across the Book of Mormon. He read it and was baptized by Oliver Cowdery. In the fall of 1830,

71 Alexander Campbell founded the Disciples of Christ with three other men—Thomas Campbell, Barton Stone, and Walter Scott. These men believed that Christianity needed to be "restored" to its primitive state.

Oliver, Parley, Peter Whitmer Jr., and Ziba Peterson were called to go on a mission to preach to the Lamanites on the western border of the United States. While enroute, they passed through Mentor and decided to pay a visit to Sidney. He and hundreds of his congregants were baptized as they received a testimony of the truthfulness of the Book of Mormon. In December 1830, Sidney and his friend Edward Partridge, who had not been baptized yet, traveled to New York to meet Joseph Smith. Soon after their meeting, Joseph received a revelation that the Saints should gather to Ohio.[72]

Sidney would become one of Joseph's closest associates. He would serve as first counselor in the First Presidency until Joseph's death in 1844. He helped Joseph with his translation of the Bible and with the Lectures on Faith. He is mentioned at least twenty times in the Doctrine and Covenants. He saw the vision of the three degrees of glory with Joseph in 1832.[73] A month later, he and Joseph were assaulted and tarred by a mob in Hiram, Ohio. They moved their families to Missouri in 1838. They were incarcerated together in Liberty Jail in the winter of 1838–39. Sidney became very sick in Liberty Jail and was released early because the jailers did not want to have a dead man on their hands. Sidney really never recovered from his experience in Liberty Jail, and his relationship with Joseph became very strained during the Nauvoo period.

In 1843, Joseph tried to have Sidney released as First Counselor, but Church members voted that he remain in the position. Sidney and his family moved back to Pennsylvania shortly thereafter. Sidney remained in Pennsylvania until he heard about the death of Joseph and Hyrum. There he had a "revelation" that he was to become "guardian" of the Church. On August 3, 1844, Sidney arrived back in Nauvoo and met with William Marks and other local Church leaders. He announced his revelation and asked that the membership of the Church be assembled to vote on appointing him guardian of the Church. He asked that the meeting be held on August 6, 1844, but William Marks changed the date to August 8. Brigham Young and the rest of the Twelve Apostles arrived the evening of August 6. At the meeting two days later, Brigham and Sidney both made their cases. The majority of the Church voted to follow the Twelve Apostles. Sidney returned to Pennsylvania and founded the Church of Christ. He died on July 14, 1876, having maintained his testimony in the Book of Mormon until the end.

In addition to serving in the First Presidency, Sidney served in the Nauvoo City Council, the Nauvoo Masonic Lodge, and the Council of the Fifty. He served as the postmaster of the City of Nauvoo from February 24, 1841 until

72 See Doctrine and Covenants 37.

73 See Doctrine and Covenants 76.

he left Nauvoo. The house currently standing was built in the early 1840s. It served as both the Rigdon home[74] and the Nauvoo Post Office. Charlotte Haven, a resident of Nauvoo, described this post office in a letter to her parents, dated March 5, 1843: "We enter a side door leading into the kitchen, and in a corner near the door is a wide shelf or table on which against the wall is a sort of cupboard with pigeon-holes or boxes. This is the post office. In this room, with the great cooking stove at one end, the family eats and sits. Mrs. Rigdon when I go for the mail always invites me to stop and rest, which after a cold long walk I am glad to do."[75]

Other Significant Locations in Nauvoo

William Marks Home

The William Marks Home is not open for tours. William Marks joined the Church in 1835 at Portage, New York, where he was baptized and ordained a priest. On June 3, 1836, he was ordained an elder. Shortly after his ordination, William moved his family to Kirtland, Ohio, to gather with the Saints. While in Kirtland, William operated a successful book and stationery store.

Soon after his arrival in Kirtland, on September 3, 1837, William was called to be on the Kirtland high council. Two weeks after, he was called to serve as an "agent" to Bishop Newel K. Whitney. On March 29, 1838, Joseph saw William in a vision being pursued by enemies. When it appeared the enemies were going to catch him, the Prophet saw "a chariot of fire [come], and near the place, and the angel of the Lord put forth his hand unto Bro Marks and said unto him, 'Thou art my son, come here,' and immediately he was caught up in the chariot and rode away triumphantly out of their midst. And again the Lord said I will raise thee up for a blessing unto many people."[76]

In a July 8, 1838 revelation given to the Joseph, William was commanded to close his business in Kirtland and travel to Missouri, for he was to "preside in the midst of my people in the city of Far West" (Doctrine and Covenants

74 Several additions have since been made to the original home.

75 William Mulder and A. Russell Mortensen, eds., *Among the Mormons* (New York: Alfred A. Knopf, 1969), 119–120, as quoted in Holzapfel and Cottle, *Old Mormon Nauvoo*, 166.

76 Joseph Smith History, vol. B-1, 786, JSP.

117:10). Compliant to the revelation, William closed his book and stationery store in Kirtland and was on his way to Missouri when mobs drove the Latter-day Saints from Far West. William changed his route and joined the Saints in Quincy, Illinois.

During the October 1839 general conference in Commerce (later Nauvoo), William was called to preside over the Saints in Nauvoo as stake president. Soon after, he was also appointed a city alderman, regent of the University of Nauvoo, and an associate justice of the municipal court. William struggled to fill each of these roles. He began to publicly complain and find fault with Church leaders, especially with Joseph. Because of his prominence as a leader in Nauvoo, he began to negatively influence many people.

Their relationship eventually soured so much that Joseph categorized William in the same league as the apostate William Law: "What can be the matter with these men [Law and Marks]? Is it that the wicked flee when no man pursueth? That hit pigeons always flutter? That drowning men catch at straws? Or that Presidents Law and Marks are absolutely traitors to the Church . . . ?"[77]

At the October 1844 general conference, a few months after Joseph's death, Latter-day Saints voted to reject William Marks as the Nauvoo stake president for his support of Sidney Rigdon's claims to become the President of the Church. William then joined with the Strangite movements and was appointed president pro tempore of the Strangite high priests quorum, a bishop, an Apostle, and a counselor to James J. Strang, the movement's president. Yet in 1849, William withdrew his affiliation with the Strangites.

For a time, William became sympathetic toward the religious views of Charles B. Thompson and John E. Page. He finally found a permanent home in June 1859 when he affiliated with and became prominent in the RLDS Church. He was one of three men to ordain Joseph Smith III as president of the RLDS Church. In March 1863, he was called to be First Counselor to President Joseph Smith III. William died on May 22, 1872, in Plano, Illinois, at age seventy-nine.[78]

---

77 Joseph Smith History, vol. E-1, 1857, JSP; spelling and capitalization standardized.

78 "William Marks," Doctrine and Covenants Central, accessed October 29, 2022, https://doctrineandcovenantscentral.org/people-of-the-dc/william-marks/.

The Times and Seasons Building Foundation

The foundation of Nauvoo's publication house is located at the northeast corner of Water and Bain Streets. The *Times and Seasons* was published here from 1839–41. The third edition of the Book of Mormon was printed here in 1840.[79] During the time the Church was in Nauvoo, the *Times and Seasons* served as the primary printed periodical for the Church. The motto of the paper was "truth will prevail." The *Times and Seasons* was launched in April 1839 with Ebenezer Robinson and Don Carlos Smith (brother of Joseph Smith) as editors. In May 1841, Robert B. Thompson joined as an editor. In January 1842, the Prophet took over as owner of the print shop, though the day-to-day operations of the paper were overseen by Apostles John Taylor and Wilford Woodruff. In November 1842, John became the primary editor, and the office was eventually sold to him in January 1844.

The *Times and Seasons* first published a number of crucial documents, some of which were later canonized as part of the scriptures used by The Church of Jesus Christ of Latter-day Saints. These included the King Follett Discourse, excerpts from the translation of the Book of Abraham, and Joseph Smith's letter to John Wentworth which included the Articles of Faith. The Prophet's personal history, now partially found in the Pearl of Great Price, and the announcement of the deaths of Joseph and Hyrum Smith, now found in Doctrine and Covenants 135, first appeared in the *Times and Seasons*.[80]

Aaron Johnson Home

The Aaron Johnson Home is not open for tours. Aaron Johnson was a Justice of the Peace and member of the Nauvoo high council. Aaron owned a farm across the Mississippi River in Iowa. He kept a boat tied up at a small dock in front of his home. Aaron's "leaky" boat is known for helping Joseph Smith, Porter Rockwell, and Willard Richards cross the river to Montrose, Iowa, on June 23, 1844, just days before the Prophet's martyrdom.

---

79 For more information about the Church's printing operations in Nauvoo, see the section on the print shop in the "Nauvoo Main Street" chapter of this book.

80 Peter Cawley, *A Descriptive Bibliography of the Mormon Church*, vol. 1, *1830–1847* (Provo, UT: Brigham Young University Religious Studies Center, 1997), 91–96.

Ownership of the Joseph Smith Historic Site

After the Saints departed from Nauvoo, Emma Smith stayed behind with her children. She was married to Lewis Bidamon in 1846. Joseph Smith III, the oldest son in the Smith family, grew up in Nauvoo. He worked on the family farm, studied law, and was eventually elected justice of the peace. In 1860, Joseph III felt prompted to address a gathering of the RLDS Church. Shortly after, he was ordained as president of the RLDS Church. With Joseph serving as president, all of the properties owned by the Smith family in Nauvoo went into the hands of the RLDS Church (hence why many Historic Nauvoo sites are owned today by Community of Christ) and eventually became part of the Joseph Smith Historic Site. Members of Community of Christ share many beliefs in common with The Church of Jesus Christ of Latter-day Saints, but they also have many differences.[81] Today, the guides at the Joseph Smith Historic Site provide a respectful and fascinating glimpse into these crucial locations in Nauvoo.

Mini-Devotional—A Family Home

It is easy to look at these buildings in Nauvoo and forget why they were built. They were not built to be museums or to act as Church office buildings. They were built to be homes for families. As you tour the homes and shops of Historic Nauvoo, try not to think of them as merely historic sites. Try to see them as homes in which families lived and where children played.

- Think about what it would be like if you became famous and your home became a historic site someday. What would you want people to know about how you lived? How would you want them to see your house? How would you want them to act in your house?
- We think of these homes in Historic Nauvoo as holy places. How can you make your home a holy place?

81 See Andrew Bolton and Casey Paul Griffiths, eds., *Restorations: Scholars in Dialogue from Community of Christ and The Church of Jesus Christ of Latter-day Saints* (Provo, UT: Brigham Young University Religious Studies Center, 2022).

Joseph Smith's Red Brick Store

The Joseph Smith Red Brick Store in Nauvoo. Photo by Casey Paul Griffiths.

Significant events at this location:

- The store was built in 1841, demolished in the 1890s, and rebuilt by Community of Christ in 1978–79.
- The Relief Society was organized in the Red Brick Store on March 17, 1842.
- Joseph Smith prepared the translation of the Book of Abraham for publication in this store during March 1842.

- In this store, Joseph Smith received Doctrine and Covenants 127, 129, and 132 and wrote the Wentworth Letter containing what is now the Articles of Faith.
- The first temple endowments were introduced and administered by Joseph Smith on the second floor of the store on May 4, 1842.
- Dry goods stores and Bishop Newel K. Whitney's office were on the first floor. The Assembly Hall and Joseph Smith's office were on the second floor.
- The store served as an economic hub which allowed Nauvoo citizens to make loans and buy city lots. The store also took collections for the construction of the Nauvoo Temple.
- Today, the main floor serves as a museum and includes a general store that sells items similar to those sold in the 1840s.

The city of Nauvoo, where Latter-day Saints began to settle in 1839, quickly grew into an important cultural and economic power in Illinois. Continuous rise in population welcomed business owners of many kinds, including many store owners, bringing the total number of Nauvoo general stores to thirty-five in the 1840s. Among these was Joseph Smith's Red Brick Store, a two-story brick building whose construction began during the fall of 1841[82] and opened for business on January 5, 1842.[83] The main floor was stocked with all kinds of merchandise, providing comforts for Nauvoo citizens, many of whom were too poor to purchase from other stores. Joseph wrote the following about the opening day:

> I rejoice that we have been enabled to do as well as we have, for the hearts of many of the poor brethren and sisters will be made glad, with those comforts which are now within their reach. The store has been filled to overflowing, and, I have stood behind the counter all day, dealing out goods as steady as any clerk you ever saw, to oblige those who were compelled to go without their usual Christmas and New Years dinners for the want of a little sugar, molasses, raisins, &c. &c. and to please myself also,

---

82 Roger D. Launius and F. Mark McKiernan, "Joseph Smith, Jr.'s Red Brick Store," 1985, 11, Americana Collection, BX 8677.73.L371j, L. Tom Perry Special Collections, Harold B. Lee Library, Brigham Young University, Provo, Utah.

83 Joseph Smith, Journal, January 1, 5, 1842, The Joseph Smith Papers, accessed June 30, 2022, https://www.josephsmithpapers.org/paper-summary/journal-december-1841-december-1842/9.

> for I love to wait upon the Saints, and be a servant to all, hoping that I may be exalted in the due time of the Lord.[84]

Interior of the first florr of the Red Brick Store. Photo by Casey Paul Griffiths.

Joseph waited on the Saints in his store, which became an important part of Nauvoo economically, socially, and spiritually.

Joseph Smith described the interior of his store as follows:

> The principal part of the building below, which is ten feet high, is devoted exclusively to shelves and drawers except one door opening back into the space, on the left of which are the cellar and chamber stairs, and on the right the counting rooms; From the space at the top of the chamber stairs opens a door into the large front room of the same size with the one below, the walls lined with counters, covered with reserved goods. . . . In front of the stairs opens the door to my private office, or where I keep the sacred writings, with a window to the south, overlooking the river below, and the opposite shore for a great distance, which, together with the passage of boats in the season thereof, constituted a peculiarly interesting situation, in prospect, from the bustle and confusion of the neighborhood and city, and altogether is a place the Lord is pleased to bless.

84 Joseph Smith History, vol. C-1, addenda, 51, The Joseph Smith Papers, accessed June 9, 2022, https://www.josephsmithpapers.org/paper-summary/history-1838-1856-volume-c-1-addenda/51.

A preserved original daybook gives valuable information about the items sold in the store as well as other business transactions. Not only was the store a place for selling goods, it also acted as a bank, where many asked for loans, and was the location for real estate transactions in Nauvoo. In addition, it housed the offices for Church headquarters and was where the bishop collected tithes, the temple construction crew received their wages, and members subscribed to the Church newspapers. Taxes were collected and city employees were paid at the store as well.

Joseph Smith's generosity often cost him a lot of money as "the prophet's business was built on too much credit and too little cash."[85] When poor Saints could not afford various goods, Joseph often gave it to them for free or a reduced price, allowing them to pay him back later. For instance, James Leech told of when he and his brother-in-law asked Joseph for employment. Joseph hired them to dig a ditch in exchange for provisions. When they finished, Joseph gave each of them two of his largest and best pork or ham as well as a sack of flour. When they expressed that they were willing to do more work for the amount of food, Joseph replied: "If you are satisfied, boys, I am."[86] Such generosity extended to many living in Nauvoo.

Jane Elizabeth Manning, a freeborn Black convert, recalled that Joseph and Emma Smith gave her clothing from the store and a place to stay after an eight-hundred-mile journey to Nauvoo that left her with nearly nothing. Jane had trekked from Connecticut with her mother, four siblings, two in-laws, and her son. She wrote, "When I went there [Nauvoo] I only had two things on me, no shoes nor stockings, wore them all out on the road." She sent her trunk of clothes ahead by water, but they were stolen in St. Louis. "One morning, . . . I had been up to the landing and found all my clothes were gone. Well, I sat there crying. [Joseph] came in and looked around. . . . To Sister Emma, he said, 'go and clothe her up.' Sister Emma did. She got me clothes by the bolt. I had everything."[87]

As further evidence of the Prophet's unprofitable business practices, later on Brigham Young spoke about establishing a similar store in Salt Lake City:

> Why does not our Church keep a store here? Many can answer that question who have lived . . . in Nauvoo. . . . Let me give you a few reasons . . . why Joseph could not keep a store, and be a merchant. . . .

85 Launius and McKiernan, "Red Brick Store," 15–16.

86 "Recollections of the Prophet Joseph Smith," *Juvenile Instructor 27* (March 1, 1892): 152–53.

87 "Joseph Smith, the Prophet," *The Young Woman's Journal* 16, no. 12 (December 1905): 552.

> Joseph goes to New York and buys 20,000 dollars' worth of goods, comes into [Nauvoo] and commences to trade. In comes one of the brethren, "Brother Joseph, let me have a frock pattern for my wife." What if Joseph says, "No, I cannot without the money." The consequence would be, "He is no Prophet." . . . After a while, in comes Bill and sister Susan. Says Bill, "Brother Joseph, I want a shawl, I have not got the money, but I wish you to trust me a week or a fortnight." Well, brother Joseph . . . lets Bill have a shawl. Bill walks off with it and meets a brother. "Well," says he, "what do you think of brother Joseph?" "O he is a first-rate man, and I fully believe he is a Prophet. See here, he has trusted me with this shawl." Richard says, "I think I will go down and see if he won't trust me some." In walks Richard. "Brother Joseph, I want to trade about 20 dollars." "Well," says Joseph "these goods will make the people apostatize; so over they go, they are of less value than the people." Richard gets his goods. Another comes in the same way to make a trade of 25 dollars, and so it goes.[88]

Joseph Smith oversaw the store himself until he realized the time and economic commitment was too much for him alone to bare, and he delegated running the store to someone else.

Nauvoo's Social and Education Center

The Red Brick Store was also Nauvoo's main hub for almost all the social activity in Nauvoo, where members gathered both officially and unofficially. The University of the City of Nauvoo, authorized in the Nauvoo Charter signed December 1840, was organized on February 3, 1841. Though an official campus was never built because of lack of funds, an informal campus emerged, which included the Red Brick Store. It also housed the Masonic Hall, the Seventies Hall, the Concert Hall, and some private residences. The university offered mathematic courses taught by Orson Pratt and language and literature classes taught by Sidney Rigdon. Though there are no records of official degrees granted by the university, there were several honorary degrees granted.[89] Joseph Smith was a huge proponent of the university and declared that it was

88 Richard S. Van Wagoner, ed., *The Complete Discourses of Brigham Young* (Salt Lake City: Smith-Pettit Foundation, 2009), 601.

89 Donald Q. Cannon, "Joseph Smith and the University of Nauvoo" in *Joseph Smith: The Prophet, The Man*, ed. Susan Easton Black and Charles D. Tate Jr. (Provo, UT: Brigham Young University Religious Studies Center, 1993), 287, 292–93.

"necessary for the great work of the last days."[90] He was willing to use his store to further the education of Nauvoo's residents.

For some time, the store's upper assembly room housed school classes for children. Joseph C. Cole, who served as a teacher along with his daughter, taught subjects such as geography, chemistry, reading, writing, and astronomy.[91] Eventually, having a school above the store was troublesome because the students would often disturb the clerks. One of the Prophet's sons, Joseph Smith III, recalled: "As schoolboys we had good reason to remember Doctor Willard Richards [one of the clerks], for often in going down the stairway from the schoolroom we were noisy, which seemed to annoy him considerably. . . . He cautioned us to be more quiet. Doubtless we were annoying as we trampled and jostled, crowing the steps and surging through the door. He especially scolded the larger children. We learned it was better to go quietly than to cause such real distress."[92] After enough complaints from the clerks, in November 1843 Joseph Cole was asked to move his school, though he ignored the request. Finally, months later in February 1844, the Prophet demanded that Joseph move the school to another location because the assembly room was needed for other purposes. The upper room was regularly used, since it was the only place big enough to hold large gatherings, such as debates, dramatic performances, schools, talent shows, political gatherings, and public speeches.

The Red Brick Store also became home to the Nauvoo Masonic Lodge. After considerable effort, on October 15, 1841, the grandmaster of the Illinois Lodge allowed a chapter to be established in Nauvoo. Initially, the Nauvoo Masons met in whatever space they could find, but after Joseph Smith was inducted in March 1942, the Masons met in the upper room of the Red Brick Store. Their chapter quickly became the largest in Illinois, larger than all other chapters in the state combined.[93]

Mini-Devotional—Seek Learning by Study and Faith

Education has always been an important aspect of The Church of Jesus Christ of Latter-day Saints, for in Doctrine and Covenants 93:36 it states that

90 G. Homer Durham, *Joseph Smith: Prophet-Statesman,* (Salt Lake City: Deseret Book, 1944), 90, cited in Cannon, "University of Nauvoo," 286.

91 Launius and McKiernan, "Red Brick Store," 20.

92 Mary Audentia Smith and Bertha Audentia Anderson Hulmes, eds., *Joseph Smith III and the Restoration,* (Independence, MO: Herald House, 1952), 28.

93 Launius and McKiernan, "Red Brick Store," 21, 23, 28.

"the glory of God is intelligence, or, in other words, light and truth." Doctrine and Covenants 88: 118 also commands that we "seek learning even by study and also by faith." Even before the Nauvoo Temple was completed, there were informal classrooms dotting Nauvoo. The University of Nauvoo and other public classes held at the Red Brick Store show that the Saints emphasized education in Nauvoo. The emphasis on education continued as the Saints crossed the plains and settled in Utah. Today, it has continued as the Church establishes schools, universities, seminaries, and institutes.

- How have you learned by study and also by faith?
- What can you do to emphasize education in your life?

Origins of the Relief Society

The second floor of the Red Brick store is where the Relief Society was organized. Photo by Casey Paul Griffiths.

While the Nauvoo Temple was under construction, the women of Nauvoo expressed interest in aiding in its construction by sewing new clothing for the men who worked on the temple. While sewing together, the women discussed the idea of forming a "Ladies' Society" and decided to have Eliza R. Snow write a constitution for such a society and present it to Joseph Smith. When Joseph saw the document, he told the women it was the best he had ever seen; however, he instructed: "Tell the sisters their offering is accepted of the Lord, and he has something better for them than a written constitution. . . . I will organize the women under the priesthood after the pattern of the priesthood."[94]

On March 17, 1842,[95] Joseph Smith organized "a select Society separate from all the evils of the world, choice, virtuou[s] and holy,"[96] stating that the purpose of the Society is "not only to relieve the poor, but to save souls."[97] His wife, Emma Smith, was unanimously voted to be the president, and she chose Elizabeth Ann Whitney and Sarah Cleveland to be her counselors and Eliza Snow to be her secretary.

The name "Female Relief Society of Nauvoo" came about after much consideration by members of the Society. Joseph Smith and John Taylor wanted to include the word *benevolent* in the name, because it was a popular word found in ladies' societies of the time. However, Emma objected, explaining that "the *popularity* of the word benevolent is one great objection—no person can think of a word as associated with public Institutions, without thinking of the Washingtonian Benevolent Society which is one of the most corrupt Institutions of the day. [I] do not wish to have it call[e]d after other societies in the world." Instead, the women were in favor of the term *relief*, though Joseph worried that *relief* suggested "some great calamity—that we intend appropriating on some extraordinary occasions instead of meeting the common occurrences." To this, Emma replied "We are going to do something *extraordinary*—when a boat is stuck on the rapids with a multitude of Mormons on board, we shall consider *that* a loud call for *relief*—we expect extraordinary occasions and pressing calls." With that, the Female Relief Society of Nauvoo was organized.[98]

94 Sarah M. Kimball, "Auto-biography," *Women's Exponent* 12, no. 7 (September 1, 1883): 51.

95 Nauvoo Relief Society, Minute Book, March 17, 1842, The Joseph Smith Papers, accessed June 30, 2022, https://www.josephsmithpapers.org/paper-summary/nauvoo-relief-society-minute-book/29.

96 Joseph Smith, Discourse, March 31, 1842, p. 22, The Joseph Smith Papers, accessed June 30, 2022, https://www.josephsmithpapers.org/paper-summary/discourse-31-march-1842/1.

97 Minutes and Discourse, June 9, 1842, p. 63, The Joseph Smith Papers, accessed June 30, 2022, https://www.josephsmithpapers.org/paper-summary/minutes-and-discourse-9-june-1842/3.

98 Nauvoo Relief Society, Minute Book, March 17, 1842, p. 8, 11–13, The Joseph Smith Papers, accessed June 30, 2022, https://www.josephsmithpapers.org/paper-summary/nauvoo-relief-society-minute-book/31.

Mini-Devotional—Turning the Key

On March 17, 1842, when the Female Relief Society of Nauvoo was organized, Joseph Smith declared: "I now turn the key to you in the name of God and this Society shall rejoice and knowledge and intelligence shall flow down from this time—this is the beginning of better days."[99] We might ask what kind of key the prophet was referring to. Elder M. Russell Ballard defines: "Those who have priesthood keys . . . literally make it possible for all who serve faithfully under their direction to exercise priesthood authority and have access to priesthood power."[100]

Joseph Smith was turning a priesthood key so that women could also exercise priesthood authority and have access to priesthood power. In October 2019, President Russell M. Nelson declared:

> Every woman and every man who makes covenants with God and keeps those covenants, and who participates worthily in priesthood ordinances, has direct access to the power of God. Those who are endowed in the house of the Lord receive a gift of God's priesthood power by virtue of their covenant, along with a gift of knowledge to know how to draw upon that power.
>
> The heavens are just as open to *women* who are endowed with God's power flowing from their priesthood covenants as they are to men who bear the priesthood.[101]

Elder Dallin H. Oaks explained how women can also exercise priesthood authority: "We are not accustomed to speaking of women having the authority of the priesthood in their Church callings, but what other authority can it be? . . .Whoever functions in an office or calling received from one who holds priesthood keys exercises priesthood authority in performing her or his

---

99 Joseph Smith, Discourse, April 28, 1842, p. [40], The Joseph Smith Papers, accessed July 25, 2022, https://www.josephsmithpapers.org/paper-summary/discourse-28-april-1842/6.

100 M. Russell Ballard, "Men and Women and Priesthood Power," *Ensign*, September 2014, https://www.churchofjesuschrist.org/study/ensign/2014/09/men-and-women-and-priesthood-power?lang=eng.

101 Russell M. Nelson, "Spiritual Treasures," *Liahona*, November 2019, https://www.churchofjesuschrist.org/study/liahona/2019/11/36nelson?lang=eng.

assigned duties. Priesthood authority, therefore, is given to both women and men, based on their callings."[102]

- How have you as a Relief Society sister exercised priesthood authority?
- How do men and women both access priesthood power?

The Nauvoo Relief Society in the Red Brick Store

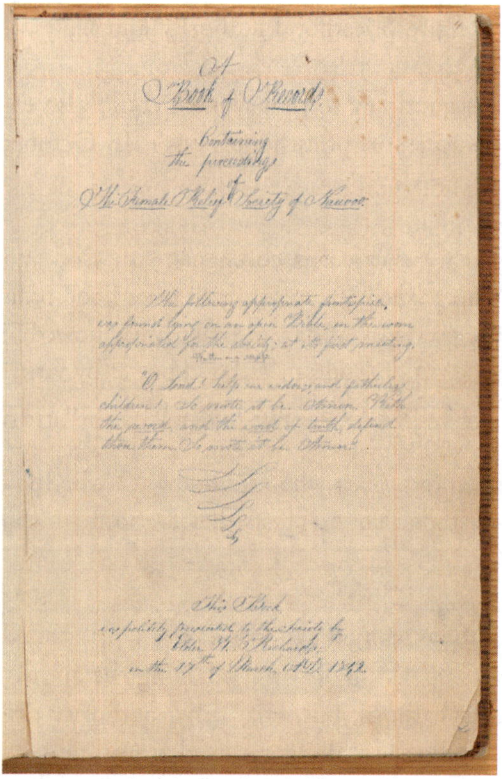

A Book of Records Containing the proceedings of The Female Relief Society of Nauvoo

Minute book of the Female Relief Society of Nauvoo. Courtesy Joseph Smith Papers.

True to her word, Emma Smith led the Relief Society housed in the Red Brick Store to do extraordinary things. Members of the Relief Society ensured that the women they served received relief: "Motherless children found homes, a bushel of wheat donated weekly went to feed a needy family, two widows with young children had money to pay for their schooling, elderly women's gardens were plowed, shoes appeared in poor homes, and a family without bedding received blankets."[103]

Records of the early days of the Relief Society can be credited to Eliza Snow's minute book which she kept from the first day the Relief Society was organized. Joseph Smith encouraged her and other women to be diligent about keeping records: "The minutes of your meetings will be precedents for you to act upon—your Constitutio[n] and law." The women kept a careful record of their thirty-three total meetings, creating a

102 Dallin H. Oaks, "The Keys and Authority of the Priesthood," *Ensign*, May 2014, https://www.churchofjesuschrist.org/study/ensign/2014/05/priesthood-session/the-keys-and-authority-of-the-priesthood.html?lang=eng.

103 Linda King Newell and Valeen Tippets Avery, *Mormon Enigma: Emma Hale Smith* (Urbana: University of Illinois Press, 1994), 117.

book with 127 pages of meeting minutes, notes, membership names, and records of donations. Nearly two years after the Relief Society was founded, the women met for the last time on March 16, 1844, before the Saints were driven from Nauvoo because of Church-wide persecution.[104] When an organized Relief Society was refounded twenty-two years later in the Salt Lake Valley, Eliza used the minute book to teach Relief Society members and leaders—sometimes reading directly from it—thus fulfilling Joseph's statement years earlier that her minutes would become precedent for others to act upon.

The founding of the Relief Society in the Red Brick Store is significant because as Joseph Smith declared, "The Church was never perfectly organized until the women were thus organized."[105] Since its establishment in 1842, the Relief Society has provided physical and spiritual aid to thousands of people across the globe, fulfilling their simple purpose of relieving the poor and saving souls. Incredibly, the organization has withstood the test of time. As General Relief Society President Belle Spafford (1945–1974) observed, "Relief Society has been just as constant in its purpose as truth is constant. The purposes that were important for a handful of women in Nauvoo are still important to women world-wide. That is the miracle of Relief Society."[106]

Mini-Devotional—By Small and Simple Things

Anciently, Alma taught that "by small and simple things are great things brought to pass" (Alma 37:6). The establishment of the Relief Society is evidence that Alma's words are true. The Society began in the upper room of the Red Brick Store with only 20 women present; two months later there were 600 members; two years later there were 1,300 members; nearly two hundred years

---

104 Nauvoo Relief Society, Minute Book, pp. 8, 125, The Joseph Smith Papers, accessed June 30, 2022, https://www.josephsmithpapers.org/paper-summary/nauvoo-relief-society-minute-book/31.

105 Kimball, "Auto-biography," 51.

106 "Reaching Every Facet of a Woman's Life: A Conversation with Belle S. Spafford, Relief Society General President," *Ensign*, June 1974, https://www.churchofjesuschrist.org/study/ensign/1974/06/reaching-every-facet-of-a-womans-life?lang=eng.

later, there are more than 7.1 million members worldwide,[107] making the Relief Society the oldest and largest women's organization in the world.[108]

Latter-day Saints see the establishment of the Relief Society not just as the beginning of better days for women in Nauvoo, Illinois, but for all women. In July 1848, just six years after the Society was founded, the first women's rights convention was held in Seneca Falls, New York, beginning a seventy-two-year campaign for woman suffrage. President George Albert Smith declared, "When the Prophet Joseph Smith turned the key for the emancipation of womankind, it was turned for all the women of the world, and from generation to generation the number of women who can enjoy the blessings of religious liberty and civil liberty has been increasing."[109]

- How in your life has the Lord used small and simple things to bring to pass great things?
- How can you use the small and simple things that the Lord provides to bring to pass great things?
- How has the key that Joseph Smith turned blessed all women everywhere?

Translation of the Book of Abraham and Other Revelations

Papyri fragments associated with the Book of Abraham. Courtesy Joseph Smith Papers.

107 Church of Jesus Christ of Latter-day Saints, "Relief Society in Action, March 20, 2020," March 20, 2020, The Church of Jesus Christ of Latter-day Saints: Newsroom, https://newsroom.churchofjesuschrist.org/article/relief-society-in-action-march-20-2020.

108 Sheri L. Dew, "Something Extraordinary," *Ensign*, March 1992, 52, https://www.churchofjesuschrist.org/study/ensign/1992/03/something-extraordinary?lang=eng.

109 George Albert Smith, "Address to the Members of the Relief Society," *Relief Society Magazine,* December 1945, 717.

Joseph Smith prepared the Book of Abraham for publication in his Red Brick Store. Tradition states that the record of Abraham—a revered prophet in three great religions—was written on ancient Egyptian papyri that Joseph Smith had bought. The Book of Abraham shares a glimpse of Abraham's life and the sacrifices that he had to make: "Abraham wrote about his life, covenant, vision, and other experiences with God" and gifted us with a book that offers important lessons that transcend time. The papyri were passed to several people before it finally reached the hands of Joseph Smith who used it to translate the Book of Abraham.[110]

Somehow, the papyri that Abraham owned made its way to Egypt—whether it was there during the time of Abraham, or his descendants took it to Egypt, we do not know. Eventually, a part of this papyri got into the hands of an Egyptian priest named Hor, who "would have been among the most educated of Egypt's priests and thus one of the most knowledgeable people in the world." When he died, Hor was buried with religious texts that were important to him, which makes it likely that the papyri found in his tomb contained the Book of Abraham. There the papyri stayed for thousands of years.

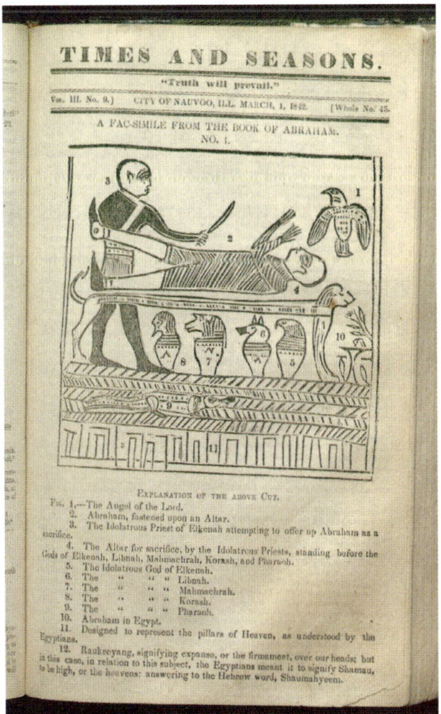

TIMES AND SEASONS.

"Truth will prevail."

Vol. III. No. 9.] CITY OF NAUVOO, ILL. MARCH, 1, 1842. [Whole No. 45.

A FAC-SIMILE FROM THE BOOK OF ABRAHAM.
NO. 1.

EXPLANATION OF THE ABOVE CUT.

FIG. 1.—The Angel of the Lord.
2. Abraham, fastened upon an Altar.
3. The Idolatrous Priest of Elkenah attempting to offer up Abraham as a sacrifice.
4. The Altar for sacrifice, by the Idolatrous Priests, standing before the Gods of Elkenah, Libnah, Mahmachrah, Korash, and Pharaoh.
5. The Idolatrous God of Elkenah.
6. The " " " Libnah.
7. The " " " Mahmachrah.
8. The " " " Korash.
9. The " " " Pharaoh.
10. Abraham in Egypt.
11. Designed to represent the pillars of Heaven, as understood by the Egyptians.
12. Raukeeyang, signifying expanse, or the firmament, over our heads; but in this case, in relation to this subject, the Egyptians meant it to signify Shamau, to be high, or the heavens: answering to the Hebrew word, Shaumahyeem.

The Book of Abraham was first printed in the Times and Seasons. Courtesy Joseph Smith Papers.

Antonio Lebolo was an Italian antiquities dealer that pursued a hobby of discovering and exporting Egypt's ancient treasures. He or someone who worked for him discovered a cache of mummies that included the papyri once owned by Hor. Antonio sent it to the United States where it came into the possession of Michael Chandler, who claimed to be Antonio's nephew. Michael traveled throughout the United States exhibiting the mummies and eventually made his way to Kirtland, Ohio, in July 1835. Joseph Smith visited with Michael, asked to study the papyri more closely, and translated several pages that day. Michael, impressed by Joseph's work and enthusiasm, subsequently sold the

110 Kerry Muhlestein, interview by Afton Beard, transcription in the possession of author, June 28, 2022.

collection of mummies and papyri to Joseph. Though his work was often interrupted by other responsibilities and the constant threat of mob violence, Joseph continued to translate the papyri when he had the time. After being driven out of Ohio and Missouri, the Saints finally settled in Illinois where Joseph finished his translation.

When the Prophet opened up his Red Brick Store, he used the office at the top of the stairs to work on the papyri, which many people reported viewing. Eventually, what we have of the Book of Abraham and Facsimiles 1–3 was published in *Times and Seasons* in March 1842. Though Joseph Smith intended to translate and publish more of the Book of Abraham, he was never able to do so.[111] The location of the Red Brick Store was significant because it allowed Joseph Smith to work on publishing the translation with minimal interruption. Book of Abraham expert Kerry Muhlestein observed, "Joseph Smith always felt so pressed for time. . . . I don't think it's a coincidence that it's not long after he has an actual office that is close to his home and close to the printing press that suddenly he can work on it. I think it's partially because he has an office where he can work, close to his home, and close to the printing press, so that it is not hard for him to squeeze in the time to do this."[112] The proximity of these important buildings in Nauvoo was what helped Joseph translate as much as he did of the papyri. Because of this arrangement, Church members today have access to the revealed truths found in the Book of Abraham.

The Red Brick Store was also the place where Joseph Smith wrote the Wentworth Letter, which contains what is now identified as the Articles of Faith. The letter, written for John Wentworth, was previously published in *Times and Seasons* on March 1, 1842. This letter contained the first account of the First Vision that Joseph himself published. Along with the account, it also contained Joseph's testimony of the gospel, a brief Church history, and a declaration of the Church's future.[113] Joseph also received several revelations in Nauvoo, and they were written down while in the Red Brick Store. These revelations are now found in the Doctrine and Covenants, including section 127, which provides more instruction on baptisms for the dead; section 129, which details how to discern between a good and evil spirit; and section 132, which reveals the new and everlasting covenant of marriage.

---

111 Kerry Muhlestein, *Let's Talk about the Book of Abraham* (Salt Lake City: Deseret Book, 2022), 5, 9, 13, 16, 24, 26–34.

112 Muhlestein, interview.

113 "The Wentworth Letter," *Teachings of Presidents of the Church: Joseph Smith*, https://www.churchofjesuschrist.org/study/manual/teachings-joseph-smith/chapter-38?lang=eng.

The Red Brick Store Becomes a Temple

Visualization of interior of the Red Brick Store arranged to perform the first endowments. Courtesy Doctrine and Covenants Central.

Before the Nauvoo Temple was completed, the Red Brick Store's upper rooms also served as a temporary location for performing sacred temple ordinances. Brigham Young recalled that Joseph Smith, along with five or six other people, labored diligently to prepare the room for the ordinances, decorating the room in such a way to resemble "the interior of a temple as much as the circumstances would permit."[114] On May 4. 1842, several Church leaders gathered to receive their temple endowments with Joseph officiating.[115] Joseph wrote that he instructed the men present "in the principles and order of the Priesthood . . . and so on to the highest order of the Melchizedek Priesthood. . . . And the communications I made to this Council were of things spiritual and to be received only by the spiritual minded: and there is nothing made known to these men, but what will be made known to all the Saints of the last days, so soon as they were prepared to receive, and a proper place is prepared

114 Lucius N. Scovil, *Deseret News: Semi-Weekly*, February 15, 1884, p. 2, as cited in Launius and McKiernan, "Red Brick Store," 29; see also L. John Nuttall, *The Journal of L John Nuttall*, February 7, 1877, https://archive.org/details/TheJournalOfLJohnNuttall/page/n3/mode/2up.

115 Launius and McKiernan, "Red Brick Store," 29.

to communicate them."[116] Later, Joseph endowed more than sixty people,[117] including Joseph's personal secretary, William Clayton, who asked the Prophet for the blessings of the endowment ordinance. Clayton wrote of his experience: "This is one of the greatest favors ever conferred on me and for which I feel grateful. May the God of Joseph preserve me & mine house to walk in the paths of righteousness all the days of my life & oh that I may never sin against him or displease him For thou oh God knowest my desire to do right that I may have eternal life."[118]

Mini-Devotional—Temple Blessings

When Joseph Smith was officiating temple ordinances in the Red Brick Store, he prophesied that "there is nothing made known to these men, but what will be made known to all the Saints of the last days, so soon as they were prepared to receive, and a proper place is prepared to communicate them."[119] Latter-day Saints of our generation have prepared to receive all that was given first in the Red Brick Store. Ponder your own feelings about the temple, about your experience as you received your own endowment, and about your experiences as you have attended the temple afterwards.

- How do you think you might have felt if you had been among the first who received their endowments in the Red Brick Store?
- Why are temples a source of joy?
- How can you demonstrate your gratitude to the Lord for temples?

116 "History of Joseph Smith," *Millennial Star* 19, no. 25 (June 20, 1857): 391–92.

117 Donald Q. Cannon, "Illinois," in *Ohio and Illinois, Sacred Places: A Comprehensive Guide to Early LDS Historical Sites*, ed. LaMar C. Berrett (Salt Lake City: Deseret Book Company, 2002), 3:41.

118 William Clayton, Journal, February 3, 1844, quoted in James B. Allen, *Trials of Discipleship: The Story of William B. Clayton, a Mormon* (Urbana: University of Illinois Press, 1987), 114, https:// archive.org/details/WilliamClaytonJournal/page/n137/mode/2up.

119 "History of Joseph Smith," *Millennial Star* 19, no. 25 (June 20, 1857): 391–92.

Deterioration and Reconstruction

Front view of the Red Brick Store. Photo by Casey Paul Griffiths.

After the Prophet Joseph Smith's death, his wife, Emma Smith, inherited ownership of the Red Brick Store. To increase her financial stability, she extended an offer to rent out the Red Brick Store to her friend, Joseph Heywood,[120] though whether Heywood accepted the offer or not is unknown. Regardless, by 1846, the store was officially closed.

In 1848, Emma Smith and her second husband, Lewis Bidamon, made plans for fifteen-year-old Joseph Smith III to reopen the Red Brick Store. Earlier that year, Joseph III had received a job as a clerk at a nearby store. When the Emma and Lewis determined that Joseph III was ready to take care of the Red Brick Store on his own, they invested $2,000 to renovate the store and buy new supplies. Unfortunately, the venture was unsuccessful and did not last more than a year.

For the next decade, little is known of what happened to the store, but in 1860, the store was used for some time as the meeting place for an official branch of the Reorganized Church of Jesus Christ of Latter Day Saints, now known as Community of Christ. The branch, commonly called the "Olive Branch," was led by Joseph Smith III and his brothers until they moved away, after which attendance slowly decreased until the branch was disbanded in 1875.[121]

After Emma's death, the store was deeded to her sons and the building fell into decline. After years of disuse, the Smith family allowed the building to be torn down in 1890, and they sold the bricks to be used in the construction

120 Scott C. Esplin, *Return to the City of Joseph: Modern Mormonism's Contest for the Soul of Nauvoo* (Urbana: University of Illinois Press, 2018), 33.

121 Launius and McKiernan, "Red Brick Store," 33–35, 38.

of other buildings in Nauvoo, leaving nothing but the foundation remaining. In 1919, Frederick M. Smith, son of Joseph Smith III and leader of the Reorganized Church, gave what was left of the store to his church, whose goal was to eventually rebuild it.

In 1959, Kenneth E. Stobaugh became the leader of the Joseph Smith Historic Center, an organization within Community of Christ who were tasked to rebuild historic Nauvoo. He, working with F. Mark McKiernan, asked the University of Missouri to perform summer archeological digs in Nauvoo beginning in 1970. Attention fell on the Red Brick Store after McKiernan discovered a listing for the store's original daybook, located in the Masonic Library in Cedar Rapids, Iowa. In 1972, the University of Missouri performed an archaeological dig at the store, finding many items that would be useful in rebuilding the store and Nauvoo. Their dig provided them with information about the size of the store, measurements of the rooms, placement of shelves, color of the interior, and size and type of bricks used.[122]

At the same time, Stobaugh and McKiernan searched for photographic evidence of the Red Brick Store to determine exactly how it looked during its time under Joseph Smith's care. They found three photographs and one painting, which gave them visuals of each side of the store. A few years later in 1977, when presented with the idea for a reconstruction project to celebrate the Reorganized Church's sesquicentennial anniversary in 1980, McKiernan expressed the idea of reconstructing the Red Brick Store because of its significant to the Reorganized Church, which "contained [Smith's] office and was the location of the founding of the Women's Relief Society."[123] In order for the project to succeed, the Church needed to raise $300,000 dollars in three years to fund the project. The solution was to ask twelve people, the "Friends of the Red Brick Store," to donate to the effort. Each Friend donated $30,000.

Construction efforts included rebuilding the foundation with the original stones and painting the interior the red color found on the original plaster, all so that the Red Brick Store was reconstructed with as much historical accuracy as possible. When putting the glass windows in the store, McKiernan bought glass to match the shimmery poured glass of 1842, but the windows ended up looking distorted. Replacing the windows accurately would require an additional $1,800 for them to be exported from France. Irwan Fender, leader of the

---

122 Launius and McKiernan, "Red Brick Store," 33–44; Esplin, *Return to the City of Joseph*, 37–41, 111.

123 McKiernan to Booth, February 9, 1977, in McKiernan, "Historic Site," 122, cited in Esplin, *Return to the City of Joseph*, 110.

construction company for the project, purchased the windows himself—ensuring historical accuracy. In another incident, a construction crew member found a key that had been used at the store. The committee searched for an authentic lock that fit the key but could not find anything that worked. Irwan then contracted with a company to recreate a lock that resembled the one used during the store's heyday and placed it on the door of the store.

The new Red Brick Store opened for visitors in 1980, reconstructed with striking resemblance to the original. As intended, the interior walls were reproduced in the red color that gave the store its name, and the store was furnished with reproductions of items sold in the store, based on the daybook. Community of Christ even included the original desk used by Bishop Newel K. Whitney.[124]

Although Community of Christ owned the property, they generously allowed The Church of Jesus Christ of Latter-day Saints to contribute to commemorating the establishment of the Relief Society. With permission, the Church put an eight-foot-tall memorial next to the store to celebrate the founding of the Relief Society. Eventually, because of some confusion about the two sects, the monument was removed.[125] In another instance, Community of Christ allowed Relief Society members from the Nauvoo Ward of The Church of Jesus Christ of Latter-day Saints to meet in the upper room of the building on March 17, 1992, to celebrate the 150th anniversary of the founding of the Relief Society.[126]

"The gift of the Red Brick Store . . . is to all people, especially those who trace their religious heritage to Joseph Smith, Jr., and the movement he founded," wrote C. Eugen Austin Sr., member of Community of Christ's Council of Twelve Apostles (1976–1994) and chairman of the executive committee for the reconstruction of the Red Brick Store. Joseph Smith and his Red Brick Store left behind a powerful legacy, including the establishment of the Relief Society, the beginning of the temple endowment, and the location of sacred translations and revelations, all of which are continually appreciated today by the many visitors who experience the reconstructed Red Brick Store.

---

124 Launius and McKiernan, "Red Brick Store," 46–48; Esplin, *Return to the City of Joseph*, 112.

125 Esplin, *Return to the City of Joseph*, 54–56.

126 Sheridan R. Sheffield, "Relief Society Birthday Noted at Site of Origin," *Church News*, March 28, 1992, https://www.thechurchnews.com/archives/1992-03-28/relief-society-birthday-noted-at-site-of-origin-145086.

The Nauvoo Temple and Related Sites

The rebuilt Nauvoo Temple with the rebuilt Edward Hunter home in the foreground.. Photo by Casey Paul Griffiths.

The heart of the city of Nauvoo was the temple. Located on a bluff that rose above the city, this massive edifice was the focal point of the lives and labors of the people of Nauvoo. The commandment to build the temple came in 1841, when in a revelation given to Joseph Smith the Lord declared, "I command you, all ye my saints, to build a house unto me" (Doctrine and Covenants 124:31). From that time on, the Saints devoted their resources and time to the construction of the temple. The temple was not completed before the deaths of Joseph and Hyrum Smith in June 1844, but the Saints pressed on, performing ordinances in the temple even as it was still under construction. The temple was finally completed in May 1846, after many Saints had already begun their exodus from the city. Soon the rest of the Saints left the temple behind to follow their Prophet into the wilderness and later learned of the temple's destruction by arson.

Today, the Nauvoo Illinois Temple has been rebuilt and serves as both a monument to the early Saints and a functional temple, where sacred ordinances are carried out. Visitors to Nauvoo can have the opportunity to perform baptisms for the dead, endowments, and other ceremonies in the very place where the early Saints made those same covenants. The story of the building of the temple is complex and interweaves itself among the stories of the people of Nauvoo. Close to the temple are several historic homes that belonged to Church members who lived in Nauvoo and assisted in different ways in the construction of the temple. Each of these homes shows visitors the importance of the temple in the lives of the Nauvoo Saints and explains why temples are so sacred to the Saints of our time.

The Nauvoo Temple

Front view of the Nauvoo Temple. Photo by Casey Paul Griffiths.

Significant events at this location:

- Construction on the original Nauvoo Temple took place from 1840 to 1846.
- Before leaving Nauvoo, over six thousand Saints received their blessings inside the temple.
- The original Nauvoo Temple was dedicated on May 1, 1846.
- The temple was burned by an unknown arsonist in 1848, and the surviving structure was destroyed by a tornado in 1850.
- In 1999 President Gordon B. Hinckley announced that the Nauvoo Illinois Temple would be rebuilt in the same location as the original building.
- The rebuilt Nauvoo Illinois Temple was dedicated in June 2002.

Like the previous cities of Kirtland, Independence, and Far West built by the Saints, the city of Nauvoo was centered on the house of the Lord. Land for the Nauvoo Temple was secured in 1840, and plans were laid for a much larger and more impressive structure than the previous temples planned and built by the Saints. The construction of the temple was a consecrated effort by all the Church members in Nauvoo. Men, women, and children all worked to finish the building. The history of this time records, "Scores of brethren in this city have offered to board one and two laborers each, till the Temple is completed; many have volunteered to labor continually, and the brethren generally are giving one tenth part of their time, or one tenth part of their income, according to circumstances; while those sisters who can do nothing more, are knitting socks and mittens and preparing garments for the laborers, so that they may be made as comfortable as possible during the coming winter."[127]

The design for the temple called for a three-story gray limestone edifice, 128 feet in length and 88 feet in width. The pattern for the temple also featured ornamental moonstones, sunstones, and five-pointed starstones carved into the exterior of thirty pilasters. A clock tower dome with a gilded weathervane and an angel was drawn. The use of sunstones, moonstones, and starstones suggests to most modern Latter-day Saints the three degrees of glory found in the afterlife, but statements left by the early Saints suggest a different symbolism for these celestial bodies. Wandle Mace, who served as the foreman for the

127 Joseph Smith History, 1838–1856, vol. C-1 [2 November 1838–31 July 1842], 1236, JSP.

framework done on the Nauvoo Temple, drew a direct connection between the sun, moon, and stars and the visions of John in the book of Revelation, particularly the vision of the Church of God found in Revelation 12. The passage in Revelation describes "a woman clothed with the sun, and the moon under her feet, and upon her head a crown of twelve stars" (Revelation 12:1). The Joseph Smith Translation of Revelation 12 identifies the woman as "the church of God" (Joseph Smith Translation, Revelation 12:1–17, JST appendix).

Details of the Sunstones and Starstones on the rebuilt Nauvoo Temple. Photo by Casey Paul Griffiths.

Mace connected the image of this woman in John's revelation to the symbolism of the temple, stating, "The order of architecture [on the Nauvoo Temple] was unlike anything in existence; it was purely original; being a representation of the Church, the Bride, the Lamb's wife. John the Revelator, in the 12th chapter [and] first verse of [the book of Revelation] says, 'And there appeared a great wonder in heaven; a woman clothed with the sun, and the moon under her feet, and upon her head a crown of twelve stars.' This is portrayed in the beautifully cut stone of this grand temple."[128]

The five-pointed stars, many of them inverted, which decorate the temple are also tied to the book of Revelation. When the Logan Utah Temple was dedicated, an article published by the Church explained that the inverted, five-pointed stars were a symbol of "the star of the morning," a title given to Jesus Christ in the New Testament (Revelation 22:16).[129] Other commentators have suggested that the inverted stars with their five points symbolize the five wounds Jesus received during his Crucifixion. Inverted, five-point stars are found in numerous Christian buildings dating back to hundreds of years before the construction of the Nauvoo Temple. Large, inverted stars were featured in Notre Dame Amiens Cathedral in France and in the Marketirche Church in Germany. The inverted star was also an important symbol in the

128 Wandle Mace, autobiography, n.d., 207, L. Tom Perry Special Collections Library, Brigham Young University, Provo, Utah.

129 *Deseret Evening News*, August 20, 1880, p. 3.

early American republic. It was found on various early versions of the American flag, including the famous Star-Spangled Banner that flew over Fort McKinley in the War of 1812. A five-point, inverted star is still featured on the Medal of Honor, the highest award given in the United States military.[130]

The rich symbolism found on the exterior of the temple was only possible because of the consecrated workers who labored on the structure. Faithful volunteers tithed by giving one day in ten to cut and haul limestone blocks to the temple site. Even Joseph Smith was part of the workforce for the temple. Byrum Bybee, one of the temple volunteers, recalled when he "hitched his team to his wagon and with his son had gone to the quarry to load a large stone into the wagon" and "their wagon became stuck in a mud hole." Joseph Smith "waded in mud halfway to his knees and [got] his shoulder covered with mud to help" Byrum get his wagon free.[131] Another worker, Luman Shurtliff, wrote, "We labored ten hours a day and got something to take to our families for supper and breakfast. . . . I mention this not to find fault or to complain, but to let my children know how the temple of Nauvoo was built, and how their parents as well as hundreds of others suffered to lay a foundation on which they could build and be accepted of God."[132]

While some workers cut limestone for the temple, others traveled to Wisconsin to cut lumber needed for the temple. Women in Nauvoo labored by making clothing for the temple workers, collecting pennies to purchase building supplies, and bartering household goods to provide further materials. "Every talent and exertion [was] peculiarly needed for the erection of the Temple," Luman Shurtliff recalled.[133] Every worker on the temple saw it as their legacy. Wandle Mace remembered, "Men were as thick as blackbirds busily engaged upon the various portions" of the temple.[134] No one who was willing and able was turned away, even when they lacked tools. From the baptismal font resting on twelve carved oxen to the tower with the gold-leaf weathervane (also borrowing symbolism from the book of Revelation, representing "another angel flying in the midst of heaven" [Revelation 14:6]), all parts of the temple

130 "History of the Nauvoo Temple Star Windows," Temple House Gallery, https://templehousegallery.com/nauvoo-temple-star-window-history/.

131 T. Edgar Lyon, "Recollections of 'Old Nauvooers' Memories from Oral History," *BYU Studies* 18 (Winter 1978): 148.

132 Luman Shurtliff, autobiography, 1807–1884, Church History Library, Salt Lake City.

133 Maureen Ursenbach, "Eliza R. Snow's Journal," *BYU Studies* 15 (Summer 1975): 405–6.

134 Wandle Mace, autobiography, 1809–1890, Church History Library, Salt Lake City.

were a labor of love. The Saints of Nauvoo wanted their temple to glorify God and stand as a testimony of their faith in Jesus Christ.

The death of Joseph and Hyrum Smith in June 1844 did not halt construction on the temple. It continued steadily, with milestones along the way. On May 24, 1845, Church members watched as the capstone on the temple was put in place by Brigham Young. Speaking to the assembled crowd, Brigham said, "The last stone is now laid upon the temple, and I pray the Almighty, in the name of Jesus, to defend us in this place, and sustain us until the temple is finished." The assembled Saints shouted, "Hosanna! Hosanna! Hosanna! to God and the Lamb, amen! amen! and amen!"[135] Men and women wept to see their temple nearly completed. For Brigham Young, that day seemed "like a foretaste of celestial enjoyment and Millennial glory."[136]

Sunstones, Star Windows, and Starstones on the Nauvoo Temple. Photo by Casey Paul Griffiths.

But even as they continued building the temple, the Saints knew they would eventually have to abandon it. Joseph Smith had prophesied that the Saints would "suffer much affliction and be driven to the Rocky Mountains."[137]

135 Joseph Smith, *History of the Church*, 6:417–18.

136 Brigham Young, quoted in Arrington and Bitton, *The Mormon Experience: A History of the Latter-day Saints*, 65.

137 Smith, *History of the Church*, 5:85.

Even while work on the temple continued, Brigham Young began to urge the Saints to prepare to leave the city. In the fall of 1845, Nauvoo became "one vast mechanic shop, as nearly every family was engaged in making wagons."[138] While the Saints prepared to depart, they also raced to finish the temple to begin receiving their endowments and sealings. The attic of the Nauvoo Temple was completed in November 1845, and the Saints immediately began to receive their endowments. The temple was operating around the clock to ensure that all the Saints who desired and were worthy could receive their blessings. Temple records indicate that over six thousand Saints received the ordinances of the temple before they departed from the city.[139]

View of the Nauvoo Temple from the William and Caroline Weeks home. Photo by Casey Paul Griffiths.

With the temple's primary purpose accomplished, Brigham Young and the Twelve made the decision to sell the temple to raise funds to assist the needy Saints departing for the West. While a few groups showed mild interest in purchasing the structure, ultimately the Church abandoned this plan. On October 9, 1848, a fire gutted the temple. With the Saints gone, a local historian described the scene:

138 Edward Tullidge, *The Women of Mormondom*, 21.

139 "The Nauvoo Temple: Destruction and Rebirth," Church History, https://history.churchofjesuschrist.org/content/museum/museum-treasures-nauvoo-temple-in-ruins-lithograph?lang=eng.

> About 3 o'clock (in the morning) fire was discovered in the cupola. It had made but little headway when first seen, but spread rapidly, and in a very short period the lofty spire was a mass of flame, shooting high in the air, and illuminating a wide extent of country. It was seen for miles away. The citizens gathered around, but nothing could be done to save the structure. It was entirely of wood except the walls, and nothing could have stopped the progress of the flames. In two hours, and before the sun dawned upon the earth, the proud structure, reared at so much cost—an anomaly in architecture, and a monument of religious zeal—stood with four blackened and smoking walls only remaining.[140]

In 1849 a communal group from France called the Icarians purchased the charred remains of the temple, hoping to renovate it to use as a school. Before they could begin work, a tornado ripped through Nauvoo on May 27, 1850, virtually destroying the remains of the temple. A local newspaper recorded, "There now remains nothing of the gigantic work of the Mormons, except the west face."[141]

This model of the interior of the rebuilt Nauvoo Temple is found in the Latter-day Saints Visitor Center.. Photo by Casey Paul Griffiths.

140 "The Nauvoo Temple: Destruction and Rebirth," Church History.
141 "The Nauvoo Temple: Destruction and Rebirth," Church History.

In time, the remains of the original temple were completely dismantled and used in a number of other structures in Nauvoo. In 1937 the Church began acquiring the land the temple was built on, eventually purchasing all of it. The location of the temple became a site of pilgrimage for Saints, with thousands visiting it every year. At the April 1999 general conference, President Gordon B. Hinckley announced plans to reconstruct the temple.[142] Over the next few years, the temple was lovingly recreated as an exact replica to the original Nauvoo Temple on the outside, save a modern depiction of the angel on the spire. Much of the interior mirrored the original temple as well, though it was given a modern set of endowment and sealing rooms, where the original temple only had an attic for those ordinances.

President Boyd K. Packer commented on the symbolism of the temple's reconstruction, stating, "The temple was destroyed and burned, and the stones of the temple were scattered like the bones had been cremated, and the temple, in effect, was dead. . . . So the temple died. But now, this day, it has come to a resurrection. The Temple stands here again."[143] President Hinckley saw the restoration of the temple as a symbol of the sacrifices of the early Saints:

> Today, facing west, on the high bluff overlooking the city of Nauvoo, thence across the Mississippi, and over the plains of Iowa, there stands Joseph's temple, a magnificent house of God. Here in the Salt Lake Valley, facing east to that beautiful temple in Nauvoo, stands Brigham's temple, the Salt Lake Temple. They look toward one another as bookends between which there are volumes that speak of the suffering, the sorrow, the sacrifice, even the deaths of thousands who made the long journey from the Mississippi River to the valley of the Great Salt Lake.[144]

Today, a majestic temple still stands as sentinel over the city of Nauvoo. The work the early Saints engaged in on that spot is still carried out by Saints today who serve within the temple's sacred walls. The temple is by far the most striking structure in Nauvoo. And just down the hill from the temple stand several homes of people who played a vital role in the construction, life, and rebirth of the Nauvoo Temple.

142 Gordon B. Hinckley, *Conference Report*, April 1999.

143 Robert Freeman, "Nauvoo Temple Milestones," *Ensign,* July 2002, 10.

144 Hinckley, "O That I Were an Angel, and Could Have the Wish of My Heart," October 2002, General Conference.

William and Caroline Weeks Home

The William and Caroline Weeks Home. Photo by Casey Paul Griffiths.

Significant events at this location:

- William Weeks was chosen as the architect of the Nauvoo Temple shortly after its construction was announced.
- William Weeks worked closely with Joseph Smith on the design and plans of the temple.
- The Weeks family played a critical role not only in the construction of the original temple but also in the reconstruction of the temple in the twenty-first century.

Located near the corner of Young and Partridge Streets stands the restored home of William Weeks, the architect of the Nauvoo Temple. William was born in 1813 in Martha's Vineyard and was raised in the Quaker faith.

He later joined the Church while working in the southern United States. He was among the Saints who became refugees when they were driven out of Missouri. While the Saints were regrouping in Quincy, Illinois, William married Caroline Allen on June 11, 1839. In August 1840, Joseph Smith announced at Nauvoo, "The time has now come, when it is necessary to erect a house of prayer, a house of order, a house for the worship of our God, where the ordinances can be attended to agreeably to His divine will."[145]

A competition was held to determine who would serve as the architect of the temple, and William's plans were chosen. A relative of William's recalled that "several architects presented their plans, but none seemed to suit [Joseph] Smith. So when [William] went in and showed his plans, Joseph Smith grabbed him, hugged him and said 'you are the man I want.'"[146] Copies of William's plans for the temple are on display in the Weeks home and show what a superb architect he was.

William became the architect of the temple, but his plans were subject to approval by the Prophet. In a revelation given to Joseph, the Lord declared, "I will show unto my servant Joseph all things pertaining to this house" (Doctrine and Covenants 124:42).[147] Joseph Smith also told William that he had seen the temple in vision. The design of the temple was a collaborative work between Joseph Smith and William. In February 1844 Joseph provided instructions for a set of "circular windows designed to light the office in the dead work of the arch between stories." William told the Prophet that "round windows in the broad side of a building were in violation of all the known rules of architecture" and argued that the windows should be semi-circular because the building was too low for round windows." Joseph insisted on the round windows, even if it meant the building would have to be ten feet higher than originally planned. He then told William, "I wish you to carry out <u>my</u> designs. I have seen in vision the splendid appearance of that building illuminated, and will have it built according to the pattern show me."[148] In the end Joseph and William compromised by making the upper circular windows smaller than the lower ones to fit better into the architectural plans.[149]

---

145 "Letter to Saints Scattered Abroad, September 1840," vol. 7 of the Documents series of *The Joseph Smith Papers*, 178–79.

146 Quoted in J. Earl Arrington, "William Weeks, Architect of the Nauvoo Temple," *BYU Studies* 19, no. 3 (1979): 2.

147 "Revelation, 19 January 1841 [D&C 124]," vol. 7 of the Documents series of *The Joseph Smith Papers*, 6.

148 Joseph Smith History, 1838–1856, vol. E-1 [1 July 1843–30 April 1844]," 1875–76, The Joseph Smith Papers (emphasis in original).

149 Arrington, 5.

On other occasions, William influenced Joseph Smith. According to one tradition, the Prophet turned down the idea of a lightning rod on the temple, believing "if God, who now holds the lightnings in his hands choose to direct a thunderbolt against those solid walls and demolish the building, it is his affair."[150] But the first drawings of the plans for the temple show a lightning rod on the steeple; later, it became a weather vane with an angel on it.[151]

After the martyrdom of Joseph and Hyrum Smith in 1844, work on the temple continued. William continued as architect and builder under the direction of the Twelve Apostles, led by Brigham Young. Under the direction of the Twelve, William also submitted plans for the Nauvoo House, a boarding house meant to complement the temple. In early 1846 William's work on the temple came to sudden end when he was called to join the thousands of Saints leaving the city. Responsibility for finishing the temple was handed over to Truman O. Angell. On February 13, 1846 William singed a note, officially appointing, as it read, "Truman Angell to be my successor as superintendent over the finishing of the Temple & Nauvoo House in the City of Joseph according to the plans and designs given by me to him."[152]

These recreations of the Nauvoo Temple Blueprints are on display in the William Weeks Home. Photo by Casey Paul Griffiths.

150 *Nauvoo Rustler,* March 10, 1891, quoted in Arrington, 6.

151 Arrington, 6.

152 Quoted in Arrington, 10.

William and Caroline left Nauvoo, traveled to Winter Quarters, and were among the first Saints to reach the Salt Lake Valley, arriving in September 1847. Shortly after his arrival in the valley, William's relationship with the Church began to sour. The reasons for his disaffection are not completely known. William and Caroline may have struggled with the idea of pioneering another new settlement in the wilderness. They had lost four of their five children while they were in Nauvoo and had lost another child in April 1847 at Council Bluffs. By the time they had arrived in the Salt Lake Valley they had buried five of their six children.[153] There may have been problems with the new Church leadership. His obituary, written years after his arrival in Salt Lake, reads, "He was not a follower of Brigham Young and did not believe in polygamy but was a great admirer of Joseph Smith."[154]

In early 1848 William and Caroline moved their family to the midwestern United States, and at the October 1848 general conference they were both excommunicated from the Church. The family returned to Utah in 1852, and some sources indicate that William was rebaptized. He worked for a short time building a sugar mill, a chapel, and a water wheel for Brigham Young's gristmill in Salt Lake City. In 1857 the Weeks moved to San Bernardino, California. They remained there when Brigham Young asked all the Saints in Southern California to return to Utah during the 1857 conflict with the United States government. William remained in Southern California for the rest of his life until his death in 1900.[155]

William and Caroline Weeks reentered the Nauvoo Temple's story in 1948. That year two young missionaries, Vern C. Thacker and Frank Gifford, knocked on the door of their grandson, Leslie Marion Griffin. Griffin told the missionaries that he was not a member of the Church but mentioned that he was a grandson of the architect of the Nauvoo Temple. The two elders developed a good relationship with the Griffin family and taught them several discussions, though it was clear the family knew little about William Weeks or his religion. When Griffin learned that Elder Thacker was about to return home, he wanted to offer him a going away present. Elder Thacker later recalled:

> On our last visit to Mr. Griffin he excused himself for a few minutes and went into the rear part of his house. He returned with a large roll of papers about three feet long, ten inches in diameter, secured with a rubber band. He explained, "These are the original architect's drawings for

153 Arrington, 11.

154 Quoted in Marjorie Hopkins Bennion, "The Rediscovery of William Weeks' Nauvoo Temple Drawings," *Mormon Historical Studies* 3, no. 1 (Spring 2002), 79.

155 Bennion, 79.

> the Nauvoo Temple. They have been in my family for 100 years, handed down from my grandfather, William Weeks." He opened the bundle and showed the plans to us. There were exterior drawings, some interior, an angel on a weather vane, pencil sketches for circular stairways, circular windows, archways, etc. Even the measurement for various details of the temple were included in William's handwriting. They were yellowed with age but [in] amazingly good condition. Mr. Griffin knew I was returning home in a few days. He asked me if I would do him a favor of carrying these plans to the headquarters of the Church in Salt Lake City, Utah. I assured him that it would be a great honor for me to do so.[156]

When the decision was made to rebuild the Nauvoo Temple, William's original drawings became an invaluable resource in ensuring the accuracy of the reborn temple. One historical researcher later commented, "While representing only a fraction of William Weeks' drawings that must have existed, those remaining have been of inestimable value in showing very precisely a great many of the details features of the temple."[157] By the time the Nauvoo Temple was being rebuilt in 1999 to 2002, several descendants of William and Caroline had joined the Church. They were invited to meet with the Church historical department and see the designs for themselves. Keith B. McMullin, then a member of the Presiding Bishopric of the Church, later stated, "The manner in which the Nauvoo Temple has been reconstructed would not have been possible without these original plans."[158]

156 Quoted in Bennion, 81.
157 Quoted in Bennion, 85–86.
158 Quoted in Bennion, 87.

Edward and Ann Hunter Home

The rebuilt Edward and Ann Hunter home. Joseph Smith wrote Doctrine and Covenants 127 and 128 in this location. Photo by Casey Paul Griffiths.

Significant events at this location:

- The Prophet Joseph Smith hid from Missouri officials here in the fall of 1842.
- The Prophet wrote all or part of Doctrine and Covenants 127 and 128 here on September 6, 1842.

Located a short walk away from the Nauvoo, Illinois Temple is the Edward Hunter home. Edward Hunter was born in Pennsylvania in 1793. He married Ann Stadley in 1830. The Hunters were prosperous Quaker farmers when they joined the Church. Edward was baptized into the Church by Apostle Orson Hyde on October 8, 1840. The couple's influence was so great, it is said, that over two hundred people joined the Church in the wake of their baptism.[159] Edward, Ann, and their family moved to Nauvoo in 1842. Edward was a member of the Masonic lodge. He served in the Nauvoo Legion, on the Nauvoo city council, and as a regent in the University of Nauvoo. From 1844 to 1846, Edward served as bishop of the Nauvoo Fifth Ward. Upon the death of Newel K. Whitney in 1851, Edward served as the Presiding Bishop of the Church until his death in 1883. Some sources say Edward made his living by manufacturing and selling iron goods, such as nails, kettles, pans, and ovens. Edward prospered at his work. In a single year, he donated fifteen thousand dollars to the Church.[160]

On May 6, 1842, an assassination attempt was made on Lilburn W. Boggs, the former governor of Missouri. While Boggs was in his study, an unknown assailant fired a gun at him through a nearby window, and Boggs was hit by large buckshot in the head and neck. Initially he was not expected to survive, though he eventually did recover. Immediately after the assassination attempt, accusations began to fly that Joseph Smith had arranged for someone to kill Boggs in retaliation for the extermination order issued against the Saints in 1838. In the controversy that followed, the Saints in Nauvoo began to fear that Joseph might be extradited to Missouri, where his life would be in grave danger.[161]

Edward was a close friend of the Prophet Joseph Smith. In the fall of 1842, Joseph hid in Edward's home while Missouri officers were trying to arrest him on charges related to the attempted murder of Governor Boggs.[162] While staying with the Hunters, the Prophet wrote part (some sources say all) of his revelation on baptism for the dead (Doctrine and Covenants 128).[163] Edward is quoted as saying: "Brother Joseph was hid up in my house from his enemies from Missouri. During that time, Joseph revealed the last part of the

159 "Historic Buildings: Hunter Home," Nauvoo Historic Sites, https://www.nauvoohistoricsites.org/buildings/hunter/, accessed July 18, 2022.

160 La Mar C. Berrett, *Sacred Places: Ohio and Illinois*, eds. Keith W. Perkins and Donald Q. Cannon (Salt Lake City, UT: Deseret Book, 2002), 121.

161 Benjamin E. Park, *Kingdom of Nauvoo,* 2020, 123–25.

162 Lilburn Boggs was the Missouri Governor who in 1838 issued the infamous "extermination order," which declared that all "Mormons" were to be driven from the state or exterminated. In May 1842 while Boggs was sitting in his home, an unknown gunman shot him through an open window. Given the animosity Boggs had with the Latter-day Saints, many people quickly jumped to the conclusion that the "Mormons" had something to do with it. For more information, see *Church History in the Fulness of Times Student Manual*, 2nd ed (Salt Lake City, UT: The Church of Jesus Christ of Latter-day Saints, 2003), 275–77.

163 Berrett, 121.

[instruction regarding] baptism for our dead. I was present with William Clayton."[164] Edward would become one of Joseph's trusted "life guards," or bodyguards as we would say today. During this time Joseph was forced into hiding to avoid arrest or abduction. Doctrine and Covenants 127 and 128 consist of letters about baptism for the dead that Joseph Smith wrote to the Saints during this time of hiding.

Joseph wrote Doctrine and Covenants 127 and 128 to encourage the Saints and to provide further instructions on the practice of baptism for the dead. The doctrine of proxy baptisms for the deceased was first taught in August 1840. Soon after, Latter-day Saints began performing these baptisms in the Mississippi River. However, a revelation given to Joseph Smith instructed the Saints to only perform proxy baptisms for the dead in the font inside the temple (Doctrine and Covenants 124:29–36), which was then under construction. The Saints were so anxious to continue these ordinances that they dedicated the basement of the unfinished temple on November 8, 1841, and performed baptisms for the dead almost exclusively in the temple font after it was dedicated.[165]

The Saints enthusiastically embraced the doctrine of baptisms for the dead when it was introduced on August 10, 1840. A few weeks after Joseph Smith introduced the ordinance, he wrote to the Twelve Apostles in England to explain the new practice: "The saints have the privilege of being baptized for those of their relatives who are dead, who they feel to believe would have embraced the gospel if they had been privileged with hearing it, and who have received the gospel in the spirit through the instrumentality of those who may have been commissioned to preach to them while in the prison. Without enlarging on the subject you will undoubtedly see its consistency, and reasonableness, and [it] presents the gospel of Christ in probably a more enlarged scale than some have received it."[166]

We do not know precisely when the first proxy baptisms took place in Nauvoo, but the first documented baptism for the dead was performed on September 12, 1840. Jane Neyman requested that Harvey Olmstead baptize her on behalf of her son Cyrus Livingston Neyman, who was deceased. Vienna Jacques served as a witness for the baptism by riding her horse into the water

164 Richard N.Holzapfel and T. Jeffery Cottle, *Old Mormon Nauvoo and Southeastern Iowa,* (Santa Ana, CA: Fieldbrook Productions Inc, 1990), 61.

165 Historical Introduction, "Letter to 'All the Saints in Nauvoo,'" 1 September 1842 [D&C 127], The Joseph Smith Papers.

166 "Letter to Quorum of the Twelve," 15 December 1840, 6, The Joseph Smith Papers.

so she could hear and watch the ordinance. Shortly after the baptism was performed, Joseph Smith gave his approval of the ordinance.[167]

As with any new practice, the Saints soon encountered questions that required refinements to how baptisms for the dead were performed. In a revelation received in January 1841, the Lord instructed that baptisms for the dead be performed inside the temple (Doctrine and Covenants 124:30–39). However, while the temple was under construction, the Saints were allowed to perform baptisms in the nearby Mississippi River. These first baptisms were carried out in a haphazard and unsystematic manner. Wilford Woodruff later recalled going to the river along with Joseph Smith and other Church members to perform baptisms for the dead. They baptized hundreds of people, but no one was assigned to record the names of the deceased who were baptized. President Woodruff later remembered, "The Lord told Joseph that he must have recorders present at these baptisms—men who could see with their eyes and hear with their ears, and record these things. Of course, we had to do the work over again. Nevertheless, that does not say that work was not of God."[168]

A discourse on August 21, 1842, to the Nauvoo Relief Society records, "Pres[ident]· S[mith] said he had one remark to make respecting the baptism for the dead—to suffice for the time being, until he has opportunity to discuss the subject to greater length—that is, all persons baptized for the dead must have a Recorder present, that he may be an eyewitness to testify of it. It will be necessary in the grand Council, that these things be testified—let it be attended to from this time, but if there is any lack[,] it may be at the expense of our friends—they may not come forth."[169] From this small beginning in Nauvoo, Church members have since labored to create a record of all the proxy ordinances performed in this dispensation. In section 127, Joseph recorded these words of the Lord: "I am about to restore many things to the earth, pertaining to the priesthood" (Doctrine and Covenants 127:8). Baptism for the deceased represented only the beginning of the great work of redeeming the dead.

167 See Alexander L. Baugh, "'For This Ordinance Belongeth to My House': The Practice of Baptism for the Dead outside the Nauvoo Temple," *Mormon Historical Studies* 3, no. 1 (2002): 48.

168 *Millennial Star,* June 29, 1891, p. 405.

169 "Minutes and Discourse, 31 August 1842," 83, The Joseph Smith Papers.

Upstairs bedroom in the Edward and Ann Hunter home. This is Likely the location where Joseph Smith penned his epistles on baptisms for the dead. Photo by Casey Paul Griffiths.

In his first letter from the Hunter home, Joseph Smith had promised the Saints further instructions on the subject of baptism for the dead (Doctrine and Covenants 127:10). His second letter, now Doctrine and Covenants 128, expounds on the scriptural background of the practice of baptism for the dead. Joseph commonly shared how the practice of proxy ordinances for the dead is an essential part of the plan of God, "prepared before the foundation of the world" (Doctrine and Covenants 128:5). In an article published in *Times and Seasons* on April 15, 1842, Joseph Smith taught:

> The great Jehovah contemplated the whole of the events connected with the earth, pertaining to the plan of salvation, before it rolled into existence, or ever the "morning stars sung together for joy," the past, the present and the future, were, and are with him one eternal now. . . . He comprehended the fall of man, and their redemption; he knew the plan of salvation, and pointed it out; he was acquainted with the situation of all nations; and with their destiny; he ordered all things according to the council of his own will, he knows the situation of both the living, and the dead, and has made ample provision for their redemption,

according to their several circumstances, and the laws of the kingdom of God, whether in this world, or in the world to come."[170]

Joseph Smith taught of "a power which records or binds on earth and binds in heaven" (Doctrine and Covenants 128:9). This power, commonly referred to in the Church today as the *sealing power*, is not exclusive to this dispensation. It has been exercised by prophets in all dispensations whenever the keys of the Melchizedek Priesthood have been present on the earth. The word *seal* appears many times in the scriptures. Jesus Christ was "sealed" by God the Father (John 6:27). Paul taught the Saints of his day that God had anointed and sealed them (2 Corinthians 1:21–22). When Paul wrote to the Saints in Ephesus, he spoke of them being "sealed by that holy Spirit of promise" (Ephesians 1:13). In the book of Revelation, John spoke of God's servants being sealed "in their foreheads" (Revelation 7:3). The power to seal was promised to the Apostle Peter when the Savior told him, "I will give unto thee the keys of the kingdom of heaven: and whatsoever thou shalt bind on earth shall be bound in heaven: and whatsoever thou shalt loose on earth shall be loosed in heaven" (Matthew 16:19).

The sealing power gives the Lord's servants who hold it power to perform certain acts on earth that are validated (or sealed) in heaven. The sealing keys were given to Joseph Smith by the ancient prophet Elijah when he appeared in the Kirtland Temple (Doctrine and Covenants 110:13–16). Today, the President of the Church holds and directs the use of sealing keys. When new members of the Quorum of the Twelve are called, they are given the sealing keys (though the Twelve act under the direction of the President of the Church in using those keys). The sealing power is also given to a select number of officiators who serve in temples around the world and perform sealing ordinances. The sealing authority is the power by which "all covenants, contracts, bonds, obligations, oaths, vows, performances, connections, associations, or expectations" receive "efficacy, virtue, or force in and after the resurrection from the dead" (Doctrine and Covenants 132:7).[171]

As a member of the Nauvoo city council, Edward Hunter met with Governor Thomas Ford to seek protection for the Saints as well as Joseph and Hyrum. When the governor's "protection" failed, Edward was one of the men who went to Carthage and escorted the martyrs' bodies home. He also helped bury them in the unfinished basement of the Nauvoo House.

---

170 *Times and Seasons,* April 15, 1842, p. 760 (emphasis in original).

171 "Sealing Power," in *Encyclopedia of Mormonism* (1992), 1288.

Other Church leaders, including Brigham Young, would use the Hunter home as a safe haven when area authorities began issuing arrest warrants to pressure the Saints into leaving Illinois. In 1846 Edward and his family left Nauvoo and settled in Winter Quarters. He led a company of Saints into the Salt Lake Valley in 1847. There he served as bishop of the 13th Ward until he became the Presiding Bishop of the Church. Edward died in 1883. Ann preceded him in death in 1855.

Mini-Devotional—No Greater Love

The Savior said, "Greater love hath no man than this, that a man lay down his life for his friends" (John 15:13). Edward hunter loved the Prophet Joseph Smith and risked his life on multiple occasions to protect him.

- Joseph Smith did not take any of his bodyguards with him when he went to Carthage. How do you think Edward Hunter felt when he learned the news that Joseph had been killed? as he escorted the bodies back to Nauvoo? as he helped bury the bodies of his dear friends?
- How did Edward's continued faithfulness to the Church show his love for the Prophet?
- It is highly unlikely that any of us will ever be asked to serve as a bodyguard for a prophet, but how can we show our love and appreciation for the prophets of God?

William and Esther Gheen Home

William and Esther Gheen home near the Nauvoo Temple. Photo by Casey Paul Griffiths.

Significant events at this location:

- William and Esther Gheen moved to Nauvoo in 1841 and worked diligently to construct the temple.
- William Gheen died from a severe illness in July 1845.
- William and Esther were sealed by proxy in the Nauvoo Temple in February 1846.

The home of William and Esther is a good place to make a final stop during a tour of the sites related to the Nauvoo Temple. If the William Weeks home highlights the physical architecture of the temple and the Edward Hunter home highlights the doctrinal nature of temple ordinances, then the

Gheen home highlights why the temple mattered so much to Latter-day Saints then and why it continues to matter so much now.

William and Esther Gheen were baptized in 1840 in Chester County, Pennsylvania. A year after joining the Church they sold their home, leaving their lives in Pennsylvania behind to gather with the Saints in Nauvoo. They brought eight children along with them on their journey to Nauvoo. Once they arrived in Nauvoo, William worked construction shifts and helped raised funds to build the Nauvoo Temple.[172] The Gheens looked forward to entering the temple together when it was completed, but their plans were shattered when William passed away on July 15, 1845 following a severe illness. Suddenly Esther was left alone to raise and care for their large family.[173]

The temple opened the way for William and Esther's marriage to endure even after his death. On December 18, 1845, just a few months after William's passing, Esther entered the Nauvoo Temple and received her endowment. She returned to the temple on February 2, 1846, where she was sealed to William by proxy for time and all eternity. Just a few months later she packed up her children and her belongings and began the lonely walk out of the city. It is easy to imagine Esther shepherding her children out of the city but pausing to look back at the temple. She might have reflected on how the covenants she made in the temple gave her an assurance that her family relationships would endure beyond death and how she was promised a reunion with her husband in the eternities. Esther was just one of over six thousand Saints who received their blessings in the Nauvoo Temple and then left the temple behind to journey into the wilderness.[174]

Esther and her younger children lived in the Salt Lake Valley until her passing in 1858. She left two children behind in the eastern United States—a daughter, Margaret, who remained with her family, and a son, Thomas, who fought and died for the Union in the Civil War. Because of the sealing ordinance, these family members were not lost. When other temples were built, the descendants of William and Esther performed the ordinances needed for all their family members.[175]

The Gheen home stood for many years as a reminder of the sacrifices the family made for the gospel and the blessings they received in the temple.

172 Sarah Jane Weaver, "What Is the Temple District of Nauvoo and Why Does It Matter to Latter-day Saints?" *Church News,* May 30, 2021, https://www.thechurchnews.com/2021/5/30/23217628/what-is-the-temple-district-of-nauvoo-elder-cook-dedication.

173 James W. Petty, "A Walk Down Parley Street," *Ensign,* August 2003.

174 Petty, "A Walk Down Parley Street."

175 Petty, "A Walk Down Parley Street."

When the restored home was dedicated in 2021, Elder Quentin L. Cook of the Quorum of the Twelve Apostles gave the prayer. During the ceremony he commented, "This family faced their house to the temple. The view was not important. It was the ordinances of the temple that mattered most."[176] Elder Cook also added that though the Gheens are not mentioned in many major history books, "they are just as important"[177] as other more prominent Saints of that time.

The story of William and Esther drives home why the temple was so important for the early Saints and why it remains central to the lives of modern Latter-day Saints. Every person faces the uncertainty of mortality. Those we love can be here one day and then gone the next. But the temple provides an assurance that they are not gone forever. In Nauvoo where death and disruption were constant, Saints like William and Esther found peace in knowing that death was not the end of the love they shared with the people in their lives. Places like the Gheen home demonstrate how the vision Joseph Smith had for the temple became real. Through the Atonement of Jesus Christ and the ordinances of His temple, the Gheens' love endures throughout the eternities.

176 Weaver, "What Is the Temple District of Nauvoo?"
177 Weaver, "What Is the Temple District of Nauvoo?"

Mini-Devotional—"It Was the Ordinances of the Temple that Mattered Most"

The Nauvoo Temple at sunset. Photo by Casey Paul Griffiths.

The stories of William and Caroline Weeks, Edward and Ann Hunter, and William and Esther Gheen show how central the temple was in the lives of the early Saints. They sacrificed nearly all that they had to build the temple and receive its ordinances. In return they received the assurance that the covenants they made in the temple would help them be with their loved ones for eternity. Take a few moments to ponder or write about the following questions:

- What sacrifices have you made to receive the blessings of the temple?
- How does the temple give you an assurance that your family can be together forever?

Homes of the Prophets

The restored Brigham Young home in Nauvoo. Photo by Casey Paul Griffiths.

As part of the restoration of Nauvoo, many of the homes that belonged to the Saints who lived here have been restored to their 1840s appearance and opened for the public to visit. The sheer number of places to visit can be overwhelming. To help visitors, the home in Nauvoo can be placed into several groups the present similar themes. For instance, some homes near the Nauvoo temple focus on the development of temple doctrines. In this chapter we have grouped together the homes where presidents of the Church lived. Depending on the time of year, these homes will be open for tours and have missionaries present to guide you through each home and familiarize you with former residents of each home. Only one of these men, Brigham Young, served as president of the Church while the Saints were in Nauvoo. But John Taylor and Wilford Woodruff both later served as Church presidents during some of the most tumultuous times in the history of the Church. Understanding their stories gives you not only a window into the struggles of the people of Nauvoo, but also the development of Church practices and doctrines throughout the 19th century.

Brigham and Mary Ann Angell Young Home

The rebuilt Brigham and Mary Ann Angell Young home. Photo by Casey Paul Griffiths.

Significant Events at this location . . .

- Mary Ann Angel, the second wife of Brigham Young moved their family into a partially completed log home on this property while Brigham Young was serving a mission to the British Isles.

- After Brigham returned home from England he began work on a brick home in the same location, where he and his family lived during the remainder of their time in Nauvoo.
- Doctrine and Covenants 126, a revelation received by Joseph Smith for Brigham Young, was given in this location.
- While Brigham Young lived in Nauvoo, prayer meetings and ordinances were performed in this home.

On July 1, 1841, Brigham Young, Heber C. Kimball, and John Taylor returned in Nauvoo after completing two years of missionary labors in the British Isles. Called to serve in Europe by a revelation given in 1838 (D&C 118), Brigham and his fellow apostles left their families in destitute conditions when departed on their mission. Brigham later described how difficult it was for him to leave his family in an 1854 discourse:

> When I left my family to start for England, I was not able to walk one mile, I was not able to lift a small trunk, which I took with me, into the wagon. I left my wife and my six children without a second suit to their backs, for we had left all our property in possession of the mob. Every one of my family were [sic] sick . . . Joseph said, "If you will go, I promise you, that your family shall live, and you shall live, and you shall know that the hand of God is in the calling for you to go and preach the Gospel of life and salvation to a perishing world." . . . My family lived . . . As for being cast down, or at all discouraged, or even such thoughts entering in my heart as, "I will provide for my family, and let the world perish," these feelings and thoughts never once occurred to me . . . When I was ready to start, I went and left my family in the hands of the Lord, and with the brethren.[178]

Under Brigham's leadership the Quorum of the Twelve Apostles converted thousands during their service in Great Britain. Their mission also played a key role in forging the Twelve into an effective priesthood body.

During their service in England, the Apostles formally sustained Brigham Young as the President of the Quorum of the Twelve.[179] It was a time of vital growth and development for the Twelve, and they returned to Nauvoo united and with a strong group of converts who brought enthusiasm and

---

178 Brigham Young, in *Journal of Discourses,* 2:19.

179 James B. Allen, Ronald K. Esplin, David J. Whittaker, *Men with a Mission, 1837–1841: The Quorum of the Twelve Apostles in the British Isles,* 1992, 134.

optimism to the American Saints. Summarizing the missionary labors of the Twelve, Brigham later recorded, "Through the mercy of God we have gained many friends, established churches in almost every noted town and city in the Kingdom of Great Britain, baptized between seven and eight thousand souls, printed 5000 Books of Mormon, 3000 Hymn Books, 2500 volumes of the *Millennial Star,* and 50,000 tracts."[180]

For as much as his mission to England blessed the Church, it also left Brigham in a difficult position when he returned home. He later recalled his poor financial situation when he returned to his family in Nauvoo: "I returned again in two years, and found that I had spent hundreds of dollars, which I had accumulated on my mission, to help the brethren to emigrate to Nauvoo, and had but one sovereign left . . . I said I would buy a barrel of flour with that, and sit down and eat it with my wife and children, and I determined I would not ask anybody for work, until I had eaten it all up. Brother Joseph asked me how I intended to live. I said, 'I will go to work and get a living.'"[181]

On July 9, 1841, just a few days after Brigham returned from his mission, Brigham received a visit from the Prophet Joseph Smith. In Brigham's home, Joseph received a revelation on Brigham's behalf that is now Doctrine and Covenants 126. The revelation reads in part, "Dear & well beloved Brother, Brigham Young, Verily thus saith the Lord unto you my servant Brigham it is no more required at your hand to leave your family as in times past for your offering is acceptable to me I have seen your labor and toil in journeyings for my name. I therefore command you to send my word abroad and take special care of your family from this time henceforth and forever, Amen. Given to Joseph Smith this day."[182] Willard Richards copied this revelation into the "Book of the Law of the Lord" on December 17, 1841. It was first placed into the 1876 edition of the Doctrine and Covenants by Orson Pratt under the direction of President Brigham Young.[183]

The Lord's comforting words to Brigham that "it is no more required at your hand to leave your family as in times past, for your offering is acceptable to me" (D&C 126:1) shows the increasing importance of the steady leadership of Brigham and the other Apostles in Nauvoo. In the next few years Brigham and most of the Twelve were among the first to receive the ordinances of the temple and became close confidants of Joseph Smith. At a conference held a few months after section 126 was received on behalf of Brigham, Joseph Smith

180 Quoted in Joseph Fielding McConkie and Craig J. Ostler, *Revelations of the Restoration,* 1999, 990.

181 Brigham Young, in *Journal of Discourses,* 2:19.

182 "Revelation, 9 July 1841 [D&C 126]," p. 26, JSP.

183 Robert J. Woodford, *Historical Development of the Doctrine and Covenants,* 3:1664.

declared "that the time had come when the Twelve should be called upon to stand in their place next to the First Presidency, and attend to the settling of emigrants and the business of the church at the stakes, and assist to bear off the kingdom victorious to the nations; and as they had been faithful and had borne the burden in the heat of the day that it was right that they should have an opportunity of providing something for themselves and families."[184]

In the months following, Brigham Brigham labored to build a better home for his family. Almost two years after he arrived home from his mission in England, the home was complete. On May 31, 1843 Brother Brigham "moved out of my log cabin into my new brick house, which was 22 feet by 16, two stories high, and a good cellar under it, and felt thankful to God for the privilege of having a comfortable, though small habitation."[185] Brigham left on another mission in the Spring of 1844 to assist in Joseph Smith's presidential campaign. Mary Ann was in this home when she wrote the letter to Brigham informing him that Joseph and Hyrum Smith were killed in Carthage Jail.[186]

When Brigham Young found out about the martyrdom of the Prophet he recalled, "the first thing I thought of was whether Joseph had taken the keys of the kingdom with him from the earth." He was in the company of "Brother Orson Pratt [who] sat on my left, we were both leaning back on our chairs. Bringing my hand down my knee, I said, the keys of the kingdom are right here with the Church."[187]

Arriving back in Nauvoo on August 6, Brigham found the Latter-day Saints still in a state of shock over the deaths of the Joseph and Hyrum. Even in the midst of their grief, questions began to circulate over who would take Joseph's place as the leader of the Church. Some Church members began advocating for the Council of Fifty to take the reigns of leadership. In early August, Sidney Rigdon, who had been living in Pennsylvania, reappeared in Nauvoo. Sidney claimed to be "a guardian through whom Joseph will speak to the people . . . as a god to this dispensation."[188] In the midst of these discussion Brigham spoke out, declaring, "I do not care who leads the Church. But one thing I must know, and that is what God says

184 Discourse, 16 August 1841, as Reported by *Times and Seasons*, p. 522, JSP.

185 *Manuscript History of Brigham Young*, 1801-1844, ed. Elden Jay Watson (Salt Lake City: Smith Secretarial Service, 1968).

186 "Brigham Young Home, Nauvoo, Illinois," Ensign Peak Foundation, https://ensignpeakfoundation.org/brigham-young-home/

187 *Manuscript History of Brigham Young*, 171.

188 William Huntington Diary, August 4, 1844.

about it" adding, "I have the keys and means of obtaining the mind of God on the subject."[189]

To settle the question of succession, on August 8, 1844, both Sidney and Brigham addressed the Church. In the morning Sidney Rigdon spoke to a large congregation, presenting his claim to Church leadership. When Sidney finished, Brigham Young declared his intention to also address the crowd at 2 o'clock in the afternoon. Seeing the Saints gathering for the afternoon meeting, Brigham took the stand along with other members of the Quorum of the Twelve, excepting John Taylor who was still recovering from his wounds received in the attack on Carthage Jail. Brigham arose and spoke to the crowd, asking, "Who has stood next to Joseph and Hyrum? I have, and will stand next to him. We had a head, and that head is the Apostleship . . . You cannot appoint a prophet, but if you will let the Twelve remain and act in their place, the keys of the kingdom are with them and they can manage the affairs of the church and direct all thing aright."[190]

Later recording the event, Brigham wrote simply, "I arose and spoke to the people my heart was swollen with compassion towards them and by the power of the holy ghost even the spirit of the prophets I was enabled to comfort the hearts of the saints in the afternoon."[191] Many of the people present in the crowd, however, recalled receiving a spiritual manifestation while Brigham spoke. Many of the people present recorded hearing the voice of Joseph Smith while Brigham was speaking, some even remembered jumping to their feet, believing the Prophet had returned.

There are over a hundred-and-twenty recorded accounts of Brigham Young's transformation. The witnesses of this even transcend categories of age, experience, and gender. While the accounts do not always agree as to the exact time when the "Mantle of Joseph" experience took place, they are consistent in describing a spiritual event for many in the congregation. Some remembered it occurring when Brigham stood up following Sidney Rigdon's address in the morning. Other witnesses testified that it occurred during Brigham's speech in the afternoon. One of the earliest accounts of the event was written by Caroline Barnes Crosby:

---

189 Brigham Young quote, in "History of the Church," *Millennial Star*, April 4, 1863, 216.

190 "History, 1838–1856, volume F-1 [1 May 1844–8 August 1844]," p. 299, JSP.

191 Brigham Young Diary August 8, 1844; Jesse, "The Writings of Brigham Young," *Western Historical Quarterly*, July 4, 1973, 284.

> Sidney Rigdon came to the stand and tried to show to the people that he was the rightful successor of Joseph. And his arguments were so powerful that many were almost persuaded to believe him such. But as soon as the twelve apostles with bro Brigham Young at their head took the stand it was shown conclusively where the power rested. It was the first time that I ever thought he [Brigham] resembled bro Joseph. But almost every one exclaimed that the mantle of Joseph had fallen on Brigham. For one I never had any doubts afterward.[192]

Another firsthand witness, George Romney, added, "I testify to you in all fervor, before God, that the mantle of Joseph Smith fell upon Brigham Young. It was Joseph's voice and manner, as Brigham Young addressed the people and told them who should be their leader. Now this is no fiction; this is true as I stand here after so many years, passing from the year 1844 up to the present time."[193] Aurelia Spencer Rogers recorded the testimony of her sister Ellen: "Brigham Young, who was President of the Quorum of Apostles, arose to speak, when 'The Mantle of Joseph' fell upon him, and he was like one transformed; his countenance, voice and form were like those of the late Prophet. Many in the congregation, even children saw this miracle; it satisfied the people and decided the question who was to be the leader."[194] George Q. Cannon wrote, "If Joseph had risen from the dead and again spoken in their hearing, the effect could not have been more startling than it was to many present at that meeting; it was the voice of Joseph which was heard, but is seemed in the eyes of the people as if it were the very person of Joseph which stood before them." [195] While most of the accounts of Brigham's transfiguration were collected by Church historians years after the event, there are also contemporary witnesses.Tthe *Times and Seasons* reported on September 5, 1845, "that just before the sustaining vote at the afternoon session of the August meeting, 'every saint could see that Elijah's mantle had truly fallen upon the 'Twelve.'"[196]

With the support of the Saints, Brigham Young became the leader of the Church, first as president of the Quorum of the Twelve, and then later reestablishing the First Presidency in 1847. Following his dramatic conflict

192 Caroline Barnes Crosby, "Memoirs Begun at Tubuai, Society Islands, 1851," as quoted in Jorgensen and BYU Studies Staff, "The Mantle of the Prophet Passes to Brother Brigham: A Collective Spiritual Witness," *BYU Studies*, 1996, 158.

193 George Romney typescript account of testimony, quoted in Jorgensen, 132.

194 Rogers, *Life Sketches of Orson Spencer and Others*, 332.

195 George Q. Cannon quote, in Roberts, *Comprehensive History*, 2:418.

196 *Times and Seasons*, September 5, 1845, 650.

with Sidney Rigdon, Brigham's home became a hub of activity for the Church, as plans were laid for the exodus. The Young family remained in this home until 1846, when they set out to find a new home in the West. The home was among the first buildings restored in the 1970s. It was dedicated by President Spencer W. Kimball on May 25, 1973.[197]

John and Leonora Taylor Home

The John and Leonora Taylor Home on Main Street in Nauvoo. Photo by Casey Paul Griffiths.

Significant Events at this location:

- On May 9, 1836, John Taylor and his wife, Leonora Cannon, are baptized members of the Church of Jesus Christ of Latter-day Saints

197 "Brigham Young Home, Nauvoo, Illinois," Ensign Peak Foundation, https://ensignpeakfoundation.org/brigham-young-home/

- John Taylor is ordained a member of the Quorum of the Twelve Apostles on December 19, 1838 and leaves for a mission in Great Britain with the rest of the Quorum the next year.
- John Taylor is appointed editor-in-chief of the Church newspaper the *Times and Seasons.*
- On April 13, 1845, John Taylor purchases a lot In Nauvoo for his home and a print shop. The Taylors move into their new Nauvoo home on May 10, 1845.

Born in 1808 in Milnthorpe, Westmoreland, England, John Taylor lived his life as a man of God long before joining the Church of Jesus Christ of Latter-day Saints. He wrote, "Often when alone, and sometimes in company, I heard sweet, soft, melodious music, as if performed by angelic or supernatural beings." For much of his childhood, John was a member of the Church of England. As a young man, he saw an angel playing a trumpet to declare the truth to all nations, which led him to search for the Church with the fullness of truth. When he was sixteen, he joined the Methodist Church and became an exhorter the next year. While walking with another Methodist member, John suddenly stopped and told his companion, "I have a strong impression on my mind, that I have to go to America to preach the gospel!" With that, he decided to immigrate to Canada. During the voyage, there was a dangerous storm that warranted distress—even the ship's captain worried it would capsize. However, John was at peace the entire time: "So confident was I of my destiny," he wrote, "that I went on deck at midnight, and amidst the raging elements felt as calm as though I was sitting in a parlor at home. I believed I should reach America and perform my work." The ship made it to the New York harbor safely and John traveled on to Toronto.[198]

In Toronto, Canada, John continued to preach the lessons of the Bible to a study group that met several times a week for two years. He recalled,

> A number of us met together for the purpose of searching the scriptures, and we found that certain doctrines were taught by Jesus and the apostles, which [none] of the religious sects taught. We concluded that if the Bible was true, the doctrines of modern Christendom were not true; or if they were true, the Bible was false. …

198 B. H. Roberts, *The Life of John Taylor* (Salt Lake City: Deseret Book, 2002), 21, 28-29.

> We rejected every man's word or writing, and took the word of God alone. ... We made it a rule to receive no doctrine until we could bring no scriptural testimony against it.[199]

The study group also believed in a restoration of the principles and organization found in the Bible, complete with apostles and prophets. When leaders of the Methodist Church learned of this they held a hearing, and then stripped John of his office, but still allowed him to retain his Methodist membership. After this the study group continued to pray for the fullness of the Gospel.[200] The answer to their prayers would come from Parley P. Pratt.

In April of 1836 on his way to his Toronto mission, Elder Parley P. Pratt arrived in Hamilton, Ontario, Canada. Having no friends, family, or money—and no means to travel on to Toronto— his options were to walk around Lake Ontario or to pay to go across it. Parley recorded, "If I went by land I would have a circuitous route, muddy and tedious to go on foot." But, he continued, "I was an entire stranger in Hamilton . . . and money I had none."[201] Unsure of what to do, he offered a prayer in a nearby forest asking for guidance, and returned to Hamilton, when he recorded, "I had not tarried many minutes before I was accosted by a stranger, who inquired my name and where I was going. He also asked me if I did not want some money. I said yes. He then gave me ten dollars."[202] He was then able to pay to travel by steamer to Toronto.

In Toronto, he immediately went to John Taylor's home, presenting John with a letter of introduction given to Parley by a stranger he had met on the way. John had heard negative things about the Church of Jesus Christ of Latter-day Saints and was uninterested in what this missionary had to preach, so he turned Pratt away. Discouraged, he still knew his course was right, and he clung to fellow apostle Heber C. Kimball's prophetic words. He prophesied: "Thou shalt go to Upper Canada, even to the city of Toronto, the capital, and there thou shalt find a people prepared for the fullness of the gospel, and they shall receive thee, and thou shalt organize the church among them, and it shall spread thence into the regions round about, and many shall be brought to the knowledge of the truth and shall be filled with joy." Despite the initial rejection, Pratt returned to the Taylor's home. This time the Taylor's had a visitor, Isabella Watson, who offered Pratt a room and a place to preach. As

199 John Taylor, *The John Taylor Papers: Records of the Last Utah Pioneer*, (Redwood City, CA: Taylor Trust, 1984), 10.

200 Roberts, *Life of John Taylor*, 31-33.

201 Taylor, *The John Taylor Papers*, 8.

202 Parley P. Pratt, *Autobiography of Parley Parker Pratt,* 5th ed., edited by Parley P. Pratt, Jr. (Salt Lake City: Deseret Book Company, 1961), 134-135.

Parley began to preach the Bible, many of Taylor's study group began to attend. Eventually, John Taylor, the leader of the group, also began to attend Parley's meetings.[203]

John quickly realized that Parley's knowledge of the Bible was impressive. He came to see that his initial impression of the new Church was wrong, and John became an active learner in Parley's lessons. John found that Parley's teachings aligned with those of the Bible but he was unsure about the authenticity of the other books of scriptures Parley used, the Book of Mormon and the Doctrine and Covenants. At one lesson, John stood and declared,

> We are here, ostensibly in search of truth. Hitherto we have fully investigated other creeds and doctrines and proven them false. … This gentlemen, Mr. Pratt, has brought to us many doctrines that correspond with our own views. We have endured a great deal and made many sacrifices for out religious convictions. We have prayed to God to send us a messenger, if He has a true Church on earth. Mr. Pratt has come to us under circumstances that are peculiar; and there is one thing that commends him to our considerations; he has come amongst us without purse or scrip, as the ancient apostles traveled; and none of us are able to refute his doctrine by scriptures or logic. I desire to investigate his doctrines and claims to authority, and shall be very glad if some of my friends will unite with me in this investigation. But if no one will unite with me, be assured I shall make the investigation alone. If I find his religion true, I shall accept it, no matter what the consequences may be; and if false, then I shall expose it.

John later wrote, "I made a regular business of it for three weeks and followed Brother Parley from place to place." John stated that after learning about the Restored Church, he had "never doubted any principle of Mormonism since." His investigation found the religion to be true, and just as he had promised, John accepted the Restored Gospel. John and his wife, Leonora, were baptized by Parley on May 9, 1836.[204]

After his baptism, John was ordained an Elder in the Priesthood and began to preach the Restored Gospel. In 1837, when he visited Kirtland to meet the Prophet Joseph Smith, Jr., he found that many Latter-day Saints, including some members of the Quorum of the Twelve Apostles, had bitter feelings toward the Prophet and had left the Church. These included Parley P. Pratt, who

203 Francis M. Gibbons, *John Taylor: Mormon Philosopher, Prophet of God*, (Salt Lake City: Deseret Book, 1985), *John Taylor*, 2-3.

204 Roberts, *Life of John Taylor*, 37-38.

was caught up in the spirit of apostasy, declaring that Joseph was not a true prophet. John told Parley,

> I am surprised to hear you speak so, Brother Parley. Before you left Canada you bore a strong testimony to Joseph Smith being a Prophet of God, and to the truth of the work he has inaugurated; and you said you knew these things by revelation, and the gift of the Holy Ghost. You gave to me a strict charge to the effect that though you or an angel from heaven was to declare anything else I was not to believe it. Now Brother Parley, it is not man that I am following, but the Lord. The principles you taught me led me to Him, and I now have the same testimony that you then rejoiced in. If the work was true six months ago, it is true today; if Joseph Smith was then a prophet, he is now a prophet.

John's convictions that the Gospel was true led him to convert that man who had converted him. These words resonated with Parley, who eventually re-joined the Church.

John and Leonora

Profile photo of John Taylor. Courtesy Church History Library.

While in Toronto, John met Leonora Cannon, who was in his new congregation. Leonora, born October 6, 1796 on the Isle of Man, was as much religiously inclined as her future husband. She often prayed about seeking a religion in which she could freely worship. She also eventually joined the Methodist Church and felt she allowed the Lord to "direct all of her movements." When Leonora was sixteen years old, she had the opportunity to journey to Canada after a friend, Mr. Mason, asked her to accompany his wife on the voyage. She did not make a hasty decision to join the voyage, but made it a matter of fervent prayer, after which she opened her bible to Genesis 12:1, which reads, "Get thee out of thy country, and from thy kindred and from thy father's house, into a land that I will shew thee." [205] This verse convinced her that "it was the will of God that she should make the voyage" and left for Canada with the Mrs. Mason in May of 1832.[206]

Even on the voyage, Leonora strived to preach the Gospel:

> "27th Sunday I got up early it was a fine morning I took my Bible on Deck the passengers were all sitting talking, I went and got my tracts and testaments and gave them—They all began reading and a good many fetched there [sic] Bibles it was a very pretty sight to see children and all as quiet as possible[.] about twelve Cleargyman [sic] read prayers and the deacons on Deck[. ...] Lord help me to be thankful that I am what I am and whom I am."

As, John and Leonora were in the same congregation, the two became fast friends. He "confided in [her the] revelation in his youth through which he knew he would preach the gospel in America, and it was a message of greater import and power than he then had."[207] John's friendship with Leonora eventually bloomed, though she was unimpressed with John as a suitor and not interested in turning their relationship into a romance, and when John proposed, she immediately rejected it.[208]

John did not to give up, as he prayed, asking the Lord to soften Leonora's heart, a prayer that was answered by a dream: in Leonora's dream, she saw "herself associated with [John] in his life-work, and from this spiritual manifestation she became convinced that John Taylor was to be her husband." She accepted the dream as revelation and recorded in her journal, "The Lord often led me by a way that I knew not and in a path that I naturally did not wish to go, every sweet had its bitter, the way seemed to me narrower every day without his almighty power to me I cannot walk in it to whom shall I go or look for succor but unto thee my Father and only Friend."[209] Two months later, John proposed again, this time with success. They were married on January 28, 1833 in the Episcopal Church in Toronto by Reverend Lockheart.[210] Their love for one another never wavered.

---

205 Mary Alice Cannon Lambert, "Leonora Cannon Taylor," *The Young Women's Journal*, 19: 345-346.

206 Brigham H. Roberts, *Comprehensive History of The Church of Jesus Christ of Latter-day Saints* (Salt Lake City: Deseret News Press, 1930), 1:255.

207 Roberts, *Life of John Taylor*, 472-473

208 Gibbons, *John Taylor*, 11.

209 Roberts, *Life of John Taylor*, 474

210 Note in Taylor Family Bible in "President John Taylor and His Wives," *Our Pioneer Heritage*, 1964, Vol. 7, 219

Mission in Great Britain

John Taylor was called to the Quorum of the Twelve Apostles on July 8, 1838—though evidence suggests he knew about the calling a year earlier—and was ordained as an apostle a few months later on December 19, 1838 by Brigham Young and Heber C. Kimball. The calling was officially announced in Doctrine and Covenants 118 along with a prophesy that the Twelve were to leave from Far West, Missouri on April 6, 1839 for their mission to Great Britain. John, being a humble man, knew of his "own weakness and littleness" when he was called to the Apostleship, but wrote that he "felt determined, the Lord being my helper, to endeavor to magnify it. When I first entered upon Mormonism, I did it with my eyes open. I counted the cost. I looked upon it as a life-long labor, and I considered that I was not only enlisted for time, but for eternity also, and did not wish to shrink now, although I felt my incompetency."

With the prophecy, John journeyed to Far West from Canada. However, his stay in Far West did not last long, because the Saints had been driven from Missouri into the neighboring state of Illinois. Though their enemies attempted to stop the prophesy from being fulfilled, members of the Quorum of the Twelve did begin their missions from Far West on April 16, 1939.

While John was on his mission arranged to leave his family in old log barracks in Montrose, just outside of Nauvoo. The conditions of his family caused him great anxiety, though he trusted in the Lord:

> The thought of the hardships they had just endured, the uncertainty of their continuing in the house they then occupied—and that only a solitary room—the prevalence of disease, the poverty of the brethren, their insecurity from the mobs, together with the uncertainty of what might take place during my absence, produced feelings of no ordinary character. These solicitations, paternal and conjugal, were enhanced also by the time and distance that was to separate us. But the thought of going forth at the command of the God of Israel to revisit my native land, to unfold the principles of eternal truth and make known the things that God has revealed for the salvation of the world, overcame every other feeling.[211]

John left Montrose on August 8, 1839, leaving behind his wife and children ill with malarial fever. While on his way to England, John also became seriously

211 B.H. Roberts, *The Life of John Taylor,* 67-68.

ill himself, forcing him to postpone his travels. He was treated with kindness by his friends in Indiana and continued to trust in God. After a few weeks, his condition improved and he was able to continue on his journey.

John returned to Nauvoo on July 1, 1841, but quickly learned that his wife was bed-ridden and near death in the small barracks where she had lived for the past two years. She had not informed John of her declining condition in any of the letters she sent to England to keep him from being distracted while he was performing the Lord's work. John asked twenty Elders to give her a blessing and the next morning she was much improved.[212] In response to his wife's close encounter with death and unsuitable living conditions, John purchased a lot on which he built a house, and the Taylors moved into their new home in Nauvoo on October 1, 1841.

The Print Shop and the Taylor's Home

The Printing Office located next to the John and Leonora Taylor home. Photo by Casey Paul Griffiths.

In Nauvoo, John's focus shifted from missionary work to city and Church affairs. He was "elected a member of the City Council, made a member of the Board of Regents for the Nauvoo University, and chosen Judge Advocate

212 Gibbons, *John Taylor*, 47-48.

with the rank of colonel in the Nauvoo Legion, a position that made him the responsible adviser of the court and also the public prosecutor in affairs military." In addition to these positions, he was helping to gather Zion, including building the Nauvoo temple.

In February of 1842, Joseph Smith, editor-in-chief, asked John to be the associate editor of the Church newspaper the *Times and Seasons.* He was the associate editor for about a year, and then became editor-in-chief for four years until the Saints were driven out of Nauvoo.[213] The *Times and Seasons* had previously been edited by Don Carlos Smith, Joseph Smith's brother who edited 31 issues of the paper until his death in 1841, and Ebenezer Robinson, who is credited with securing the Book of Mormon's stereotype and arranging for its printing in Ohio. Ebenezer also participated in the printing of the first edition of the Doctrine and Covenants as well as the second and third editions of the Book of Mormon.[214] After Don Carlos's death, Joseph Smith became the editor.[215]

He also became the editor of the *Nauvoo Neighbor,* which had previously been called the *Wasp,* a paper devoted "to the dissemination of useful knowledge of every description—the arts, science, religion, literature, agriculture, manufactures, trade, commerce and the general news of the day."[216] The *Wasp* was previously edited by William Smith, another one of Joseph's brothers, who used the paper to defend the Church and criticize its enemies. William decided to run for the legislature, which opened up the position of editor that John filled. John had it renamed the *Nauvoo Neighbor.*[217]

John wrote many editorials in these two papers defending the Church and the Prophet Joseph Smith.[218] For instance, after the Prophet and Patriarch's martyrdom in 1844, John wrote in the *Times and Seasons,*

> The idea of the church being disorganized and broken up because of the Prophet and Patriarch being slain, is preposterous. This church has the seeds of immortality in its midst. It is not of man, nor by man—it is the offspring of Deity: it is organized after the pattern of heavenly beings, through the principles of revelation; by the opening of the heavens, by the ministering of angels, and the revelations of Jehovah. It is not affected by the death of one or two, or fifty individuals. . . . Times

213 Roberts, *Life of John Taylor*, 102-103.

214 "Autobiography of Ebenezer Robinson," in *The Return* 1 [1889].

215 Gibbons, *John Taylor*, 49.

216 Roberts, *Life of John Taylor*, 102-103.

217 Gibbons, *John Taylor*, 49-50.

218 Roberts, *Life of John Taylor*, 102-103.

> and seasons may change, revolution may succeed revolution, thrones may be cast down, and empires be dissolved, earthquakes may rend the earth from centre to circumference, the mountains may be hurled out of their places, and the mighty ocean be moved form its bed; but amidst the crash of worlds and the crack of matter, truth, eternal truth must remain unchanged, and those principles which God has revealed to his Saints be unscathed amidst the warring elements, and remain as firm as the throne of Jehovah.[219]

John had a distinctive style of writing with a "wry sense of humor" used to defend the Church. He did not always write satires or caricatures, however, and in most instances "was conservative in his reporting and editorializing … in his usual objective, dignified, and highly literate style." He partnered with Wilford Woodruff, who acted as the business manager of the publications, and the two of them used the money generated to support their families, though it was not always enough. As a solution, they turned to job printing and bookbinding, eventually delving into selling books, boots, and seeds.[220]

On April 13, 1845, John Taylor purchased a new home and a print shop in Nauvoo. He recorded his purchase of the property:

> A man of the name of James Ivins has considerable property, and wished to part with it[. …] He had a first rate large brick house, brick store, and large pine board barn, on a half acre of land on Main street, corner of Kimball, which he had offered to me for three thousand two hundred dollars although the buildings had cost twice that sum. I asked the brethren what their counsel was upon the subject; they said go ahead and get it. I took measure forthwith to procure it, not that I wanted to build myself up; but my idea in getting it was to keep it out of the hands of our enemies, as it was offered so cheap; and I thought the store would suit us for a Printing Office. My feelings after I had traded for this were the same as ever, I felt like sacrificing all things when called upon, my heart is not set upon property, but the things of God: I care not so much about the good things of this life, as I do about the fellowship of my brethren, and to fulfilling the word the Lord has called me to do; and the

---

219 *Times and Seasons* 5:744, December 15, 1844, cited in Gordon B. Hinkley, "Dedication of the John Taylor Building," *BYU Speeches,* 14 September 1982, https://speeches.byu.edu/talks/gordon-b-hinckley/dedication-john-taylor-building/.

220 Gibbons, *John Taylor*, 49-50.

favor of the Lord, and securing to myself, my family, and friends an inheritance in the Kingdom of God."[221]

The Taylors moved into the house on May 10, 1845 and remained there until the Saints left for Winter Quarters, Nebraska. The printing press John bought was similar to those throughout the country during this period of time, which applied paper and ink to moveable type. The shop contained two large presses along with smaller presses.

Mini-Devotional — "The Love of a Father"

Wooden rocking horse in the John and Leonora Taylor home. Photo by Casey Paul Griffiths.

The John Taylor Home found in Nauvoo today displays a small wooden rocking horse. Family legend tells that when the Taylor's were forced to leave Nauvoo by a mob, the family left their home, the rocking horse, which John had carved for his children, was left behind. The weight of unnecessary items was too much to bear on a wagon which had to journey hundreds of miles to the Rocky Mountains. To make room for essentials, the Taylor family had to

221 John Taylor, *John Taylor Nauvoo Journal,* (Provo, UT: Grandin Book Co., 1996), 55.

leave behind such things as toys and other comforts. Saying goodbye to this rocking horse caused especially great disappointment to John's son, Joseph. When Joseph could not be comfort aged about the loss of the toy which was so precious to him, John returned to a hostile Nauvoo to retrieve the horse. The journey required crossing the icy Mississippi River and avoiding angry mobs. Still, John risked all of this to return a wooden rocking horse that was so dear to his son.[222]

The love that our Heavenly Father has for us is far beyond even the love that John showed for his son, Joseph, by even risking his life. The story of the rocking horse serves as a gentle reminder that just as John loved Joseph, we, too, are loved by our Heavenly Father.

- When have you made a significant sacrifice to help someone else in need?
- When has someone else made a sacrifice to help you?
- When have you felt God's love for you in your life?

John Taylor was declared by Brigham Young to be the "most powerful editor and writer in the Church."[223] His dedication to the Gospel of Jesus Christ and to the Prophet Joseph Smith shone through his words, both in his speech and his writing. He had an unwavering testimony of the Church of Jesus Christ of Latter-day Saints. John Taylor went on to become the third president of the Church of Jesus Christ of Latter-day Saints.

---

222 A primary source for this story has yet to be found. See Amie Jane Leavitt, "The Love of a Father," *The Church of Jesus Christ of Latter-day Saints,* https://www.churchofjesuschrist.org/study/friend/2010/03/the-love-of-a-father?lang=eng.

223 Gibbons, *John Taylor,* 26.

The Wilford and Phebe Woodruff Home

The Wilford and Pheobe Woodruff home in Nauvoo. Photo by Casey Paul Griffiths.

Interior of the Wilford and Pheobe Woodruff home. Photo by Casey Paul Griffiths

Significant Events at this location:

- On July 22, 1839, Wilford Woodruff took Joseph Smith's handkerchief to administer and heal Latter-day Saints suffering from cholera.
- Wilford Woodruff leaves Nauvoo for Mission to England from August 1839 to August 1841.
- Wilford Woodruff leaves Nauvoo for a Mission to the Eastern States March 1844.
- Wilford Woodruff and Phebe Carter are sealed for Time and all Eternity, November 11, 1842.
- Wilford Woodruff completes his home in Nauvoo in 1844 and only lives there for 64 days as he is chased out by a mob.
- Wilford Woodruff's home sells for $675 as he heads west.

Wilford Woodruff, fourth president of the Church of Jesus Christ of Latter-day Saints, was born in 1807 in Farmington, Connecticut. His childhood was filled with accidents, one of which involved a bite from a rabid dog and another involving a plunge into boiling water.[224] On the day of his baptism, "his horse kicked the hat off his head, narrowly missing what could have been a fatal or seriously damaging blow. Ten minutes later, as he left the baptismal pond, he was thrown from a sled beneath the feet of a team of horses and was dragged for some distance." He reported at least twenty-three major accidents, many of which could have taken his life. [225] Despite his adversities, he wrote, "The repeated deliverances from all these remarkable dangers I ascribe to the mercies of my Heavenly Father."[226] His unwavering faith and persistent efforts allowed him to touch the lives of thousands of people.

Although Wilford did not learn of the Church of Jesus Christ of Latter-day Saints until the age of twenty-three, before finding the church he believed that the world lacked the fullness of Christ's gospel. These beliefs were heavily influenced by Robert Mason, a mentor who told him that the Lord would soon raise up a church like the one during Christ's time. Mason, known as Old Prophet Mason by people in Connecticut, had a vision in the year 1800

224 Matthias F. Cowley, *Wilford Woodruff, Fourth President of the Church of Jesus Christ of Latter-day Saints. History of His Life and Labors, as Recorded in His Daily Journals*, (Salt Lake City: Bookcraft, 1964, 5, 11

225 Francis M. Gibbons, *Wilford Woodruff: Wondrous Worker, Prophet of God,* (Salt Lake City: Deseret Book Co., 1988), 3-4.

226 Cowley, *Wilford Woodruff,* 5, 11.

depicting Christ's restored Church as fruit. Mason told Wilford of this vision thirty years later—the year the church was organized—on their last visit, prophesying, "I shall never partake of this fruit in the flesh; but you will, and you will become a conspicuous actor in that kingdom." Mason's vision was fulfilled, for while Wilford was able to partake of the fruit of Christ's Gospel, Mason died before getting the chance. Wilford remembered Mason's vision and continued to read the scriptures and pray often, fully believing that God would guide him "in the way of salvation."[227]

Ironically, he first learned of the Church of Jesus Christ of Latter-day Saints from an anti-Mormon news article, though he refrained from making judgements until he could learn more. In fact, he was impressed by the Church's belief in modern revelation, prophets, and apostles, and since reading the article he wanted to meet members of the new Church. A year later in December of 1833, Wilford and his brother Azmon purchased a farm and sawmill in New York and had the opportunity to attend a sermon taught by Latter-day Saints Zera Pulsipher and Elijah Cheney. The Elders had visited the Woodruff's home while Wilford and Azmon were absent. When the returned home, Azmon's wife told them that missionaries had visited and would be teaching a sermon at a local schoolhouse that day. Wilford recalled, "I immediately turned out the horses and started for the schoolhouse without waiting for supper. On my way I prayed most sincerely that the Lord would give me His spirit, and that if these men were the servants of God I might know it, and that my heart might be prepared to receive the divine message they had to deliver." During the sermon the Spirit confirmed to Wilford that the words the missionaries spoke were of God. Afterwards, the Elders invited those in the congregation to share their thoughts about the words spoken. Wilford recalled, "Almost instantly I found myself upon my feet. The spirit of the Lord urged me to bear testimony to the truth of the message delivered by these elders." Azmon also bore testimony similar to that of Wilford's. Wilford immediately read the Book of Mormon and knew it to be true. Wilford and Azmon were baptized two days later on December 31 by Elder Pulsipher. Of his experience Wilford observed, "The snow was about three feet deep, the day was cold, and the water was mixed with ice and snow, yet I did not feel the cold."[228]

---

227 Wilford Woodruff, *Leaves from My Journal*, (American Fork, UT: Covenant Communications, Inc., 2005), 2-4.

228 Cowley, *Wilford Woodruff*, 33-34.

Mini-Devotional – Following Promptings from God

In 1832, when Wilford was making plans to move to New York to buy a farm with his brother Azmon, Wilford had a strong impression that he needed to go to Rhode Island instead. He told Azmon before their move to New York, "I wonder what the Lord wants of me in Rhode Island! The spirit of the Lord has rested upon me for two weeks and said, 'Go to Rhode Island.'" An hour later, his brother Azahel came to visit and almost immediately said, "I wonder what the Lord wants of me in Rhode Island! The spirit of the Lord has been upon me for two or three weeks and has told me to go to Rhode Island." Wilford explained, "This caused us to marvel exceedingly. We had not seen each other for several months. My brother Azmon thought that as we were ready to go to New York, we better not go to Rhode Island. To this we consented with great reluctance. I felt sure it was our duty to go there, although at that time it was a mystery." After accepting the gospel in New York the next year, Wilford learned that Elders Orson Hyde and Samuel H. Smith were on a mission to Rhode Island the year before. Had they gone to Rhode Island, they would have joined the Church a year earlier and gone directly to Kirtland, Ohio, rather than purchasing a farm in New York. Wilford learned from this experience of the importance of heeding promptings.

- Have you ever ignored a prompting that you later learned would have blessed your life had you followed? What did you learn from the experience?
- When have you followed a prompting immediately after receiving it? What blessings did you receive from your obedience?
- How do you receive guidance from the Spirit? What in your life do you do, or can you do, to better listen to the Spirit?

Wilford Woodruff's as a Missionary

When Wilford joined the Church, he desired to preach the Gospel, however he knew he would need to wait patiently to be called to serve. When he was ordained to the office of a Teacher, he went into the woods to pray to God that the path would open for him to preach. The Lord then confirmed to Wilford that he would have an opportunity to serve a mission. As he walked home from the woods, he met a High Priest whom he knew, who told Wilford, "The Lord has revealed to me that it is your privilege to be ordained, and to go and preach the gospel." Wilford replied, "I told him I was willing to do whatever the Lord required of me. I did not tell him I had just asked the Lord to let me go and preach." His first mission was to Arkansas and Tennessee.[229] He would eventually serve eight missions for the Church—several in the Eastern States and England—and baptize more than two thousand people.[230]

Wilford did not let anything get in the way of his service to the Lord. When he was called on his first England mission, he struggled with poor health. Before leaving, while talking to the Prophet Joseph Smith, he felt and looked "more like a subject for the dissecting room than a missionary." To this Joseph replied, "What did you say that for? Get up, and go along; all will be right with you." Wilford obeyed and served his mission, despite his illness, allowing many in England to join the Church.

While on his mission to England, Wilford wrote of an experience he had preaching at a farm down the road from a parish church. Many listened to his sermon while the parish church just had fifteen attendees. The rector of the parish sent a constable to arrest Wilford for preaching, but Wilford was able to show he had a license to preach as evidence that he was doing nothing wrong. He then invited the constable to listen to the sermon, promising that they could talk after the meeting. Wilford recorded,

> He took my chair and sat beside me. I preached the first principles of the everlasting gospel for an hour and a quarter. The power of God rested upon me, the Spirit filled the house, and the people were convinced.
>
> At the close of the meeting I opened a door for baptism, and seven offered themselves. Among the number were four preachers and the constable. [...] The constable went to the rector and told him if he wanted Mr. Woodruff taken up for preaching the gospel, he must go himself and serve the write, for he had heard him preach the only true gospel sermon he had ever listened to in his life.
>
> The rector did not know what to make of it, so he sent two clerks of the Church of England as spies, to attend our meeting, and find out what we did preach.
>
> But they were both pricked in their hearts and received the word of the Lord gladly and were baptized and confirmed members of the Church of Jesus Christ of Latter-day Saints.

---

229 Cowley, *Wilford Woodruff*, 17-18, 30-35.

230 Donald Q. Cannon "Illinois," in *Ohio and Illinois, Sacred Places: A Comprehensive Guide to Early LDS Historical Sites*, ed. LaMar C. Berrett, (Salt Lake City: Deseret Book Company, 2002), vol 3, 167.

> The rector became alarmed and did not dare to send anybody else.[231]

Wilford continued to have success baptizing hundreds of people within three months.

In March 1844, just a few months before the Prophet and Patriarch's martyrdom, Wilford was assigned to serve again in the Eastern States. Wilford remarked that "This was the last mission the Prophet ever gave to the Twelve Apostles in this dispensation." He wrote of his encounter with Joseph Smith before he departed from Nauvoo to begin his mission:

> The Prophet then turned to me and said: 'Brother Woodruff, I want you to go, and if you do not you will die.' His words rested with mighty weight upon me when he spoke, and I have often thought since, in contemplation of the awful tragedy of his and Hyrum's martyrdom, how truly his words would have been verified had I remained. [...] I took the parting hand of Hyrum and Joseph, at their own dwellings. Joseph stood in the entry of his door when I took his hand to bid him farewell. [...] As he took me by the hand, he said: 'Brother Woodruff, you are about to start upon your mission.' I answered, 'Yes.' He looked me steadily in the eye for a time without speaking a word; he looked as though he would penetrate my very soul, and at the same time seemed unspeakably sorrowful, as if weighed down by a foreboding of something dreadful. He finally spoke in a mournful voice: 'God bless you, Brother Woodruff; go in peace.' I turned and left him with a sorrowful heart, partaking of the same spirit which rested upon him. This was the last time I ever saw his face or heard his voice again—in the flesh.[232]

Joseph and Hyrum were killed in Carthage Jail on June 27, 1844. Willard Richards and John Taylor were the only members of the Quorum of the Twelve remained with the brothers and both survived. Wilford did not learn of their deaths until July 9, 1844 after reading an article in the *Boston Times.* He wrote a few days later, "I have never shed a tear since I heard of the death of the prophets untill [sic] this morning but my whole soul has felt nerved up like steel. Elder B. Young arrived in Boston this morning. I walked with him to 57 Temple st and called upon Sister Voice. Br. Young took to the bed and I the big chair, and I here veiled my face and for the first time gave vent to my grief and mourning for the Prophet and Patriarch of the Church, Joseph and

---

231 Woodruff, *Leaves from my Journals,* 124, 144-146.

232 Cowley, *Wilford Woodruff,* 204-205.

Hyrum Smith, who were murdered by a gentile mob. After being bathed by a flood of tears I felt composed."[233]

This entry comes from a journal Wilford Woodruff kept diligently for sixty-three years, starting not long after his baptism. In 1872, he reflected on his extensive journaling:

> I made a record from the first sermon I heard, and from that day until now I have kept a daily journal. Whenever I heard Joseph Smith preach, teach, or prophesy, I always felt it my duty to write it; I felt uneasy and could not eat, drink, or sleep until I did write; and my mind has been so exercised upon this subject that when I heard Joseph Smith teach and had no pencil or paper, I would go home and sit down and write the whole sermon, almost word for word and sentence by sentence as it was delivered, and when I had written it it was taken from me, I remembered it no more. This was the gift of God to me. …
>
> I seem to be a marked victim of the adversary. I can find but one reason for this: the devil knew if I got into the Church of Jesus Christ of Latter-day Saints, I would write the history of that Church and leave on record the works and teachings of the prophets, of the apostles and elders.[234]

Indeed, his diligence in keeping a journal preserved the history of the early Church and its members, a journal which became the most important record of those years of the Church. Without it, modern historians and members would lack much information about the history of the Church.

In addition to the important spiritual record, Wilford's journals blessed his immediate family. On one occasion, after keeping a journal for forty years, he and his family sat down to read the journals together. Wilford wrote, "it is now a great pleasure to me and my family to sit down and read an account of our travels, where we have been, and what we have done, and the dealings of God with us, and the many good times we have had with our friends."[235] His journals record that in the first 61 years of his membership, he traveled 172,269 miles; held 7,555 meetings; preached 3,526 discourses; established 77 preaching places in missions; organized 51 branches; assisted in confirming 8,952

233 "Journal (January 1, 1843 – December 31, 1844)," July 16, 1844 - July 17, 1844, The Wilford Woodruff Papers, accessed August 23, 2022, https://wilfordwoodruffpapers.org/documents/6e34557b-3015-4803-9a97-d913b4afd003/page/2a564cf1-267b-4db2-acfd-9cbda413969c.

234 Cowley, *Wilford Woodruff*, 478-477.

235 Gibbons, *Wilford Woodruff*, 8-9.

members; and traveled throughout England, Scotland, Wales, 6 islands of the sea, 23 states, and 5 U.S. territories.[236] These numbers demonstrate Wilford's dedication to the Church and to the Lord.

Mini-Devotional – The Importance of Keeping a Journal

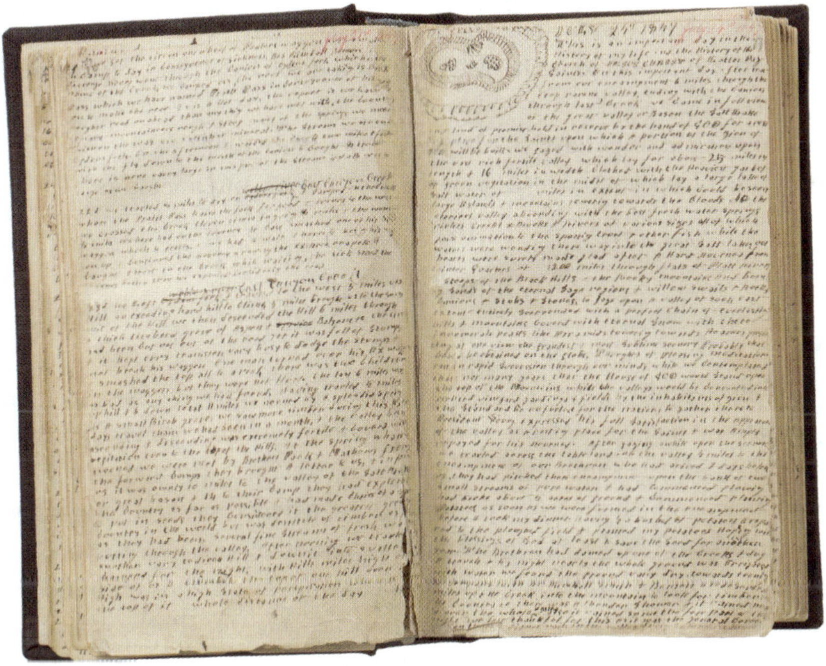

One of the journals Wilford Woodruff wrote during his lifetime. Courtesy Church History Library.

Wilford knew of the importance of keeping a journal, which has often been a commandment. For instance, the Nephites were chastised for not keeping a record of the teachings of Samuel the Lamanite (3 Nephi 23:6-13), Moses was commanded to record what he was taught (Moses 1:40). Wilford Woodruff admonished that "If men had not kept a journal in former days, we should not now have any Bible, Book of Mormon, Doctrine and Covenants or any other book." Though many are grateful for the journals of these great people of the past, they do not see them keeping their own journals as having merit or their everyday life as having any interest. Though Wilford wrote about major events, such as sermons given by the Prophet Joseph or his experience on missions, he

236 Andrew Jenson, *Latter-day Saint Biographical Encyclopedia: A Compilation of Biographical Sketches of Prominent Men and Women in the Church of Jesus Christ of Latter-day Saints,* (Salt Lake City: Western Epics, 1971), 1:26.

also recorded his everyday life: "So the journals are liberally sprinkled with entries of a prosaic nature, like digging clams, fishing, walking in the mud, sore feet, sea sickness, and so on. And some such entries open a field of thought that far transcends the particular item or incident mentioned. … Such entries provide the seasoning and variety for the extraordinary record Wilford Woodruff began after his baptism."[237] Keeping a journal, even for those moments in life that seem provincial, can provide future generations with valuable insights into the lives of those that came before.

- Do you keep a journal? What can you do to have more regular or descriptive entries?
- What blessings have you received from journaling?
- What have you learned from the journals of your ancestors?

Wilford and Phebe

Wilford Woodruff met his wife, Phebe Carter, after she had traveled to Kirtland, Ohio one year after her baptism to join with the Saints. She recalled, "In the year 1834, I embraced the Gospel, as revealed through the Prophet Joseph Smith, and, about a year after, I left my parents and kindred, and journeyed to Kirkland [sic], Ohio, a distance of one thousand miles, a lone maid, sustained only by my faith and trust in Israel's god. My friends marveled at my course, as did I, but something within impelled me on." Phebe's decision to journey to Ohio was laced with difficulty. Her mother begged her not to leave, making a hard decision much harder. Still, Phebe listened to the quiet whisperings of the Spirit:

> My mother's grief at my leaving home was almost more than I could bear; and had it not been for the spirit within I should have faltered at the last. My Mother told me she would rather see me buried that going thus alone into the heartless world, and especially was she concerned about my leaving home to cast my lot among the Mormons. 'Phebe,' she said, impressively, 'will you come back to me if you find Mormonism false?' I answered thrice, 'Yes, mother, I will.' […] When the time came for my departure I dared not trust myself to say farewell, so I wrote my good-bye to each, and leaving them on my table, ran down stairs and jumped in the

237 Gibbons, *Wilford Woodruff*, 9, 11.

> carriage. Thus I left my beloved home of childhood to link my life with the Saints of God.[238]

Despite her parent's initial objections to the Church, they were later baptized by Wilford Woodruff—her father in 1849 and her mother before her passing in 1845.[239]

Phebe's decision to join the Saints led her to meet her future husband, who she married in Joseph Smith's home in Kirtland on April 13, 1837 by Frederick G. Williams. Though Joseph was initially asked to officiate the marriage ceremony, he was forced into hiding to avoid his enemies.[240] Phebe was a great support for her husband, whose missionary duties required him to travel more than he was at home—Wilford embarked on a mission less than two months after his marriage to Phebe. She relied on her unwavering faith in God as her strength during those difficult times of separation. As evidence, on one of Wilford's missions to England from August 1839 to April 1841, Phebe wrote to him from Nauvoo: "I know that it is the will of God that you should labour in his vineyard; therefore, I feel reconciled to his will in these things. I have not been left to murmur or complain since you left me, but am looking forward to the day when you shall return home once more to the bosom of your family."[241] There were some instances when Phebe joined Wilford on his missions. For example, on Wilford's mission to the Fox Islands, Phebe made the journey from Nauvoo to visit him. After converting nearly one-hundred people, Wilford and Phebe returned home with the new Saints from the Islands. During their trek Wilford wrote of the Lord's hand in their lives:

> On the 23rd of November my wife, Phebe, was attacked with a severe headache, which terminated in brain fever. She grew more and more distressed daily as we continued our journey. It was a terrible ordeal for a woman to travel in a wagon over rough roads, afflicted as she was. . . .

238 Augusta Joyce Crocheron, "Phebe W. Carter Woodruff, Wife of Wilford Woodruff, President of the Twelve Apostles, of the Church of Jesus Christ of Latter-day Saints," *Representative Women of Deseret* (Salt Lake City: J. C. Graham and Co., 1884), 35.

239 Cowley, *Wilford Woodruff*, 337.

240 "Journal (December 29, 1833 – January 3, 1838)," April 13, 1837, The Wilford Woodruff Papers, accessed August 23, 2022, https://wilfordwoodruffpapers.org/documents/b048a7c5-6b6b-438a-bce7-262d5ba297d8/page/114d13a4-1517-423c-96d4-cb06e7fa0f2f.

241 "Late From America," *Millennial Star* 1, no. 4 (August 1840): 90.

> December 3rd found my wife very low. I spent the day in taking care of her. … She seemed to be gradually sinking, and in the evening her spirit apparently left her body, and she was dead.
>
> The sisters gathered around her body, weeping, while I stood looking at her in sorrow. The Spirit and power of God began to rest upon me until, for the first time during her sickness, faith filled my soul, although she lay before me as one dead.
>
> … I laid my hands upon her, and in the name of Jesus Christ I rebuked the power of death and the destroyer, and commanded the same to depart from her, and the spirit of life to enter her body.
>
> Her spirit returned to her body, and from that hour she was made whole.[242]

She lived for almost fifty more years, eventually returning to her Father in Heaven on November 10, 1885. Wilford and Phebe's love for one another transcended their time on the Earth. On November 11, 1842, they were sealed for time and eternity in Nauvoo by Hyrum Smith.[243]

Wilford Woodruff's Service in Nauvoo

Wilford was called to the Quorum of the Twelve Apostles on July 14, 1838 through a letter to him while on his mission to the Fox Islands. The letter did not reach him until August 9.[244] He then returned to Kirtland where he was ordained a member of the Quorum of the Twelve on April 16, 1839. After moving to Nauvoo in 1839, he was frequently in meetings and councils with the rest of the Quorum of the Twelve, working on the Nauvoo temple, or serving the people of Nauvoo. One journal entry in November 1841 shows a glimpse of a typical day for him in Nauvoo:

> The Twelve met in council at President Brigham Young's home. Afterwards there was a general meeting of the Saints who were addressed by John Taylor and Hyrum Smith. The Twelve then returned to Brigham Young's home and were occupied in counsel until four in the afternoon when they repaired to the baptismal font in the basement of the Nauvoo Temple. … It was truly an interesting scene. It was the first font built in

242 Woodruff, *Leaves from My Journal,* 91, 94, 96-97.

243 Cowley, *Wilford Woodruff,* 194, 689.

244 Gibbons, *Wilford Woodruff,* 42

> this dispensation for the glorious provision in the gospel which provided for the redeptoin [sic] of the dead. It was dedicated by President Joseph Smith and the Twelve. A large congregation assembled to witness the baptism of about forty persons by Brigham Young, Heber C. Kimball, and John Taylor. Elders Willard Richards, George A. Smith, and myself assisted in confirming them. Afterwards I passed the evening with the quorum of the Twelve at the home of Heber C. Kimball.

Wilford also worked on the Nauvoo temple, including hauling "large stones from the river to Temple Hill."

Other responsibilities included becoming a member of the city council in Nauvoo on October 30, 1841.[245] He was also in charge of the provision store for the committee of the Nauvoo House and worked as a real estate agent. In addition to his work, "Wilford and his wife, Phebe, were caught up in a satisfying and stimulating social life with frequent dinner and other entertainments shared with church and civic leaders and their companions."[246]

Joseph Smith's Healing Handkerchief

The handkerchief Joseph Smith gave to Wilford Woodruff is currently on display in the Church History Museum. Courtesy Church History Museum.

In July of 1839, a terrible sickness attacked the citizens of Nauvoo. Joseph Smith gave his house over to care for the sick as he administered to them and slept outside in a tent during the night. Eventually, Joseph himself became sick, and on the morning of July 22, awoke reflecting on the terrible circumstances. He prayed that he might be healed, and his prayer was answered, as he was able to get up and go around Nauvoo healing the citizens of the town. After healing everyone in Nauvoo, he crossed the

245 Cowley, *Wilford Woodruff*, 154-155.
246 Gibbons, *Wilford Woodruff*, 71, 73.

Mississippi River to Montrose where Brigham Young and Wilford Woodruff were staying, both of them ill. Joseph healed Brigham and then while passing by Wilford's cabin door, commanded Wilford to follow him. Joseph, Wilford, and other members of the Twelve Apostles then healed many others that day.

As the group was returning home, they ran into a man who ran a ferry boat who had heard from his passengers about the miracles they had performed. He then asked Joseph to journey two miles outside of Montrose to his home to heal his twin girls who were "sick nigh unto death." Though Joseph could not go, he asked Wilford to go in his stead, giving him a red silk handkerchief and instructing him to wipe the faces of the children with the handkerchief as he administered to them, promising that they would be healed. He also told Wilford that he could keep the handkerchief and promised by so doing that Joseph would always be with him. Wilford healed the children as counseled, keeping the handkerchief with him thereafter.[247]

Work on the *Times and Seasons*

On February 3, 1842, Wilford Woodruff was asked to leave the provision store and edit the Church newspaper, the *Times and Seasons,* along with John Taylor. Wilford took this work seriously. Recalling a time when the paper desperately needed supplies that could only be purchased in St. Louis, a long distance down the Mississippi River. Wilford made the trip by steamer, despite being ill. He wrote of what he accomplished within twenty-four hours:

> I walked till ten o'clock at night, and I went to bed weary and sick and in severe pain and did not sleep till two in the morning. I was awakened shortly after that hour with the bleeding of the nose, through which I must have lost a pint of blood. Notwithstanding my weakness from fatigue and loss of blood, I began work before breakfast the following morning. In the afternoon my supplies were all on board the boat. I ate dinner and went to bed tired and sick. The boat left at six in the evening and arrived in due time at Keokuk.

Upon his return to Nauvoo, he found that the printing press was also out of paper. Still ill, he returned to St. Louis to purchase the paper, returning home at midnight with a fever and a cold. "Since the boat had landed our freight and I had seen it distributed to the several departments, I went home

247 Woodruff, *Leaves from My Journals*, 111-116.

where I was confined to my bed and passed through the severest siege of sickness I ever had in my life." Wilford remained in his room, mostly bedridden, for the next forty days. When he felt strong enough to resume working, he attended a meeting of the Quorum of the Twelve. His strength did not last very long, however.[248] He wrote, "*I* lay down upon a bench, but had no sooner lain down that I was gone. My breath stopped. My Brethren raised me up, took me to the door into the air, and with the assistance of water and air I was brought into breath again, but not without a hard struggle between life and death."[249]

Wilford Woodruff's Gift to His Family

From the time Wilford joined the Church he was seldom home, being away about four-fifths of the time. In fact, until Nauvoo "during all the years of his labor in the Church he had been without a home of his own."[250] When the Woodruff family first moved to Nauvoo, they stayed in army barracks in the nearby town of Montrose. It would not be until 1841 that Wilford had the opportunity to buy a home for his family. Wilford bought a home for $85 and almost immediately began working to make it more comfortable. The house was small, making it no more than a shack. He "cut two loads of wood and drew it to the door," spent three days "mowing and drawing hay" for their cows, and furnished the house with furniture that had been stored away. On his first night in his new home, he wrote, "I felt to rejoice to spend a night with my family under a roof of my own, it being the first time that I have ever enjoyed such a privilege since we were married." After moving in, he still worked to improve the home, he purchasing brick and mortar to build a chimney and an oven, laying new flooring in the bedroom and lathing and plastering its walls.

Though grateful for the opportunity to own a home, Wilford realized that this house was not the most comfortable home that he could provide for his family, and after one especially bitter winter, he desired "to leave a house of my family to abide in and be comfortable in my absence." Wilford and other workers began construction on a two-story brick home on May 22, 1843: "I cleared away my ground and commenced digging my cellar for my house."[251] After leaving on a mission that year and returning to Nauvoo in November,

248 Cowley, *Wilford Woodruff,* 166-167

249 Gibbons, *Wilford Woodruff,* 77.

250 Cowley, *Wilford Woodruff,* 158, *177*

251 Gibbons, *Wilford Woodruff,* 47, 70-71, 77-78.

he found that nothing had been done to complete the home.[252] He finished building it and moved his family into the home on May 4, 1844. Interestingly, he included eight fireplaces, one for each room, to further enhance the comfort of his home.[253] That day he wrote in his journal, "I mooved [sic] into my new brick house & truly felt thankful to have a comfortable dwelling to leave my family in while I go on my mishion [sic]." He included a small drawing of his home underneath that journal entry.[254] Five days later, he left on a mission to the Eastern States.[255] and in one of his detailed journals, he recorded that this home had 14,574 bricks. Wilford only lived in this home for a total of sixty-four days because of his frequent travels as a missionary.[256] Though Phebe did not travel as often, she accompanied Wilford on his mission to England three months after moving into her new home, leaving her children with friends and family.

In 1846, the Saints in Nauvoo were forced by mobs to leave their homes and travel to the Rocky Mountains. Frantically attempted to sell their homes and property, many could not find buyers and had to leave their homes vacant and unsold. Wilford Woodruff's home and land sold for a meager $675 because of its quality, though it was worth more than that.[257] As a testament to Wilford's building, the home was lived in continuously thereafter until 1965,[258] when the Nauvoo Restoration, Inc. purchased it. After four years of restoration, it became the first building in Nauvoo which was authentically restored.[259]

President Wilford Woodruff was a man of great faith and an integral component to the work of the Church of Jesus Christ of Latter-day Saints. Much can be learned from his life about what it means to be a disciple of Christ, and an example that would be wise to follow. His extensive missionary efforts

252 Journal (January 1, 1843 – December 31, 1844)," November 5, 1843 - November 11, 1843, The Wilford Woodruff Papers, accessed August 23, 2022, https://wilfordwoodruffpapers.org/documents/6e34557b-3015-4803-9a97-d913b4afd003/page/ad3de4ba-7a10-49f9-8f62-6eaa1e7fcd12.

253 Loren C. Dunn, "Introduction to Historic Nauvoo," *BYU Studies Quarterly* 32, no. 1, (1992): 23-32.

254 "Journal (January 1, 1843 – December 31, 1844)," May 4, 1844 - May 7, 1844, The Wilford Woodruff Papers, accessed August 5, 2022, https://wilfordwoodruffpapers.org/documents/6e34557b-3015-4803-9a97-d913b4afd003/page/ddf06d43-65ca-4c2e-a00c-2921ec030f28.

255 Gibbons, *Wilford Woodruff,* 83.

256 Cannon, "Illinois," 167.

257 Gibbons, *Wilford Woodruff,* 90-91, 110-111.

258 "Nauvoo, Illinois," *Doctrine and Covenants Central*, https://doctrineandcovenantscentral.org/nauvoo-illinois/.

259 Cannon, "Illinois," 167

and his thorough journal-keeping facilitated thousands of people to come unto Christ and thousands more to learn about the history of the Church of Jesus Christ of Latter-day Saints.

The Homes of Church Leaders in Nauvoo

Sarah Granger Kimball Home

The Sarah Granger Kimball Home in Nauvoo. Photo by Kenneth Mays.

Significant events at this location:

- In February 1842, a preliminary meeting was held in this home for the purpose of organizing a ladies' benevolent society.

Sarah Melissa Granger was born in 1818 at Phelps, New York, located only a few miles from Palmyra, New York. Sarah's parents, Oliver and Lydia

Granger, joined the Church in 1832. Sarah joined the Church around the same time and moved with her parents to Kirtland, Ohio in 1833. While in Kirtland she was one of twenty-three women allowed to attend the School of the Prophets led by the Prophet Joseph Smith. Sarah married Hiram Kimball in 1840 and subsequently moved to Nauvoo. Hiram, a distant cousin to Heber C. Kimball, moved to Nauvoo (then called Commerce) in 1833. He established several stores, maintained a riverboat landing, and became a prosperous businessman. The boat landing would become one of the crossing points used by the Saints when they evacuated Nauvoo in 1846. Though Hiram was not a member of the Church when he married Sarah, he was eventually baptized in July 1843.

Hiram and Sarah Kimball had six children. When their firstborn son, Hiram W. Kimball, was born, Sarah wanted to donate money toward the building of the Nauvoo Temple, but she was hesitant to ask her non-member husband to make the donation. Instead, Sarah asked her husband,

> "What is the boy worth?" He replied, "O, I don't know, he is worth a great deal." I said, "Is he worth a thousand dollars?" The reply was, "Yes, more than that if he lives and does well." I said, "Half of him is mine, is it not?" "Yes, I suppose so." "Then I have something to help on the Temple." He said pleasantly, "You have?" "Yes, and I think of turning my share right in as tithing." "Well, I'll see about that." Soon after the above conversation Mr. Kimball met the Prophet Joseph Smith, President of the Church, and said, "Sarah has got a little the advantage of me this time, she proposes to turn out the boy as Church property." President Smith seemed pleased with the joke, and said, "I accept all such donations, and from this day the boy shall stand recorded, Church property." Then turning to Willard Richards, his secretary, he said, "Make a record of this, and you are my witness." Joseph Smith then said, "Major, (Mr. Kimball was major in the Nauvoo Legion) you now have the privilege of paying $500 and retaining possession or receiving $500 and giving possession."[260]

Hiram Kimball donated a piece of land to the Church as payment for the difference and retained his son.

Sarah's passion for the temple was not limited to its construction. Sarah noticed that the clothing of the temple builders wore out easily as they handled the rough stone. She had an idea to sew shirts for the workmen but did

260 Augusta Joyce Crocheron, comp., *Representative Women of Deseret: A Book of Biographical Sketches* (Salt Lake City,1884), accessed July 19, 2022, http://files.usgwarchives.net/ut/state/bios/ajc/kimball-sarahm.txt.

not consider herself a good seamstress, so she teamed up with Miss Margaret Cook. Sarah furnished the materials and Margaret sewed the shirts.

Realizing that the project was too big for just the two of them, they invited other sisters to join in. In the winter of 1842, these sisters met together in the parlor of Sarah Kimball's home for the purpose of establishing a ladies' benevolent society. Eliza R. Snow was asked to write the constitution. Eliza took the constitution to Joseph Smith who commended it but said the Lord had something better in mind for the sisters. On March 17, 1842, Joseph organized the Female Relief Society of Nauvoo with Emma Smith as its first president.[261]

When the Saints left Nauvoo in 1846, Sarah and Hiram Kimball stayed in Nauvoo to continue pursuing some of Hiram's business interests. It was not until 1851 that the Kimballs finally emigrated to Utah. Once in Utah, Sarah was called to preside over Salt Lake City's 15th Ward Relief Society. She served in that position until her death in 1898. Sarah also served in the Church-wide Relief Society when it was reorganized under the leadership of Eliza R Snow. She served as the general secretary and later as a counselor in the presidency. Sarah also became the first president of the Utah Woman's Suffrage Association and was good friends with fellow suffragist Susan B. Anthony.

Hiram Kimball died in 1863 while serving a mission for the Church. Sarah Kimball died more than two decades later in Salt Lake City on December 1, 1888. The Sarah Granger Kimball home is the original home that the Kimball family lived in during their time in Nauvoo.

Mini-Devotional—Strong Minded and Warm Hearted

The words "Strong Minded and Warm Hearted" are engraved across the top of Sarah Kimball's headstone in Salt Lake City. Sarah was both a compassionate and strong-willed person—she was not afraid to stand up for what she believed in. She took a stand when she wanted to help the temple workers in Nauvoo, and she took a stand when she believed women should have the right to vote.

- The Savior told us to be "wise as serpents, and harmless as doves" (Matthew 10:16). What do you think he meant by that?
- How does being "strong minded and warm hearted" make one a good disciple of Jesus Christ?

261 For more information on the formation of the Relief Society, see the chapter on Joseph Smith's Red Brick Store.

- In what ways can you be "strong minded and warm hearted" as you stand up for what you believe in?

Orson Hyde Home

The Orson and Marinda Hyde home in Nauvoo. Photo by Casey Paul Griffiths.

Orson Hyde was born in Connecticut in 1805. Throughout his life he held a wide variety of occupations: laborer, clerk, storekeeper, teacher, editor, businessman, and even judge.[262] He moved to Kirtland, Ohio in 1818. He was baptized in October 1831 after his former minister, Sidney Rigdon, converted to the Church. There he met and married Marinda Johnson in 1834. Also in 1834, he accompanied the Prophet Joseph Smith on the Zion's Camp expedition. In 1835, Orson was ordained as one of the original members of the Quorum of the Twelve Apostles (two of Marinda's brothers, Luke and Lyman Johnson, also served as original members of the Twelve).

262 "Orson Hyde" (biographical entry), The Joseph Smith Papers, accessed July 18, 2022, https://www.josephsmithpapers.org/person/orson-hyde.

Over the course of his lifetime, Orson Hyde would serve thirteen missions for the Church.[263] In 1837, he served a mission to England with Heber C. Kimball. In the summer of 1838, the Hyde family moved to Far West, Missouri. Shortly after arriving in Missouri, Orson became very ill and weak. His faith was deeply shaken by the persecutions the Church was facing as well as by some of the vigilante activities a small group of Church members claimed to be carrying out in Joseph Smith's name. When dissenters decided to file an affidavit accusing Church leaders of crimes against the state of Missouri, Orson signed on as a witness saying he believed the statements to be true. Orson was disfellowshipped and removed from the Quorum of the Twelve.

Orson Hyde's estrangement from the Church only lasted a few months. Realizing that he made a serious mistake, he asked Heber C. Kimball to intercede on his behalf. At a conference of the Church held on June 27, 1839, Orson confessed his error and was restored to the priesthood and as an Apostle.[264]

In March 1840, Orson Hyde had a dream in which he saw many of the great cities of the world, including Jerusalem, laid before him. In this vision, Orson was told to preach in these cities and dedicate Jerusalem for the return of the children of Abraham.[265] He told the Prophet Joseph Smith about the vision, and Joseph confirmed Orson's calling to that mission. Joseph assigned Apostle John E. Page to accompany Orson on his journey. Orson and John left Nauvoo on April 15, 1840, and embarked on the longest missionary journey ever taken (to that date) by a missionary of the Church. Orson and John would eventually split up in hopes of finding more opportunities to preach and raise money for their mission and agreed to meet up again in New York City. Orson waited for some time in the city, but John never showed up, so Orson decided it would be best for him to continue on his own.

Orson Hyde traveled through London and Rotterdam and into Germany. There he met a tutor who taught him how to speak German in eight days! Hyde attributed this accomplishment to the Spirit of the Lord.[266] He continued his travels through Constantinople and Beirut on his way to Jerusalem. Orson arrived in Jerusalem on October 21, 1841. Three days later, Orson crossed over to the Mount of Olives and dedicated Jerusalem for the return of the children of Abraham. After accomplishing his purpose, Orson returned

263 Roy B. Huff, "Orson Hyde: A Life of Lessons Learned," *Religious Educator* 3, no. 2 (2002), accessed July 18, 2022, https://rsc.byu.edu/vol-3-no-2-2002/orson-hyde-life-lessons-learned.

264 Joseph Smith, Journal, June 27, 1839, The Joseph Smith Papers, accessed July 18, 2022, https://www.josephsmithpapers.org/paper-summary/journal-1839/5.

265 Huff, "Orson Hyde."

266 Huff, "Orson Hyde."

through Egypt, Italy, and Germany. He arrived in Nauvoo on December 7, 1842, having traveled over twenty thousand miles in nearly a thousand days.

During this journey, Orson Hyde suffered many trials and hardships, including losing his missionary companion, overcoming language barriers, encountering passport issues, confronting pirates, and facing near starvation when the crew on a ship he was sailing in did not pack enough food for the journey.[267] Marinda Hyde also struggled to make ends meet while raising their two daughters when Orson was away. In 1842, friends and neighbors pitched in to build a home for the Hydes. The home was built in recognition of Marinda's sacrifices and Orson's lengthy mission.[268]

After returning to Nauvoo, Orson Hyde served as a member of the Masonic Lodge. He also served on the Nauvoo City Council and the Council of the Fifty. In 1843, the Prophet asked Orson to deliver a petition on behalf of the Church to the United States Congress. As the exodus from Nauvoo began in 1846, Orson stayed behind to dedicate the temple. On April 30, 1846, Orson offered the prayer for the public dedication of the Nauvoo Temple. The Hydes left Nauvoo and headed west in mid-May 1846, but Orson was soon called on a mission to England with John Taylor. The Twelve had received reports that things were not going well in England, so they sent Orson and John to bring the Saints and affairs of the Church in order.

When Brigham Young reorganized the First Presidency in 1847, Orson Hyde became the President of the Quorum of the Twelve Apostles and served in that capacity for twenty-seven years, the longest to serve in this dispensation. Orson presided over the Church in Kanesville, Iowa until 1852 when he was released to emigrate to Utah. He served in both the Utah Legislature and Supreme Court. He also went on a colonizing mission to Sanpete County, Utah, eventually settling there with his family. Orson and Marinda Hyde welcomed ten children to their family, but unfortunately their marriage ended in divorce in 1870. Orson died in 1878 in Spring City, Utah, and Marinda died on March 24, 1886 in Salt Lake City.

The Orson and Marinda Hyde home is one of the few frame structures remaining from the Nauvoo era. Over time, it has been used as a residence and as an office building. It was renovated by the Church in 2019.

267 Huff, "Orson Hyde."

268 "Orson & Marinda Hyde Home," Nauvoo Historic Sites, accessed July 18, 2022, https://www.nauvoohistoricsites.org/buildings/hyde-home/; see also Holzapfel, 113–14.

Mini-Devotional—The Power of Forgiveness

The affidavit that Orson Hyde signed in Missouri was one of the pieces of evidence used to arrest the Prophet Joseph Smith and hold him in Liberty Jail. It also was used to help justify the persecution heaped upon the Saints by the Missourians in 1838–39. When Orson asked for readmission to the Church, many of the Saints were angry with him.

Joseph Smith was reluctant to allow Orson Hyde to rejoin at first. The four and a half months Joseph spent in Liberty Jail and the suffering the Saints had endured made him cautious. But after being assured by Heber C. Kimball and also his brother Hyrum Smith, Joseph decided to forgive Orson and reinstate him pending the vote of the full Church. It is said that after Orson returned to the Church, Joseph ran out to greet Orson when he approached the Smith home.

- The Savior has commanded us to forgive each other: "But if ye forgive not men their trespasses, neither will your Father forgive your trespasses" (Matthew 6:15). Why do you think forgiving others is a commandment?
- After rejoining the Church, Orson Hyde completed a phenomenal mission which culminated in the rededication of Jerusalem for the gathering of the Jews. How can forgiveness—being forgiven and forgiving other people—result in great things being done for the kingdom of God?

Heber C. Kimball Home

Heber and Vilate Kimball home in Nauvoo. Photo by Casey Paul Griffiths.

Heber Chase Kimball was born at Sheldon, Vermont, in 1801. In 1811, his family moved to New York and settled in West Bloomfield. Heber lived there during the War of 1812 and recalls soldiers walking up and down the road near his house. At the age of fourteen, Heber went to work in his father's blacksmith shop and learned the trade. In 1820, he moved to Mendon, New York with his brother and learned how to make pottery. It was in Mendon that he met two people who would become his life-long friends—Brigham Young and Vilate Murray. He married Vilate in 1822.

On September 22, 1827, Heber C. Kimball was awakened by a neighbor calling him to come outside and see what was happening in the night sky. Heber said that it appeared as though an army was marching across the sky: "We could distinctly see the muskets, bayonets and knapsacks of the men, who wore caps and feathers like those used by the American soldiers in the last war with Britain. . . . This scenery we gazed upon for hours, until it began to disappear." Heber went on to say, "After I became acquainted with Mormonism, I learned that this took place the same evening that Joseph Smith received the records of the Book of Mormon from the angel Moroni, who had held those records in his possession."[269]

Sometime in late 1831, Heber C. Kimball discovered that five elders of the Church of Christ (as the Church was known at that time) were visiting at the nearby home of Phineas Young (Brigham Young's brother). Heber had heard about this new church and was curious, so he paid them a visit. That night, according to Heber, "for the first time I heard the fullness of the everlasting gospel."[270] Heber continued to investigate the Church until April 15, 1832, when he finally felt ready to be baptized. His best friend Brigham Young had been baptized the day before.

Heber C. Kimball moved his family to Kirtland, Ohio in 1833. There he met the Prophet Joseph Smith and the two became great friends. Heber participated in Zion's Camp in 1834 and then was ordained as an original member of the Quorum of the Twelve Apostles in 1835. Heber served on missions with his fellow Apostles throughout the eastern United States. However, it was a mission call he received in 1837 that changed his life: "On Sunday, the 4th day of June, 1837 . . . the Prophet Joseph came to me, while I was seated in front of the stand, above the sacrament table, on the Melchisedek [*sic*] side of the Temple, in Kirtland, and whispering to me, said, 'Brother Heber, the Spirit of the Lord has whispered to me: "Let my servant Heber go to England and proclaim my Gospel and open the door of salvation to that nation."'" The call overwhelmed Heber. He cried out to the Lord, "O, Lord, I am a man of stammering tongue, and altogether unfit for such a work; how can I go to preach in that land, which is so famed throughout Christendom for learning, knowledge and piety; the nursery of religion; and to a people whose intelligence is proverbial!"[271]

Even though he was unsure of his ability to connect with the people of England, Heber C. Kimball started his mission on June 13, 1837. He arrived in Liverpool on July 20 accompanied by Elders Orson Hyde, Willard Richards, and Joseph Fielding. It is estimated that by the time Heber left England on April 20, 1838, two thousand people had been baptized and twenty-six branches of the Church had been organized.[272] Heber had also grown to love the British people. Upon bidding farewell to one group, Heber wrote, "My

269 Orson F. Whitney, *Life of Heber C. Kimball, an Apostle: The Father and Founder of the British Mission* (Salt Lake City, 1888), 32–33.

270 Whitney, *Life of Heber C. Kimball*, 34

271 Whitney, *Life of Heber C. Kimball*, 116.

272 *Church History in the Fulness of Times: Student Manual*, 2nd ed. (Salt Lake City: The Church of Jesus Christ of Latter-day Saints, 2003), 176.

heart was like unto theirs and I thought my head was a fountain of tears, for I wept for several miles after I bed them adieu."[273]

Heber C. Kimball arrived back in Kirtland on May 22, 1838, but he would not stay there long. In Heber's absence, apostasy and persecution had ravaged the Church in Kirtland. Many Church leaders had already moved to Far West, Missouri, and Heber went to join them. He packed up his family and journeyed to Missouri, arriving at Far West on July 25, 1838. His stay in Missouri would also be brief. The persecution and apostasy in Kirtland followed the Saints to Missouri, where tensions with the Missourians had been boiling since 1833. Conflict with local militias and affidavits by disillusioned members led the governor of Missouri, Lilburn Boggs, to issue his infamous extermination order. The Saints were driven from Missouri and local Church leaders were arrested and imprisoned. Brigham Young and Heber avoided arrest and they led the effort to relocate the Saints to Illinois.

While in Far West, Heber C. Kimball also learned about a revelation Joseph Smith had received a couple of weeks before Heber arrived: "And next spring let them [the Quorum of the Twelve] depart to go over the great waters, and there promulgate my gospel, the fulness thereof, and bear record of my name. Let them take leave of my saints in the city of Far West, on the twenty-sixth day of April next, on the building-spot of my house, saith the Lord" (Doctrine and Covenants 118:4–5). At great risk to their lives, Heber, Brigham Young, and the other remaining members of the Twelve gathered at the temple site in Far West at midnight on April 26, 1839 to fulfill the prophecy.

Though their mission to England officially began at Far West, it was several months later that they departed. In the meantime, the Apostles did the best they could to make arrangements for their families to be taken care of during their missionary service. Heber and Vilate Kimball moved their family to Nauvoo in May 1839. They were destitute and first found shelter in the remains of an old stable in the back of someone else's property. After a couple of months, Heber erected a larger log cabin on a site a half mile east of where his Nauvoo home now stands.[274]

Since their departure to England had been delayed, Heber C. Kimball and Brigham Young resolved in September 1839 to continue on their mission. Just as they were about to leave, both families were stricken with malaria. Brigham was so sick that he was unable to walk without assistance. He had a friend take him to Heber's house but could go no further. Brigham left his sick wife, Mary Ann, with a three-week-old baby, and his other children in an

---

273 R. B. Thompson, comp., *Journal of Heber C. Kimball* (Nauvoo, IL, 1840), 34.

274 *The Heber C. Kimball Home* (Nauvoo, IL: Nauvoo Restoration, Inc., n.d.).

abandoned Army barracks across the river in Montrose, Iowa. Upon hearing of Brigham's plight, Mary Ann left her children in the care of neighbors and arranged for someone to take her to Heber's home so she could care for Brigham. Heber's wife and children were also sick with malaria. His only well child was five-year-old Heber P. Kimball. Little Heber did his best to carry water to his sick mother and siblings. On September 18, a wagon arrived to help Brigham and Heber begin their journey. Heber described his feelings as follows:

> "It appeared to me as though my very inmost parts would melt within me at leaving my family in such a condition, as it were almost in the arms of death. I felt as though I could not endure it. I asked the teamster to stop, and said to Brother Brigham, 'This is pretty tough, isn't it; let's rise up and give them a cheer.' We arose, and swinging our hates [sic] three times over our heads, shouted; 'Hurrah, hurrah for Israel.' Vilate, hearing the noise, arose from her bed and came to the door. She had a smile on her face. Vilate and Mary Ann Young cried out to us: 'Good bye, God bless you.' We returned the compliment, and then told the driver to go ahead."[275]

During this mission, the Church continued to grow in the British Isles. A Church newspaper, *The Latter-Day Saints' Millennial Star*, began publication, and copies of the Book of Mormon and a hymnal were also published there. The Apostles also responded to the Prophet's call to have the British Saints gather to Nauvoo (see Doctrine and Covenants 124:25). They organized and streamlined the emigration of groups of Saints who wanted to gather to Zion by chartering boats. The first group of Saints left England in June of 1840.

The success of the Apostles' mission to England continued after they returned to the United States. "Over twelve thousand converts joined the Church in the British Isles from 1837–47. More than four thousand of them went to Nauvoo in at least thirty-six companies. This accounted for approximately one-third to one-fourth of Nauvoo's population before the exodus."[276]

Heber C. Kimball and Brigham Young arrived back in Nauvoo in July 1841. They were astonished to see how quickly Nauvoo had grown: "'There were only thirty buildings in the city when we left about two years ago, but at this time there are about 1,200, and hundreds of others in progress.'"[277] Heber was happy to be reunited with his family and went to work at improving their

275 Whitney, *Life of Heber C. Kimball*, 276.

276 *Church History in the Fullness of Times*, 234.

277 Helen Mar Whitney, "Scenes in Nauvoo," *Woman's Exponent* 10, no. 7 (September 1, 1881), 50.

situation. He purchased the lot where the Heber and Vilate Kimball home now stands and built a log cabin where the family lived until their brick home was finished in 1845.

While in Nauvoo, Heber C. Kimball served as a chaplain in the Nauvoo Legion. He also served on the Nauvoo City Council and was a founding member of the Nauvoo Masonic Lodge. He was a member of the Council of the Fifty and worked on the Nauvoo Temple when he could.

In May 1844, Heber C. Kimball left with Brigham Young and other Apostles to campaign for Joseph Smith's candidacy for President of the United States. Heber was in Salem, Massachusetts, when word of the martyrdom reached him. He did not want to believe it at first, but as his fears were confirmed, he immediately began his return home, travelling day and night until he reached Nauvoo on August 6, 1844.

During the turmoil following the death of the Prophet and Patriarch, Heber C. Kimball supported Brigham Young and the Twelve as the rightful leaders of the Church. Heber supported Brigham unconditionally. After the majority of the Church voted to follow Brigham and the Twelve on August 8, 1844, the anxiety and turmoil in the Church settled down for a while.

In May 1845, Heber C. Kimball began construction of a large two-story brick home on his lot in Nauvoo.[278] After completion, the Kimball family moved in sometime in September 1845. But they only lived in their new home for a few months before anti-Mormon sentiment had risen again, and the neighboring settlers were determined to see the Saints leave Nauvoo. Unable to find a buyer, they abandoned their home on February 4, 1846 and joined the exodus to the west.

The Kimballs journeyed first to Winter Quarters and then continued on to Utah. Heber C. Kimball was part of the pioneer company that entered the Salt Lake Valley in 1847. Heber returned to Iowa with Brigham Young and was sustained as his first counselor when the First Presidency was reorganized on December 27, 1847. Heber would serve in that capacity until his death at Salt Lake City on June 22, 1868.

In 1954, Dr. J. LeRoy Kimball purchased the home of his great-grandfather, Heber C. Kimball, intending to restore it and use it as a summer home. The purchase generated a lot of excitement, and pretty soon he found that the home had become quite a tourist attraction. Realizing that he would never be able to use the home for his original purpose, he decided to restore the home

278 The one and a half stories on the east of the house were built after the Nauvoo period; See Lamar C. Berrett, *Sacred Places: Ohio and Illinois,* (Salt Lake City: Bookcraft, 1999-2007), 122.

using his own finances and donate it to the Church. The home was dedicated in 1960. "This act of foresight on the part of Dr. Kimball was the real beginning of the current restoration of old Mormon Nauvoo. He was the first to envision the possibilities of Nauvoo, who undertook such a project with his own financial resources."[279] Dr. Kimball would serve as a founder and the first president of Nauvoo Restoration, Inc.

Mini-Devotional—Answering the Call

Heber C. Kimball was thunderstruck when Joseph Smith whispered in his ear that the Lord was calling him to serve a mission in England.

- Heber's experience of not feeling qualified to serve is still felt by many in the Church. What does Heber's experience tell us about the often-quoted phrase, "God doesn't call the qualified. He qualifies the called"?

When Heber C. Kimball left on his second mission to England, he felt as though "[his] very inmost parts would melt within [him]." It must have felt like an incredible sacrifice for him to leave his sick wife and children.

- How did the Lord bless Heber and Brigham Young for making this sacrifice?
- How was the Church blessed by their sacrifice?
- Have you ever been asked to leave your family or to give up something to build the kingdom of God? If not, how would you respond if you were asked to make that sacrifice?

279 *The Heber C. Kimball Home.*

Lucy Mack Smith Home

The Lucy Mack Smith home in Nauvoo. Photo by Casey Paul Griffiths.

Lucy Mack Smith was the mother of the Prophet Joseph Smith. She was born on July 8, 1775 in Gilsum, New Hampshire. She married Joseph Smith Sr. on January 24, 1796. Lucy and Joseph had eleven children—eight boys and three girls. Lucy buried seven of her eight sons; only one, William, outlived her.

Lucy Mack Smith was a petite woman, standing only about four feet, eleven inches tall, but she was a giant in terms of faith. She had a near-death experience when she was in her late twenties that led her to rededicate her life to Christ. She taught her children how to read using the Bible and always believed one of her children would do something great in the world. When her son Joseph Smith Jr. organized the Church of Christ on April 6, 1830, Lucy was baptized that very day.

Lucy Mack Smith, or Mother Smith as she was known, believed strongly in her son's prophetic calling and did all that she could to support him. She became a prominent leader in the early Church. When the Prophet received a revelation calling for the Church to move from New York to Ohio (see Doctrine and Covenants 37), Lucy was asked to lead the Fayette group. When Lucy's group arrived in Buffalo to seek ship passage to Kirtland, Ohio (traveling by ship was much faster and cheaper than travelling by land), she found that the harbor was iced in, all the ships were booked, and many of the other groups of Saints had fallen into disarray. By calling in a favor with a ship captain that had known her family, she managed to get deck passage for her group. Deck passage meant that they would have to sleep on the deck without any shelter from the weather, but at least they could continue on their journey. She reprimanded the other groups for their lack of faith and for murmuring. She led the group in prayer that "that the ice may give way before us and we be set at liberty to go on our way, as sure as the Lord lives it shall be done." As she finished her prayer, a loud "crack" was heard, and the ice began to part just wide enough for a boat to go through. Lucy and the Fayette Saints were on their way to gather to Ohio.[280] Truly, Lucy had the faith to move mountains, or at least, icebergs!

Lucy Mack Smith traveled with her family to Ohio and then to Missouri. While living in Far West, Lucy watched both of her sons get arrested and placed in a wagon. She was told that her sons had been sentenced to death and that she would never see them again. The general who had been ordered to execute the Smiths, Alexander Doniphan, refused, so the brothers were carted off to jail instead.

In the spring of 1839, Lucy Mack Smith and her family made their way to Quincy, Illinois and then to Nauvoo. Lucy's first home in Nauvoo was a small log cabin built adjacent to the Joseph Smith Homestead. That cabin became a summer kitchen when they moved into a double-log cabin across Main Street from where the Mansion House now sits. It was in this cabin that a dying Joseph Smith Sr. gathered his wife and family around him and gave them a final blessing. He told Lucy, "Mother, do you not know that you are one of the most singular women in the world? . . . You have brought up all my children, and could always comfort them when I could not. We have often wished that we might both die at the same time, but you must not desire to die when I do, for you must stay to comfort the children when I am gone. So do not mourn, but try to be comforted. Your last days shall be your best days."[281]

---

280 Jennifer Reeder and Kate Holbrook "Lucy Mack Smith's Faith-Filled Speech That Parted the Ice on the Erie Canal," *LDS Living*, March 2, 2017, accessed July 18, 2022, https://www.ldsliving.com/lucy-mack-smiths-faith-filled-speech-that-parted-the-ice-on-the-erie-canal/s/84570.

281 *Journal of History* 12, no. 1 (January 1919): 103.

One of Lucy Mack Smith's responsibilities while living in Nauvoo was to be a caretaker for the Egyptian mummies that Joseph Smith had acquired (along with the Egyptian papyrus scrolls that served as the basis for the Book of Abraham). She displayed the mummies to visitors and bore her testimony of her son's divine mission. Sometimes she would charge admission to see the mummies at a cost of twenty-five cents.[282]

Lucy Mack Smith cared for many of the poor and sick who came to Nauvoo. Her home was frequently filled with people in need. She was also present when the Relief Society was organized on March 17, 1842 and was an active member of the Society.

Once the Mansion House was finished in 1843, Lucy Mack Smith moved in to live there with Joseph and Emma Smith. The Mansion House had a large dining room in its east wing. It was there that the bodies of Joseph and Hyrum were placed for viewing following the martyrdom on June 27, 1844. Upon seeing the lifeless bodies of her two sons, Lucy is reported to have exclaimed, "My God, My God, why hast thou forsaken this family!" But she later wrote, "As I looked upon their peaceful, smiling countenances, I seems almost to hear them say—'Mother , weep not for us, we have overcome the world by love; we carried to them the Gospel, that their souls might be saved; they slew us for our testimony, and thus places us beyond their power; their ascendancy is for a moment, ours is an eternal triumph.'"[283]

After the martyrdom, there was a great deal of clamoring about who should lead the Church. For various reasons, Emma Smith and William Smith (Lucy Mack Smith's last surviving son) did not support the leadership of the Quorum of the Twelve, but Lucy did. In the October 1845 General Conference, Lucy voiced her support for Brigham Young and the Twelve and expressed her desire to go west with the Saints. But due to her advanced age and her desire to be buried with her husband, she did not think she could make the trip.

In 1846, as a parting gift, the Church purchased the Joseph Bates Noble home for Lucy Mack Smith so that she could have a home of her own. Lucy was seventy years old when she moved in, and she ended up living there for less than a year. Rising anti-Mormon sentiment caused her to move in with her daughter, Lucy Smith Millikin, outside of Nauvoo. Lucy returned to Nauvoo around 1852 and lived with Emma Smith until her death. Lucy died on May 14, 1856. She was buried next to her husband in the Smith Family Cemetery next to the Homestead.

---

282 Josiah Quincy, *Figures of the Past: From the Leaves of Old Journals* (Boston, 1888), 387.

283 Ron E. Romig, *Lucy's Nauvoo,* (Independence, MO: John Whitmer Books, 2009), 32.

Upon hearing of Lucy Mack Smith's death, her nephew, George A. Smith, said the following: "Blessed woman! Her name and memory are engraven upon the tablets of the hearts of tens of thousands, and will be handed down to millions yet unborn, who will speak her praise and talk of her virtues and goodness, of her motherly kindness, her watchful care and administration to the sick and afflicted—the kind and affectionate mother, the beloved wife, the partner of her aged and venerable husband . . . [of] the trials and persecutions she bore for the Gospel of truth, her unvarying steadfastness to truth through all circumstances and being filled with charity to all."[284]

The house at the corner of Kimball and Hyde Streets was built by Joseph Bates Noble, a justice of the peace in Nauvoo. Joseph had joined the Church in 1832. He purchased this lot in 1841 and erected the house that still stands on it today in 1843. Church trustees purchased the house for Lucy Mack Smith in 1846.[285] Several decades later, the Church purchased the property, and the home was restored to its original design by 1972.

Mini-Devotional—Faith to Move Mountains

By all accounts, Lucy Mack Smith lived a difficult life. When she married Joseph Smith Sr., she had a sizeable dowry, but it was soon lost through bad investments. From that point on, she lived in relative poverty moving from house to house. Once Joseph Smith Jr. received his divine calling, she never wavered in her support. But she saw him hounded, tarred, arrested, and even tually martyred with his brother Hyrum. While living in Nauvoo, Lucy lost her husband and four sons. Yet her faith never wavered.

- Why do you think Lucy was able to maintain her faith despite all her hardship and loss?
- Lucy had the faith to move mountains (or icebergs). If Lucy could do it, why can't you? Is there something that keeps you from moving the icebergs in your life? Have you seen God work miracles in your life? When and how?
- What does Lucy's example teach you about maintaining your faith in the midst of difficulties and even death?

284 Romig, 113.
285 Holzapfel, 87.

Nauvoo Cemeteries

The Old Nauvoo Burial Grounds. Photo by Casey Paul Griffiths.

The Saints found joy during their time in Nauvoo, but it was also filled with challenges and loss. They arrived in Nauvoo as refugees after horrific persecution in Missouri, coming to this new place not out of desire but of necessity. Formerly known as Commerce, Illinois, Nauvoo was built by the Saints on the least expensive land they could purchase. They arrived in Commerce to find that much of the land was a malarial swamp. Already exhausted and destitute from their experiences in Missouri, scores of Saints passed away in the malarial conditions. There were several instances of miraculous healing, but nearly every family lost someone. The losses from Joseph Smith's family included his younger brother Don Carlos, an infant son, and Joseph Smith Sr., the patriarch of the family and the Church. Other faithful Saints, including many who served in crucial positions such as Apostle David Patten and Edward Partridge, the first presiding bishop, were lost in the struggles of Missouri and early Nauvoo (see Doctrine and Covenants 124:19).

In the midst of these losses, the Saints found hope in Jesus Christ. They believed that because of the Savior's sacrifice, their loved ones would be resurrected. But being constantly surrounded by death caused them to think deeply about what their lives would be like in the eternities. They grappled with the nature of eternal family relationships and how to help their loved ones who had passed on to the next life. The Lord blessed them with answers to these questions, creating the theological framework that gives hope and meaning to millions of Church members today. A visit to the cemeteries in Nauvoo is a powerful reminder of the difficult path the Saints took before they received answers from the Lord.

There are several major cemeteries in Nauvoo. The Smith family cemetery is part of the Joseph Smith Historic Site and is discussed in that chapter. Two of the other most significant cemeteries are the Old Nauvoo Burial Grounds and the Saints Peter and Paul Cemetery. Both cemeteries are found on the Eastern end of Nauvoo and contain the final resting places of several important figures of the early Restoration.

The Old Nauvoo Burial Grounds

Family Monument at the Old Nauvoo Burial Grounds. Photo by Casey Paul Griffiths.

The Old Nauvoo Burial Grounds are found approximately two miles east of Nauvoo. The grounds have no physical address, but they can be located by turning off Highway 96 onto Parley's Street and following the road east for two and half miles. The burial grounds are secluded by trees, but there is a sign on the right side of the road to direct you to the correct place. The Church of Jesus Christ of Latter-day Saints acquired the burial grounds from the Community of Christ in 1989 and maintains the property. It is open to the public during daylight hours.[286]

As many as 1,800 people died during the Saints' time in Nauvoo, and many of their graves are found in these old burial grounds. About 200 of the graves have been located, with around 150 identified by headstones or other sources. Because of the frontier conditions in Nauvoo, many of the grave markers were not made of durable material and have been weathered away. Information is still being sought about the people in the old burial grounds. Though many of the names are not known, the shaded environment of trees

286 "Old Nauvoo Burial Grounds, Nauvoo, IL," Ensign Peak Foundation, https://ensignpeakfoundation.org/nauvoo-burial-ground/.

and the peaceful atmosphere of the grounds create a good place to reflect on the sacrifices of the early settlers of Nauvoo.[287]

After the Church acquired the burials grounds in a land trade with Community of Christ, they worked to beautify and restore the grounds. A monument by Utah sculptor Dee Jay Bawden was placed on the site and depicts a mourning family. It stands as a representation of every family that left a loved one in Nauvoo. When President Gordon B. Hinckley dedicated the burial grounds, he said, "This is sacred, hallowed ground . . . this is ground that will become increasingly dear to an ever-growing number of people who, through the years, will come back to visit." He continued, "There is beauty in faith, and I think there was even beauty in death, for death, solemn and tragic as it may be, can be beautiful."[288] One of the prominent individuals laid to rest in the Nauvoo burial grounds is Edward Partridge, the first bishop of the Church.

Edward Partridge Grave

The Edward Partridge Memorial at the Old Nauvoo Burial Grounds. Photo by Casey Paul Griffiths.

287 John L. Hart, "Nauvoo Restoration Now Complete; 'Hallowed' Burial Ground Dedicated," *Church News,* October 14, 1989.

288 Quoted in Hart, "Nauvoo Restoration Now Complete."

Near the family sculpture in the burial grounds is a monument to Edward Partridge. Edward was among the earliest converts to the Church and remained a prominent figure in the Church from the time of his baptism to the end of his life. Though he was moved by the message of the missionaries, he put off baptism until he could meet Joseph Smith himself. He traveled with Sidney Rigdon over three hundred miles in the middle of winter to meet the Prophet in person. Edward went not only for himself but on behalf of others in Painesville who were interested in the new church. This group of seekers even helped pay part of Edward's expenses for the trip and chose him to be the messenger because, as they described him, "he is a man who would not lie [to save] his right arm."[289] When he arrived he sought a revelation from the Prophet, which is now section 36 of the Doctrine and Covenants.

Joseph Smith and Edward soon became close friends. The Lord commended Edward in a revelation given in February 1841, saying, "His heart is pure before me, for he is like unto Nathanael of old, in whom there is no guile" (Doctrine and Covenants 41:11). In the same revelation, Edward was called to serve as the first bishop in the Church (Doctrine and Covenants 41:9). For the next decade, Edward labored tirelessly on behalf of the Church. He worked to find homes and provide for the needs of Saints in Ohio and Missouri. When persecutions broke out in Missouri he was dragged before a mob, tarred and feathered, and then threatened with death. Edward bore this humiliation in silence, later reflecting, "I bore my abuse with so much resignation and meekness, that it appeared to astound the multitude, who permitted me to retire in silence, many looking very solemn, their sympathies having been touched. And as to myself, I was so filled with the Spirit and love of God, that I had no hatred towards my persecutors or anyone else."[290]

Bishop Partridge labored to care for Church members as they were driven from their homes by mobs in 1833. He helped the Saints find a new home in Far West, Missouri, where they were eventually again driven out of. He was arrested in Far West and given the chance to retain his property if he denied his faith, but he refused and was thrown into the Richmond Jail. Commenting on conditions in the jail, he later wrote, "We were confined in a large open room, where the cold northern blast penetrated freely. Our fires were small and our allowance for wood and fuel was scanty; they gave us not even a blanket to lie upon; our beds were the cold floors. . . . The vilest of the vile did guard us and

289 Scott H. Partridge, "Edward Partridge in Painesville, Ohio," *BYU Studies* 42, no. 1 (2003), 56.

290 "History, 1838-1856, volume A-1 [23 December 1805-30 August 1834]," 327, The Joseph Smith Papers.

treat us like dogs; yet we bore our oppressions without murmuring."[291] While Joseph Smith was in Liberty Jail, Joseph wrote a letter addressed to "Edward Partridge and the Church" meant to provide encouragement to Edward and the Saints in the midst of their trials. Excerpts from this letter were later included in the Doctrine and Covenants as sections 121, 122, and 123.[292]

Bishop Partridge was later freed from jail. He moved with his family to Quincy and then to Nauvoo, where he was appointed the bishop of the upper ward. But the physical strain of the move combined with the unhealthy conditions in Nauvoo took their toll on Edward, and he collapsed from exhaustion. He died on May 27, 1840 at the age of forty-six. When Edward died, Joseph Smith wrote a closing comment on the death of his friend, "He lost his life in consequence of the Missouri persecutions, and he is one of that number whose blood will be required at their hands."[293]

Because no one knew the precise burial place for Bishop Partridge, when the Old Nauvoo Burial Grounds (now known as the Pioneer Saints Cemetery) was obtained by the Church a monument to Edward Partridge was erected to honor the sacrifices he made for the gospel of Jesus Christ. The monument was dedicated by President James E. Faust, who noted during the dedication that the statue was meant to honor all those "who lie in unmarked graves."[294] President Faust also gave honor to the memory of the members of Edward's family who sacrificed for their testimonies, including Edwards's wife, Lydia Clisbee Partridge; their five daughters, Eliza Maria, Harriet Amelia, Emily Dow, Caroline Ely, and Lydia; and their two sons, Clisbee, who died as an infant, and Edward Partridge Jr.[295]

When he was given the chance to reflect on the life of his friend Edward, the Prophet Joseph Smith wrote, "The Spirit of the Lord strove with him a number of times, insomuch that his heart was made tender, and he went and wept; and that sometimes he went silently and poured the effusions of his soul to God, in prayer."[296] Perhaps the greatest tribute given to Edward came from the Savior, who told the Prophet in revelation that Edward had gained his exal-

291 Andrew Jenson, *Latter-day Saint Biographical Encyclopedia,* vol. 1 (Salt Lake City: The Andrew Jenson History Co., 1901–1936), 221.

292 "Letter to Edward Partridge and the Church, circa 22 March 1839," 10, The Joseph Smith Papers.

293 "History, 1838–1856, volume C-1 [2 November 1838–31 July 1842]," 1060, The Joseph Smith Papers.

294 Don and Betty Ulmer, "President Faust Dedicated Monument in Nauvoo to Bishop Partridge," *Church News,* September 6, 1997.

295 Ulmer, "President Faust Dedicated Monument."

296 "History, 1838–1856, volume A-1 [23 December 1805–30 August 1834]," 94, The Joseph Smith Papers.

tation when the Lord said He had received Edward "unto [himself]" (Doctrine and Covenants 124:19).

Mini-Devotional—"Those Who Lie in Unmarked Graves"

The Old Nauvoo Burial Grounds have hundreds of grave markers too weathered and worn to identify who they were meant to memorialize. But together they stand as a monument to the sacrifices the Saints made to settle Nauvoo and pass their faith on to the next generation. Speaking of the dead, Joseph Smith once said, "They without us cannot be made perfect—neither can we without our dead be made perfect" (Doctrine and Covenants 128:15). Take a few moments to ponder and think about the following questions:

- How have your ancestors who have already passed on impacted you?
- How can you honor people like Edward Partridge who sacrificed themselves for the gospel?

Saints Peter and Paul Cemetery

Gravestones at dusk at the Saints Peter and Paul Cemetery in Nauvoo. Photo by Casey Paul Griffiths.

The other major cemetery in Nauvoo is the Saints Peter and Paul Cemetery. It is easily found by following Nauvoo Main Street eastward. The cemetery is located on the right side of the road on the outskirts of town. This is still an active cemetery in Nauvoo, but graves here go back to the time of Joseph Smith and are where many significant figures, including Seymour Brunson and Julia Murdock Smith, were buried.

Seymour Brunson and Baptism for the Dead

Monument to Seymour Brunson in the Saints Peter and Paul Cemetery in Nauvoo. Photo by Casey Paul Griffiths.

On the south side of the cemetery is found a monument to Seymour Brunson. Seymour was a veteran of the War of 1812 and joined the Church in January 1831. He served several missions for the Church in the following years. He reported on his missionary travels to the Church newspaper *The Evening and the Morning Star* on January 25, 1832, writing:

> Dear brethren in Christ, I, for the first time, take up my pen to give you a general account of my travels. On the eleventh of March, 1832, I started with brother Luke Johnson unto the south country, and on the

> twenty second, we left our brethren at Shalersville, and began to preach and baptize, and arrived at Windsor, Lawrence county, Ohio, on the ninth of May, having witnessed several instances of the Lord's healing power. At this place we built up a church, which made in all that we had baptized, fifty-three members.[297]

Seymour settled in Lawrence, Ohio, where he later reported that he "received some persecution, such as attempts to injure persons, and destroy some property."[298] He moved with his family to Caldwell County, Missouri, around 1836 and there suffered persecution because of his faith. During the 1838 Missouri persecutions, he was called upon to rescue three families "from the mob who had without cause or provocation driven their husbands from home and threatened their lives if they returned."[299]

When the Saints moved to Nauvoo, Seymour was appointed a member of the Nauvoo High Council and served as the Prophet's bodyguard. In August 1840, Seymour fell ill and died a few days later. Vilate Kimball wrote of Seymour's death:

> Seymour Brunson is . . . dead, everything was done to save him that could be done, but the Lord had need of him. A short time before he died he told Joseph not to hold him any longer "for" said he, "I have seen David Patten and he wants me, and the Lord wants me, and I want to go." They then gave him up; at one time as Joseph entered the room, he told him that there was a light encircled him above the brightness of the sun—he exclaimed, "The room is full of angels they have come to waft my spirit home." He then bade his family and friends farewell and sweetly fell asleep in Jesus.[300]

Though he was an ordinary citizen of Nauvoo, Seymour Brunson's death served as a catalyst for one of the most important doctrinal developments in the history of the Church. At Seymour's funeral, Joseph Smith took the stand and preached a sermon. Seeing a woman in attendance who had lost her son before he could be baptized, Joseph taught the Saints that they "could now act for their friends who had departed this life" by being baptized in their behalf.

---

297 *The Evening and the Morning Star*, June 1833, 100.

298 *Messenger and Advocate*, December 1834, 46.

299 *Mormon Redress Petitions: Documents of the 1833-1838 Missouri Conflict*, ed. Clark V. Johnson (Provo, UT: Religious Studies Center, 1992), 146–47.

300 Vilate Kimball to Heber C. Kimball in Nauvoo, Illinois, September 6, 1840, MS 3276 1, Church History Library, Salt Lake City.

He then cited the teachings of the Apostle Paul, referring to baptism for the dead, and encouraged Saints by telling them "that the plan of salvation was calculated to save all who were willing to obey the requirements of the law of God."[301]

With all the losses they had suffered in Missouri and Nauvoo, the Saints received this teaching with joy. It was soon after that the first recorded baptism for the dead took place in the Mississippi River. On that occasion, Jane Neyman was baptized on behalf of her son, Cyrus, who had recently passed away. The first witness of a proxy baptism was Vienna Jaques, who rode her horse into the river to be able to closely observe the ordinance.[302] Later revelations emphasized that baptisms for the dead must take place in temples (Doctrine and Covenants 124:40) and that the baptisms must be properly recorded to be valid (Doctrine and Covenants 127 and 128).

Because Seymour Brunson's death served as an important catalyst in bringing about the practice of baptism for the dead, a monument was placed in the Saints Peter and Paul Cemetery to his memory. The monument notes that at his funeral the practice of baptism for the dead was introduced. It also notes a revelation that provides insight into the final fate of Seymour Brunson, when the Lord declared, "Seymour Brunson I have taken unto myself; no man taketh his priesthood" (Doctrine and Covenants 124:132).

---

301 Simon Baker in *Journal History,* August 15, 1840, cited in "Baptism for the Dead," *Church History Topics,* https://www.churchofjesuschrist.org/study/history/topics/baptism-for-the-dead?lang=eng.

302 Jane Neyman statement, given November 29, 1854, in *Journal History,* August 15, 1840; see also "Baptism for the Dead," *Church History Topics,* https://www.churchofjesuschrist.org/study/history/topics/baptism-for-the-dead?lang=eng.

Julia Murdock Smith, Daughter of Joseph and Emma

The grave of Julia Murdock Smith, the adopted daughter of Joseph and Emma Smith in the Saints Peter and Paul Cemetery. Photo by Casey Paul Griffiths.

Another significant grave in the Saints Peter and Paul Cemetery is the final resting place of Julia Murdock Smith, the daughter of Joseph and Emma Smith. Julia was the first Smith child to grow to full maturity. She was adopted by the Smiths in 1831 and remained a close part of their family for the rest of her life. Julia was born with her twin brother, Joseph, on April 30, 1831 to John and Julia Murdock, new converts to the Church. Six hours after her birth, Julia's mother died. John Murdock later wrote, "The children were born without any great agony or pain to the Mother, and all appeared to be doing well." John saw that his wife "appeared to look fresh and be doing well, but she told me she was going, and reached out her hand and shook hands with me and every person in the room and bid us farewell, and immediately folded her hands across her own stomach, shut her eyes, and went to sleep in Jesus."[303]

The same day that Julia Murdock died giving birth to twins, Emma Smith also gave birth to twins. Her children, also a boy and girl, only lived a few

303 Quoted in Sunny McClellan Morton, "The Forgotten Daughter: Julia Murdock Smith," *Mormon Historical Studies* 3, no. 2 (2002): 37–38.

hours. John Murdock, grieving the loss of his wife and already having five children to care for, was left with few options. John later told his daughter Julia, "Brother Joseph, hearing of the death of my wife and the two children left, sent word to me that he would take the children and raise them."[304] Joseph and Emma took the newborn twins and moved to the John Johnson Farm. While they were staying at the Johnson Farm, the twins came down with a case of measles. While Joseph was up late in the night tending to the baby boy, a mob broke into the home, dragging Joseph into the night and tarring and feathering him. The cold night air exacerbated the illness of the baby, and five days later Joseph Murdock Smith died.[305]

After the death of her brother, Julia continued to be raised by the Smiths. She was treated no differently than any of the other Smith children, though she was the only daughter raised by Joseph and Emma. Joseph Smith III, her adopted brother, wrote of her, "[She was my] adopted sister and the only sister I ever knew . . . [W]e boys . . . held her in great esteem and affectionate regard, and . . . in every respect treated her honorably and considerably – quite as we would have treated a sister born of the family."[306]

Joseph Smith loved Julia and wrote affectionately of her in his family correspondence. When he was staying in New York City on Church business, Joseph sent a letter to Emma filled with longing, writing, "The thoughts of home of Emma and Julia [M. Smith] rushes upon my mind like a flood and I could wish for [a] moment to be with them my breast is filled with all the feelings and tenderness of a parent and a husband."[307] In another letter written to Emma from Richmond Jail, Joseph spoke of his daughter, saying, "Julia is a lovely little girl, I love hir [sic] also She is a promising child, tell her Father wants her to remember him and be a good girl."[308] Julia also enjoyed a close relationship with Emma, later writing, "She ha[s] been more than a Mother to me, and loves me as one of her own."[309]

After the death of Joseph Smith and the exodus of the Saints from Nauvoo, Julia remained behind with Emma. In 1849, when she was eighteen years old, she married Elisha Dixon. Joseph III described Elisha in unfavorable terms, calling him a "magician by profession, a most successful prestidiginator, who had been traveling about as a gypsy king."[310] Emma disapproved

304 Morton, 38–39.

305 Morton, 39.

306 Quoted in Morton, 42.

307 "Letter to Emma Smith, 13 October 1832," [2], The Joseph Smith Papers.

308 "Letter to Emma Smith, 12 November 1838," [2], The Joseph Smith Papers.

309 Quoted in Morton, 43.

310 Quoted in Morton, 46.

of the marriage for a number of reasons, including the fact that Elisha was thirty-six—twice Julia's age. Emma's fears were partly justified when Elisha, who was in poor health, left Nauvoo in 1850 set out alone for Cuba, intending to restore his health. He did not take Julia with him, and a letter from Emma at the time reported that "Julia is with me and is almost as lonely as I am."[311]

Elisha only made it as far as St. Louis before his health failed and he returned to Nauvoo. In 1852, Elisha and Julia moved to Galveston, Texas, where Elisha worked doing bookkeeping and tending bar on a riverboat. His work entailed long periods of separation from Julia, who missed her family terribly. Her marriage to Elisha ended in 1853 when he died from injuries sustained when the boiler of a riverboat he was working on exploded. Julia then returned to Nauvoo a twenty-two-year-old widow.[312]

Julia remarried in 1855, this time to a man five years older than her named John Jackson Middleton. Joseph III reported that soon after the wedding Julia joined the Catholic Church, "for her husband was one [a Catholic] and he was strongly opposed to Mormonism."[313] Little is known about John Middleton except what was written about him by Joseph III, who strongly disliked him. Joseph III describes him as a violent alcoholic. He wrote about several negative encounters with John and summarized John's relationship with Julia by saying she "had been very unfortunate in her second marriage."[314] Emma commented at one point that "poor Julia has a trying life."[315] After several decades of marriage, John deserted Julia in 1877 to go to New Mexico, leaving her with only her clothing and a featherbed. Soon after his departure, Julia moved in with Emma, whose health was failing.[316]

Julia was present when Emma passed away in 1879. Afterward she went to live with the Moffitt family, an established Catholic family in Nauvoo. The Moffitts generously took care of her during the final years of her life. In 1880, she was visited by her biological brother, John Riggs Murdock, who was traveling East from Utah on business. His journal records:

> [Julia] had been very unfortunate in her second marriage. I found her at the home of Mr. Moffat, who wife took care of her with a sisterly kindness. Julia's foster mother Emma, had died, and she was left without a home under the most distressing circumstances. She was suffering from a

311 Quoted in Morton, 47.
312 Morton, 48.
313 Quoted in Morton, 49.
314 Quoted in Morton, 50.
315 Morton, 52.
316 Morton, 52.

> cancer in her right breast. This was caused by a severe blow that she had received. I remained with her about one month, but on leaving I left sufficient means to provide for her and to cover the expenses of her burial and of a tombstone. She died soon after my departure and was buried in the Catholic cemetery.[317]

Julia passed away September 10, 1880. Julia's grave is found near the graves of James and Semantha Moffitt, who cared for her during her final illness.

Though Julia's life was difficult, she retained her faith in Jesus Christ, although she never seemed to have strong connections with any particular religion. Her letters to her family contain frequent mentions of God and show her faith in a better world to come. She closed one of her letters to Emma by writing, "I bid you adieu for a time but may God in his mercy grant it may not be forever. . . . Every night I breathe a prayer to him to grant that we may all meet again in this world and he has promised that if we prayed in sincerity of heart we should receive and in this promise I trust."[318]

Mini-Devotional—"In This Promise I Trust"

Seymour Brunson and Julia Murdock Smith both lived challenging lives filled with difficulty and sorrow. But both had a hope for a better world to come. Seymour was greeted at his death by his friend David Patten. Julia expressed her hope that she would see her loved ones in the next world. The funeral of Seymour Brunson, which could have been tragic, was instead an opportunity for Joseph Smith to teach the principles of baptism for the dead. Temple work for the dead brings hope and joy to untold numbers of people on both sides of the veil. Take a few moments to ponder or write about these questions:

- How does the gospel of Jesus Christ help us see hope even in the difficult times of our lives?
- How does the teaching of work for the dead allow us to have hope for our deceased loved ones and for all humankind?

317 Quoted in Morton, 53.
318 Quoted in Morton, 53.

Ramus, Illinois

Local monument marking the foundation of the first Church built in Ramus, Illinois. Photo by Casey Paul Griffiths.

Significant events at this location:

- Here Joseph Smith gave one of his most profound discourses. Part of the discourse included his answers to questions from a congregation in Ramus, Illinois (see Doctrine and Covenants 130).
- Some of Joseph Smith's earliest teachings about eternal marriage were given at this location (see Doctrine and Covenants 131).

- Joseph Smith's sister Katherine Smith Salisbury is buried at this location. Joseph frequently visited her as well as other close friends that lived in Ramus, including Benjamin and Melissa Johnson.
- Ramus was the site of one of the first Latter-day Saint chapels in the United States.

While Nauvoo was the main hub of the Church in the 1840s, a number of small settlements surrounding Nauvoo were also sites of important Church events. Some of the most important Church events during the 1840s took place at Ramus, a small settlement located approximately twenty miles east of Nauvoo.

Ramus was settled by Ute V. Perkins and his family and was simply called the Perkins settlement. When Perkins and his family converted to the Church, a number of Church members moved to the area. Soon after, the name of the settlement was changed to Ramus, a Latin word that means "branch." Several Church members lived in Ramus, and eventually a stake of Zion was organized in Ramus under the direction of Hyrum Smith on July 9, 1840. Joseph Smith's sisters Katherine Salisbury and Sophronia and their families lived there and were frequently visited by the Prophet. Other close friends of Joseph lived in Ramus, including Benjamin and Melissa Johnson. In the spring of 1843, Joseph visited the area and gave several discourses that were important enough to later be canonized in the Doctrine and Covenants. These discourses, which were essentially question-and-answer sessions with the Prophet, reflect Joseph's mature understanding of the gospel and also his inquisitive mind. Most importantly, the Ramus discourses demonstrate the Prophet's close relationship with the Savior. At Ramus, he taught, "When the Savior shall appear we shall see him as he is. We shall see that he is a man like ourselves" (Doctrine and Covenants 130:1).

The Saints in Ramus built one of the first chapels in the Church, and several important meetings were held there. After the Saints left the region, the name of the settlement was changed to Webster. Today, it contains only a small collection of houses. The chapel built by the Saints no longer exists, but parts of its foundations remain. A Church member who lives near Webster has placed a red-painted door near the foundations of the chapel and posted historical information about the chapel. In addition, the Ute V. Perkins Family Organization, with assistance from the Ensign Peak Foundation, placed a historical marker at the chapel's foundations. Outside of these monuments and the grave of Katherine Salisbury, little of this once-promising community remains.

The Prophet Comes to Ramus

This church is not the original, but was built near the foundations of the original church building in Ramus. Photo by Casey Paul Griffiths.

Ramus, Illinois, was the home of Joseph's sisters Sophronia McCleary and Katherine Salisbury as well as some of Joseph's other friends, such as Benjamin and Melissa Johnson. On April 1, 1843, Joseph Smith traveled to Ramus, accompanied by William Clayton, who was one of his scribes, and the Apostle Orson Hyde. The morning after their arrival, Orson addressed the Saints in Ramus, drawing on 1 John 3:2 and John 14:3 as the basis for his speech. Both scriptures discuss coming into the presence of the Savior. 1 John 3:2 reads, "Beloved, now are we the sons of God, and it doth not yet appear what we shall be: but we know that, when he shall appear, we shall be like him; for we shall see him as he is." And John 14:3 declares, "And if I go and prepare a place for you, I will come again, and receive you unto myself; that where I am, there ye may be also." After sharing these scriptures, Orson stated, "It is our privilege to have the Father and Son dwelling in our hearts."[319]

Joseph Smith's history records, "We dined with my Sister Sophronia McCleary; when I told Elder Hyde that I was going to offer some corrections to his sermon this morning, he replied [that] they shall be thankfully received."[320] Joseph Smith proceeded to preach to the Saints in both their afternoon and evening meetings. Doctrine and Covenants 130:1–7 was received during the afternoon meeting, while verses 18–23 were given during his evening discourse. At some point during the day, Joseph also made several "remarks on doctrine" relating to events leading up to the Second Coming of Jesus Christ.[321] William Clayton kept notes on these sermons and other conversations held during the trip, expanding and clarifying the conversations as he wrote them down. After the trip, Willard Richards copied Clayton's notes into Joseph Smith's journal. William Clayton's original notes are no longer extant, but based on other discourses he transcribed, this is most likely an accurate account of what the Prophet taught in Ramus.[322]

One of the most important contributions of the Ramus discourses was Joseph Smith's statement that the Father and the Son are physical beings. The scriptures clarify that when Jesus was resurrected, He inhabited a body of flesh and bones (see Luke 24:39). Joseph taught that to say that Jesus is now a disembodied, ethereal being is to take away His body and confine Him to a second death. In another discourse (separate from those given in Ramus) on January 5, 1841, Joseph taught, "That which is without body or parts is nothing. There is no other God in heaven but that God who has flesh and bones. John 5:26, 'As the father hath life in himself, even so hath he given the son to have life in himself.' God the Father took life unto himself precisely as Jesus did."[323]

In Ramus, Joseph also taught that "the same sociality which exists among us here will exist among us there, only it will be coupled with eternal glory" (Doctrine and Covenants 130:2). The word *sociality*, a broad term that encompasses "socialness, or the quality of being social,"[324] captures the Prophet's vision of the afterlife.

---

319 Joseph Smith History, vol. D-1, 1510, JSP.

320 Joseph Smith History, vol. D-1, 1510, JSP.

321 Joseph Smith History, vol. D-1, 1510–11, JSP.

322 "Doctrine and Covenants 130," in *Joseph Smith's Revelations: A Doctrine and Covenants Study Companion from the Joseph Smith Papers*, eds. Matthew C. Godfrey et al. (Salt Lake City, UT: Church Historian's Press, 2020).

323 "Discourse, 5 January 1841, as Reported by William Clayton," vol. 7 of the Documents Series *The Joseph Smith Papers*.

324 "Sociality," Webster's 1828 Dictionary, webstersdictionary1828.com/Dictionary/sociality.

Often the popular conception of heaven is beings sitting on clouds, playing harps, and singing praises to God, without any kind of dynamic action or growth. Joseph taught that heaven, in order to be a meaningful, eternal home, must be more than that. One author's sentiment reflects this type of heaven:

> "Heaven is not dull; it is not static; it is not monochrome. It is an endless dynamic of joy in which one is ever more oneself as one was meant to be, in which one increasingly realizes one's potential in understanding as well as love and is filled with more and more with wisdom. It is the discovery, sometimes unexpected, of one's deepest self. Heaven is reality itself; what is not heaven is less real."[325]

Joseph Smith believed that in heaven the most real things in this life—our connections to the ones we love—endure and become even stronger than they were on earth. Parley P. Pratt captured this idea when he wrote, "It was Joseph Smith who taught me how to prize the endearing relationships of father, mother, husband, wife, brother, sister, son and daughter. It was from him I learned of marriage for eternity, that the refined sympathies and affections which endeared us to each other emanated from the fountain of divine eternal love. I had loved before[,] but I knew not why. But now I loved with the pureness and intensity of elevated, exalted feeling which would lift my soul from the transitory things of this groveling sphere and expand it as the ocean."[326] Without these connections—this sociality—heaven would not be heaven.

In Ramus, Joseph also shared his perspective about the Second Coming and the end times (see Doctrine and Covenants 130:12–17). There are some things that Joseph is certain of, such as the looming war between the Northern and the Southern states in America. The prophecy of the American Civil War, given to Joseph Smith on December 25, 1832, was fulfilled to the letter. The war began in South Carolina on April 12, 1861, about twenty-nine years after the prophecy was given, when Confederate forces fired on the Union installation of Fort Sumter (see Doctrine and Covenants 87:1–3).

Joseph also reported to friends in Ramus that the Lord told him, "Joseph, my son, if thou livest until thou art eighty-five years old, thou shalt see the face of the Son of Man; therefore let this suffice, and trouble me no more on this matter" (Doctrine and Covenants 130:15). Rather than offer a definitive interpretation of what this revelation meant, Joseph acknowledged that this

325 Jeffrey Burton Russell, *A History of Heaven: The Singing Silence* (Princeton: Princeton University Press, 1997), 3–4.

326 Parley P. Pratt, *The Autobiography of Parley P. Pratt* (Salt Lake City: George Q. Cannon and Sons, 1874), 297–98.

prophecy could be fulfilled in multiple ways. Joseph received revelations about the signs of the times (see Doctrine and Covenants 38; 45; 133), but he never claimed to know the precise time of the Savior's return to earth. One of his revelations declared that "the hour and the day [of the Second Coming] no man knoweth, neither the angels in heaven, nor shall they know until he comes" (Doctrine and Covenants 49:7). In a discourse from the final months of his life, Joseph declared, "Jesus Christ never did reveal to any man the precise time that he would come. Go and read the scriptures and you cannot find anything that specifies the exact [time] he would come, and all that say so are false teachers."[327]

The New and Everlasting Covenant of Marriage

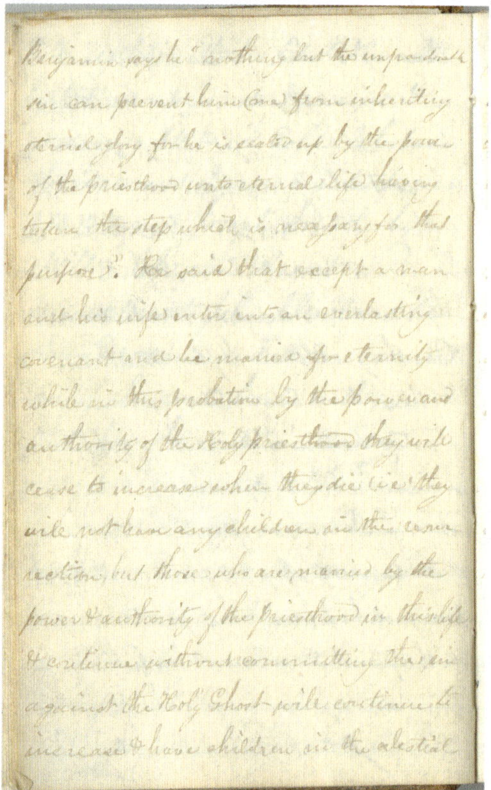
Benjamin says he "nothing but the unpardonable sin can prevent him (one) from inheriting eternal glory for he is sealed up by the power of the priesthood unto eternal life having taken the step which is necessary for that purpose". He said that except a man and his wife enter into an everlasting covenant and be married for eternity while in this probation by the power and authority of the Holy priesthood they will cease to increase when they die (i.e. they will not have any children in the resurrection, but those who are married by the power & authority of the priesthood in this life & continue without committing the sin against the Holy Ghost will continue to increase & have children in the celestial

William Clayton's notes of the instructions Joseph Smith gave to Benjamin and Melissa Johnson at Ramus, Illinois. Phto by Casey Paul Griffiths.

The teachings now found in Doctrine and Covenants 131 consist of three different items of instruction that Joseph Smith gave on three different occasions. The first part of the section, verses 1–4, consists of instructions given on May 16, 1843 in the home of Benjamin F. and Melissa Johnson, close friends who lived in Ramus. During his stay in Ramus, Joseph Smith instructed Benjamin Melissa on the eternal nature of marriage. In the months following, Joseph performed the couple's sealing, making their union eternal.[328]

Benjamin later recalled, "In the evening he [Joseph Smith] called me and my wife to come and sit down, for he wished to marry us according to the law of the Lord. I thought it a joke, and said I should not marry my wife again, unless

327 "Discourse, 10 March 1844, as Reported by Wilford Woodruff," 212, JSP.

328 "Doctrine and Covenants 131," in *Joseph Smith's Revelations.*

she courted me, for I did it all, the first time. He chided my levity, told me he was in earnest, and so it proved; for we stood up and were sealed by the Holy Spirit of promise."[329]

When talking to the Johnsons, Joseph simply taught, "In order to obtain the highest, a man must enter into this order of the priesthood." With the approval of Brigham Young, Orson Hyde later added the bracketed phrase "[meaning the new and everlasting covenant of marriage]" (Doctrine and Covenants 131:2) for clarification.[330] In bringing both Melissa and Benjamin Johnson into this order of the priesthood, Joseph was teaching of an order of the priesthood that both women and men could enter into together. In a discourse recorded in Joseph Smith's journal on August 27, 1843, he taught of "three grand orders of priesthood."[331] Most Church members are familiar with the Aaronic and Melchizedek orders of the priesthood, but Joseph, speaking of "patriarchal authority," taught of the third order, the "patriarchal order of the priesthood." He also added, "Finish that temple [the Nauvoo temple] and God will fill it with power," implying that this order of the priesthood functioned primarily within the walls of the temple.[332] Bathsheba W. Smith, another Church member from Joseph's time, later recounted that the Prophet "wanted to make us [women], as the women were in Paul's day, 'A kingdom of priestesses.'" She then explained, "We have that ceremony in our endowments as Joseph taught."[333]

During his discussion with Benjamin and Melissa Johnson, Joseph clearly connected the power to continue their marriage in the next life with a God-given covenant. William Clayton recorded, "[Joseph] said that except a man and his wife enter into an everlasting covenant and be married for eternity while in this probation by the power and authority of the Holy priesthood, they will cease to increase when they die, they will not have any children in the resurrection. But those who are married by the power and authority of the priesthood in this life and continue without committing the sin against the Holy Ghost will continue to increase and have children in the celestial

329 Benjamin Johnson, *My Life's Review* (1947), 92 (underlining in original).

330 "Instruction, 16 May 1843, as Reported by William Clayton," 15, JSP.

331 "Journal, December 1842–June 1844," Book 3, 15 July 1843–29 February 1844, 71, JSP.

332 "Journal, December 1842–June 1844," Book 3, 15 July 1843–29 February 1844, 74, JSP.

333 "Pioneer Stake," *Woman's Exponent*, July and August 1905, 34:14, quoted in Jill Mulvey Derr and others, eds., *The First Fifty Years of Relief Society: Key Documents in Latter-day Saint Women's History* (2016), xxix.

glory."[334] This new and everlasting covenant opened the way for men and women to continue the joys of family and love into the eternities.

Mini-Devotional—Eternal Families

Benjamin and Melissa Johnson were among the first Saints to experience the joy of knowing their family relationships could endure beyond death. Through their marriage they shared a priesthood that would bless generations of their children after them. The concept of eternal marriage is well-known by and normal for most Church members today, but this was a new concept for the Saints of the early Restoration. Take a moment to reflect on the importance of family relationships and how they affect your view of the world. Ponder or write about the following questions:

- How does your view of eternal family relationships affect the way your treat your family right now?
- What steps can you take to deepen and enrich the relationships you have with your family connections so that they will endure in the eternities?

The More Sure Word of Prophecy

The teachings found in Doctrine and Covenants 131:5–6 is taken from a sermon Joseph Smith preached in Ramus, Illinois on May 17, 1843. The Prophet spoke using 2 Peter 1 as his text, discoursing on the meaning of the phrases "make your calling and election sure" (2 Peter 1:10) and "a more sure word of prophecy" (2 Peter 1:19). Samuel Prior, a Methodist preacher who was in the congregation while Joseph spoke, later recalled, "He glided along through a very interesting and elaborate discourse, with all the care and happy facility of one who was well aware of his important station, and his duty to God and man, and evidencing to me, that he was well worthy to be styled 'a workman rightly dividing the word of truth,' and giving without reserve, 'saint and sinner his portion in due season.'"[335] Samuel also wrote, "I was compelled

---

334 "Instruction, 16 May 1843, as Reported by William Clayton," vol. 12 of the Documents series of *The Joseph Smith Papers*, 15.

335 Samuel Prior, "A Visit to Nauvoo," *Times and Seasons*, May 15, 1843, 4:19798, italics in original; see also 2 Timothy 2:15 and Luke 12:42.

to go away with a very different opinion from what I had entertained when I first took my seat to hear him preach."[336]

In the evening of that same day, May 17, 1843, Samuel spoke to a large group of Latter-day Saints. He later wrote of the sermons, "The congregation was large and respectable—they paid the utmost attention. This surprised me a little, as I did not expect to find any such thing as a religious toleration among them."[337] After Samuel finished his sermon, Joseph "arose and begged leave to differ from me in a few points of doctrine, and this he did mildly, politely, and affectingly; like one who was more desirous to disseminate truth and expose error, than to love the malicious triumph of debate over me. I was truly edified by his remarks, and felt less prejudiced against the Mormons than ever."[338]

Unfortunately, we do not have the text of Samuel Prior's sermon that prompted Joseph Smith's response. Part of Joseph's response, however, was later canonized in Doctrine and Covenants 131:7–8. Joseph's teachings focused on the eternal nature of both spirit and matter.

William Clayton, who was present in the Johnson home on May 16, recorded both of Joseph's May 17 sermons and later copied these teachings into his journal. These excerpts were used to create the *History of the Church*, and excerpts from this history were used in Doctrine and Covenants 131. There is evidence that Clayton copied the portions of these discourses into his journal using notes that he took during the sermons, which further lends credibility to the accuracy of his reports.[339]

In his sermon, Joseph referred to 2 Peter 1:19, in which Peter declares, "We have also a more sure word of prophecy; whereunto ye do well that ye take heed, as unto a light that shineth in a dark place, until the day dawn, and the day star arise in your hearts" (2 Peter 1:19). Peter also gives the exhortation, "Wherefore the rather, brethren, give diligence to make your calling and election sure: for if ye do these things, ye shall never fall" (2 Peter 1:10). In these passages Peter may have been quietly alluding to his experience alongside James and John on the Mount of Transfiguration (see Matthew 17:1–2).

Joseph connected Peter's "more sure word of prophecy" to being sealed up unto eternal life. In a discourse in Ramus only a few days earlier, Joseph had taught that the "more sure word of prophecy" related to "the promise of eternal [life] in the kingdom of God." Wilford Woodruff's notes regarding this discourse record Joseph's statement:

336 Samuel Prior, "A Visit to Nauvoo," 4:197–98.
337 Samuel Prior, "A Visit to Nauvoo," 4:197–98.
338 Samuel Prior, "A Visit to Nauvoo," 4:197–98.
339 "Doctrine and Covenants 131," in *Joseph Smith's Revelations*.

> Now for the secret & grand key. Though they might hear the voice of God and know that Jesus was the son of God, this would be no evidence that their election and calling was made sure that they had part with Christ and was a joint-heir with him, they then would want that more sure word of prophecy that they were sealed in the heavens and had the promise of eternal live [*sic*] in the kingdom of God. Then having this promise sealed unto them[,] it was as an anchor to the soul[,] sure and steadfast though the thunders might roll; and lightnings flash and earthquakes bellow and war gather thick around. Yet this hope and knowledge would support the soul in every hour of trial[,] trouble[,] and tribulation. Then knowledge through our Lord and Savior Jesus Christ—is the grand key that unlocks the glories & mysteries of the kingdom of heaven.[340]

A revelation given to Joseph Smith in May 1833 revealed that "the elements are eternal" (Doctrine and Covenants 93:33). In Doctrine and Covenants 131:7–8, Joseph expanded this idea, braking down the conceptual barrier between material matter and spirit by declaring them to be the same thing, only in different states. A year earlier in the *Times and Seasons,* Joseph taught: "The body is supposed to be organized matter, and the spirit by many is thought to be immaterial, without substance. With this latter statement we should beg leave to differ—and state that spirit is a substance; that it is material, but that it is more pure, elastic, and refined matter than the body;—that it existed before the body, can exist in the body, and will exist separate from the body when the body will be moldering in the dust; and will in the resurrection be again united with it."[341] In the same discourse, he added, "The spirits of men are eternal."[342]

340 "Discourse, 14 May 1843, as Reported by Wilford Woodruff," vol. 12 of the Documents series of the *Joseph Smith Papers*, 32.

341 *Times and Seasons,* April 1, 1842, Joseph Smith Papers, 745.

342 *Times and Seasons,* April 1, 1842, Joseph Smith Papers, 745.

The Grave of Katherine Smith Salisbury

The grave of Katherine Smith Salisbury, sister of the Prophet Joseph Smith. Photo by Casey Paul Griffiths.

The grave of Katherine Smith Salisbury, the younger sister of Joseph Smith, is located in the Webster cemetery. Born in 1813, Katherine was the younger sister of Joseph and was a stalwart supporter of the Prophet during his ministry. Katherine was present at some of the most momentous events in Church history and left behind reminiscences of her experiences. Katherine was only six when Joseph Smith had his First Vision and only fourteen when he received and brought home the plates that contained the Book of Mormon.

The weeks following the arrival of the plates were filled with anxiety for Katherine and the rest of the family. She remembered Joseph, exhausted and injured, thrusting the cloth-covered plates into her arms. She quickly took the plates and placed them on a nearby table, then rushed to assist Joseph, who told her of three separate attackers who assailed him as he attempted to get the plates home. The tension didn't increase in the weeks following. Katherine recalled, "We got a chest and locked the records up in the house. From that time on our house was searched all around; and our field and our wheat stacks were searched. The mob was around our house nearly every night and one night they went into father's cooper shop and tore up his floor and dug the earth up. And from that time until we went to Pennsylvania we had to keep watch for the enemy."[343]

Though she was not chosen as one of the witnesses of the Book of Mormon, Katherine hefted and handled the plates while they were wrapped in a cloth on at least three different occasions. Her grandson later said, "[Katherine] told me that while dusting up the room where the Prophet had his study she saw a package on the table containing the gold plates on which was engraved the story of the Book of Mormon. She said she hefted those plates and found them very heavy like gold and also rippled her fingers on the edge of the plates and felt that they were separate metal plates and heard the tinkle of sound that they made."[344]

Katherine and the rest of Smith family remained wholehearted believers in Joseph's mission for their entire lives. Katherine followed her family from their home in New York to Kirtland, Ohio. While she was living in Ohio, she was married to Wilkins Jenkins Salisbury, a convert to the Church who had emigrated with the Smith family to Ohio. In the years following, Jenkins, as he was called, had an uneven record of Church service. Jenkins marched with Zion's Camp in 1834 and was made a member of the Quorum of the Seventy. Jenkins was excommunicated from the Church in 1836 after charges were raised against him of neglecting his family, abusing alcohol, and being unfaithful to Katherine. After this time, Jenkins remained distant from the Church, eventually forsaking any religion and becoming an agnostic.[345]

Despite her husband's choices, Katherine remained devoted to her faith, even as her family was forced to leave Ohio and later Missouri because of persecution. When the Salisbury family settled in Ramus it was difficult for Katherine to be far away from her family, most of whom had settled in Nauvoo. Taking care of an unsteady husband and her three children was a strain, and she missed her family. She was the only Smith child who was absent when her father died on September 14, 1840. Katherine was not able to be there until two days after his funeral.[346]

Despite the distance, Katherine's family tried to include her. She remembered that "[Joseph and Hyrum] were both very kind to me, and whenever there was a church celebration or any big doings at Nauvoo they would always

343 Quoted in Kyle R. Walker, *United by Faith: The Joseph Smith Sr. and Lucy Mack Smith Family* (American Fork, UT: Covenant Communications, 2005), 311.

344 Quoted in Walker, 313.

345 Walker, 315–17.

346 Walker, 321.

send for me."[347] Joseph and Emma invited Katherine's family to join them each year at Christmas, and she recalled, "Joseph entertained us royally and gave me silk dresses and other valuable presents."[348] The family also worried over how well Jenkins provided for Katherine and her children. Willard Richards, who accompanied Joseph on a visit to see Katherine in January 1843, later said, "My heart was pained to see a sister of Joseph's almost barefoot and four lovely children entirely so, in the middle of a severe winter."[349] Apparently Jenkins was absent for long stretches of time during this period.

Katherine was in Nauvoo in mid-June 1844 when the controversy arose that would lead Joseph and Hyrum to Carthage Jail. She was present for Joseph's final sermon to the Nauvoo Legion, and Joseph promised to visit her once his legal difficulties were settled. She later remembered that while she was preparing to leave, Hyrum said goodbye "with deeper feeling than I had ever known him to entertain."[350] This was the last time she saw her two brothers alive.

After the martyrdom of Joseph and Hyrum, Katherine initially supported Brigham Young and the Twelve, but her relationship grew strained with them when her brother William began to assert his right to lead the Church. Jenkins briefly returned to Church activity and became a strong supporter of William as well. William's excommunication by the Twelve created a rift between the Salisburys and Church leadership. When the main body of the Church left Nauvoo, Katherine and her family stayed behind.[351]

The years following were difficult for Katherine. Jenkins died in 1853, leaving the family in dire financial straits. Perhaps seeking greater economic security, Katherine was married to Joseph Younger in 1857, but by 1859 he moved to Iowa, and Katherine began using the last name Salisbury again and continued to use the name to the end of her life. She was frequently visited by missionaries from Utah, including her own relatives such as George A. and Joseph F. Smith. She always greeted them warmly. She even thawed a bit in her feelings toward Brigham Young. In 1871, she wrote to Brigham, asking for two hundred dollars to build a house. Brigham sent the money, and Katherine wrote back to him, "My gratitude to you is unbounded and I shall ever pray for blessings to rest on your venerable head."[352] When George A. Smith visited Katherine after the home was completed, he reported to

347 Quoted in Walker, 321.
348 Quoted in Walker, 321.
349 Quoted in Walker, 321.
350 Walker, 322.
351 Walker, 324–25.
352 Quoted in Walker, 333 (spelling and punctuation added).

Brigham, "[Katherine] is living on the place that you furnished her means to purchase—and is apparently the happiest woman I have seen on the journey. . . . In all her [life] she has never been able to enjoy a home of her own for a single hour; her gratitude to you seems unbounded."[353]

In her later years, Katherine affiliated with the Reorganized Church (the Community of Christ). She was accepted based on her original baptism but later chose to be rebaptized in 1873. The last survivor of the children of Joseph Sr. and Lucy Mack Smith, Katherine lived to see the dawn of the twentieth century, passing away on February 2, 1900. Upon her death, Orville F. Berry, a senator from Illinois, wrote this tribute: "The writer knew her personally, has been in her house many times and has grown up from boyhood days with her sons and grandsons, and the world would be wonderfully well off if all women were as good as Katherine Smith Salisbury."[354]

Mini-Devotional—Lessons from the Life of Katherine Smith Salisbury

The story of Katherine Smith Salisbury shows that the lives of the early Saints were often filled with challenges. Katherine raised her children and maintained her faith with little help from her husband. She found the help she needed from her extended family, who visited her often and looked after her. Even after the main body of the Church left Nauvoo, her relatives visited her and secured help so that she could live in a comfortable home. Take a few minutes to ponder or write about the following questions:

- Do you have loved ones who have similar challenges to Katherine's? What can you do to help them?
- How has your family helped you in your struggles? How can you show your gratitude to them for the help they have offered?

Leaving Ramus Behind

Though little remains of the Church settlement of Ramus today, the experiences there demonstrate the complex experiences of many early Saints. Some like Benjamin and Melissa Johnson experienced the blessings of eternal

353 Quoted in Walker, 333 (spelling and punctuation added).

354 Quoted in Walker, 339 (spelling and grammar added).

marriage, knowing their family connections would endure into the next life. Some like Samuel Prior were moved by the teachings of the Prophet. Some like Katherine Smith Salisbury lived challenging lives but found joy in and security through family and through the generosity of others. Each of their lives took varied paths after Ramus, but they were each in some way influenced by the experiences they had there.

Carthage Jail

Statue of Joseph and Hyrum Smith with Carthage Jail in the background. Photo by Casey Paul Griffiths.

Significant events at this location:

- Joseph Smith Jr., Hyrum Smith, and other Church leaders were arrested after the Nauvoo City Council sanctioned the destruction of the printing press used to publish the *Nauvoo Expositor*.

- Governor Thomas Ford of Illinois promised to protect Church leaders if they agreed to stand trial in Carthage.
- Upon their arrival at Carthage, most to the Church leaders were released on bail, except for Joseph and Hyrum Smith, who were charged with treason and placed in Carthage Jail.
- After a mob broke into the jail, Joseph and Hyrum Smith were martyred on June 27, 1844.
- John Taylor was shot five times, first in his leg and then in his chest, but he and Willard Richards survived the attack and served as witnesses of Joseph and Hyrum Smith's final moments.[355]

Nauvoo Expositor

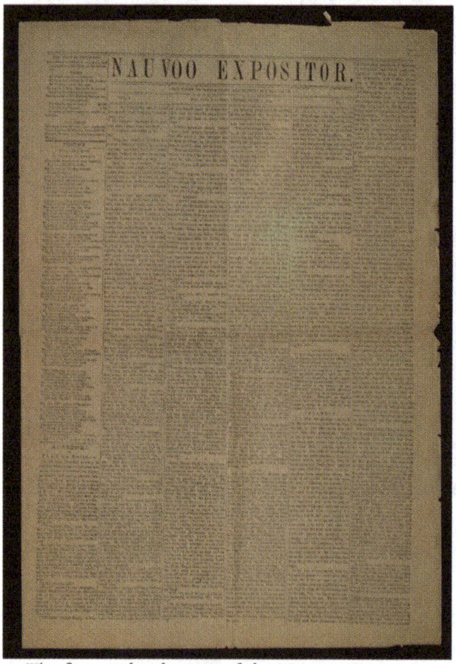
NAUVOO EXPOSITOR.

The first and only issue of the Nauvoo Expositor. Courtesy Joseph Smith Papers.

When members of The Church of Jesus Christ of Latter-day Saints began settling in Illinois in 1839 and founded the city of Nauvoo, persecution followed, including hateful speech, whipping, kidnapping, destruction of property, and false accusations. Opposition even came from government officials, who promised that if elected they would drive out or exterminate the Saints. In June 1844 dissenters among the Saints published a newspaper called the *Nauvoo Expositor*, that "put in circulation the most libelous, false, and infamous reports concerning the citizens of Nauvoo."[356] Joseph Smith, as mayor of Nauvoo, along with the

355 Firsthand accounts of the martyrdom written by Willard Richards and John Taylor are included in the appendices of this book.

356 Mark H. Taylor, *Witness to the Martyrdom: John Taylor's Personal Account of the Last Days of the Prophet Joseph Smith* (Salt Lake City: Deseret Book Company, 1999), 26, 30, 34.

Nauvoo City Council determined that the *Expositor* was a public nuisance, and they passed a bill ordering it to be shut down. The bill stated, "Resolved by the city council of the city of Nauvoo, that the printing office from whence issues the 'Nauvoo Expositor' is a public nuisance, and also of said Nauvoo Expositors, which may be, or exist in said establishment, and the Mayor is instructed to cause said printing establishment and papers to be removed without delay, in such manner as he shall direct."[357] Joseph, exercising his legal authority as mayor, ordered Nauvoo Marshal John P. Green to remove or break the press and scatter the types in the street.

The decision to destroy the Expositor press only ignited further opposition among the enemies of the Church. After the destruction of the newspaper, they accused Joseph and members of the Church of being antifreedom and against free speech: Persecutors of the Church quickly circulated these statements to surrounding cities to incite more hatred toward the citizens of Nauvoo. Though the Saints desperately attempted to publish their version of the events, they were unable to reach the surrounding cities fast enough, especially since much of their mail was intercepted and destroyed. An affidavit accused that those involved in destroying the *Nauvoo Expositor* did so illegally, so Joseph and Hyrum Smith were required to report at the Nauvoo municipal court, but they were dismissed. Public opinion outside of Nauvoo still believed the Latter-day Saints to be guilty, so to further appease the public, Church leaders consented to go before a judge outside of Nauvoo who was not a member of the Church, and they were dismissed once again.[358] In response, a mob declared that "if the law will not reach [Joseph], powder and ball must."[359]

Illinois Governor Thomas Ford Promises Protection

Church members living outside of Nauvoo continued to experience violence and harassment. Joseph Smith wrote to the governor of Illinois, Thomas Ford, and asked for guidance on how to handle the mob harassment. Governor Ford asserted that it was Joseph's duty as lieutenant-general of the Nauvoo Legion to "protect the city and surrounding country." In response, Joseph prepared the Nauvoo Legion for defending the city if an attack were to occur by

357 Joseph Smith History, vol. F-1, 85, JSP.

358 Taylor, *Witness to the Martyrdom*, 33–34, 39, 42.

359 Martyrdom Account, n.d., draft, 28, JSP.

putting Nauvoo under martial law, which prevented people from coming into the city limits.[360] Joseph wrote to the marshal of the City of Nauvoo:

> From the newspapers around us, and the current reports as brought in from the surrounding country, I have good reason to fear that a mob is organizing to come upon this city, and plunder and destroy said city, as well as murder the citizens; and by virtue of the authority vested in me as Mayor, and to preserve the city and the lives of the citizens, I do hereby declare the said city, within the limits of its incorporation, under martial law. The officers, therefore, of the Nauvoo Legion, the police as well as all others, will strictly see that no persons or property pass in or out of the city without due orders.[361]

Placing Nauvoo under martial law only added fuel to the mobs' raging hatred for Joseph and the Saints.

As tensions rose, Governor Ford's role in the matter became more prominent. He traveled to Carthage and requested by letter that both the Church leaders and the Church's persecutors present "one or more well-informed and discreet persons, who will be capable of laying before [him their] version of the matter."[362] He finished the letter by promising that the "messengers are assured the protection in person and property and will be returned to [them] safely."[363] Joseph asked Dr. J. M. Bernhisel and John Taylor to go to Carthage to meet with the governor on June 22, 1844, which they agreed to do. A later history recorded these events as follows: "During the conversation the governor expressed a desire that Joseph Smith, and all parties concerned in passing or executing the city law, in relation to the press, had better come to Carthage . . . and that, notwithstanding [their] opinions, he would recommend that the people should be satisfied." When told of concerns about Joseph's safety if he came to Carthage for trial, Governor Ford "pledged his faith as governor, and the faith of the state, that [they] should be protected, and that he would guarantee [their] perfect safety."[364]

360 Taylor, *Witness to the Martyrdom*, 39.

361 Joseph Smith History, vol. F-1, 116–17, JSP.

362 "Letter from Thomas Ford, 21 June 1844," p. [1], JSP.

363 "Letter from Thomas Ford, 21 June 1844," p. [1], JSP.

364 Joseph Smith History, vol. F-1, 116–17, JSP.

Joseph and Hyrum Smith Seek Refuge Across the Mississippi in Iowa

Joseph and Hyrum Smith, however, were not confident in the governor's protection but believed that if they left, the people of Nauvoo would be safe. As such, they decided to cross the Mississippi River heading west. John Taylor wrote, "It was Brother Joseph's opinion that, should we leave for a time, public excitement, which was so intense, would be allayed."[365] Joseph stated boldly, "If I and Hyrum were ever taken again, we should be massacred, or I was not a prophet of God." Before crossing the river, Hyrum informed Reynolds Cahoon of the situation: "A company of men are seeking to kill my brother Joseph, and the Lord has warned him to flee to the Rocky Mountains to save his life; Goodbye brother Cahoon, we shall see you again." A few moments after this interaction, Joseph passed by with tears streaming down his face and followed Hyrum without saying anything. At 2 a.m., the men finally started across the river with Orrin P. Rockwell rowing.

The Saints in Nauvoo were displeased with Joseph leaving. Some believed that it was a cowardly act to save himself from further persecution. Emma, also believing that Joseph ran from persecution, had asked Porter to convince him to return. Reynolds also did not want Joseph to leave, so he joined Porter, and they visited Joseph with a letter from Emma to persuade him to return. In response to Emma's letter, Joseph stated, "If my life is of no good to my friends then my life is of no use." Joseph asked his brother for advice on whether to return, and Hyrum suggested, "Let us go back and give ourselves up, and see the thing out." After a few moments, Joseph said, "If you go back, I will go with you, but we shall be butchered." Hyrum replied, "No, no; let us go back and put our trust in God, and we shall not be harmed; the Lord is in it; if we live or have to die, we will be reconciled to our fate." With that, Joseph and Hyrum returned to Nauvoo. [366] Emma later told a friend, "When he came back I felt the worst I ever did in my life, and from that time I looked for him to be killed."[367] As further cause for Joseph to go on trial in Carthage, Governor Ford warned that if Joseph did not give himself up, then Nauvoo and all of its citizens would be destroyed.[368]

---

365 Taylor, *Witness to the Martyrdom*, 44–51, 54.

366 Joseph Smith History, vol. F-1, 147–48, JSP.

367 Edmund C. Briggs, "Visit to Nauvoo in 1857," *Journal of History* 9, no. 1 (January 1916): 454.

368 Joseph Smith History, vol. F-1, 149, JSP.

Mini-Devotional—Dreams as Revelation

While Joseph Smith temporarily relocated himself to Iowa to keep the Saints safe, he had the following dream which he shared with W. W. Phelps:

> While I was at Jordans in Iowa the other night I dreamed that myself and my brother Hyrum went on board a large steamboat lying in a small bay near the great Ocean shortly after we went on board their was an alarm of fire and I discovered that the boat had been anchored some distance from the shore out in the bay and that an escape frome [*sic*] the fire in the confusion appeared hazardous but as delay was folly I and Hyrum jumped over board and tried our faith at walking upon the water.
>
> At first we sank in the water nearly to our knees but as we proceeded we increased in faith and were soon able to walk upon the water looking towards the burning boat in the East we saw that it was drifting towards the wharf and the town with a great flame and clouds of smoke and as if by whirlwind the town was taking fire too so that the scene of destruction and horrors of the frightened inhabitants was terrible.
>
> We proceeded on the bosom of the Mighty deep and were soon out of sight of land the ocean was still the rays of the sun were bright and we forgot all the troubles of our Mother Earth just at that moment I heard the sound of a human voice and turning round saw my Bro Samuel H. aproching [*sic*] towards us from the East we stoped [*sic*] and he came up after a moment's conversation he informed me that he had bin [*sic*] lonesome back and had made up his mind to go with me across the mighty deep.
>
> We all started again and in a short time were blest with the first sight of a city whose silver steeples and towers were more beautiful than any that I had ever seen or heard of on earth. It stood as it were upon the western shore of the mighty deep we walking on and its order and glory seemed far beyond the wisdome [*sic*] of man while we were gazing upon the perfection of the city a small boat launched of from the port and almost as quick as thought came to us in an instant they took us on board and saluted with welcome and with music such as is not of earth the next scene on landing was more than I can describe the greetings and the music from a thousand towers and the light of God, himself at the return of three of his sons soothed my soul into quiet and joy that I felt as if I were

> truly in heaven I gazed upon the splendor I greeted my friends I awoke and lo it was a dream.[369]

Joseph's dream was a prophetic revelation and as something that brought great comfort to the Prophet as he faced the end of his life at Carthage Jail.

- Have you had any dreams that could be considered revelation?
- Have you had dreams that have brought you comfort and joy?

Joseph and Hyrum Smith Travel to Carthage

Early in the morning on Monday, June 24, 1844, Joseph and Hyrum started toward Carthage accompanied by several friends. As the group passed the Nauvoo Temple, Joseph paused, looked at the temple and then at the city of Nauvoo, and said: "This is the loveliest place and the best people under the heavens; little do they know the trials that await them."[370] At 10 a.m., they arrived four miles outside of Carthage where they were met with Captain Dunn and his sixty mounted militia. Upon seeing the captain and his forces, Joseph said to his friends around him, "Do not be alarmed brethren, for they cannot do more to you than the enemies of truth did to the ancient saints—they can only kill the body."[371]

Joseph then told those who were with him, "I am going like a lamb to the slaughter, but I am calm as a summer's morning; I have a conscience void of offense toward God, and toward all men. I shall die an innocent man, and my blood shall cry from the ground for vengeance, and it shall yet be said of me 'he was murdered in cold blood.'"[372] Captain Dunn and his company then began their trip back to Nauvoo to assist in taking the weapons from the citizens of Nauvoo.

Shortly after, Captain Dunn took control of the Nauvoo Legion and requested that the citizens of Nauvoo give up their arms, pledging that Joseph and his people would be protected, even at the cost of his own life. Though the

369 W. W. Phelps, *Joseph Smith's Last Dream*, n.d., M288 P541d 1992 and MS 9040, Church History Library, Salt Lake City.

370 "Historian's Office, Martyrdom Account, Draft," p. 1, The Joseph Smith Papers, accessed October 20, 2022, https://www.josephsmithpapers.org/paper-summary/historians-office-martyrdom-account-draft/1

371 "Historian's Office, Martyrdom Account," p. 3, The Joseph Smith Papers, accessed October 20, 2022, https://www.josephsmithpapers.org/paper-summary/historians-office-martyrdom-account/3

372 "Appendix 3: Willard Richards, Journal Excerpt, 23–27 June 1844," p. [20], JSP.

citizens of Nauvoo feared that giving up their weapons would result in another massacre like at Hawn's Mill in Missouri, Joseph instructed them to obey. At 6 p.m., the Nauvoo citizens relinquished their weapons, and the group that was called to trial prepared again to go to Carthage. Joseph went back to Nauvoo "twice to bid his family farewell. He appeared solemn and thoughtful, and expressed himself to several individuals that he expected to be murdered. There appeared no alternative but that he must either give himself up, or the inhabitants of the city would be massacred by a lawless mob under sanction of the Governor."[373] Although Joseph knew that he would be killed in Carthage, he was willing to give up his life for the gospel.

Mini-Devotional—A Testimony of the Book of Mormon

On the way again to Carthage with his brother, Hyrum Smith opened his Book of Mormon to Ether 12:36–38, read it aloud, and folded the corner of the page to mark it. While in jail, Joseph Smith also demonstrated his faith in and love of the Book of Mormon by bearing witness of it to the guards stationed nearby. Of these events, Elder Jeffery R. Holland observed,

> In this their greatest—and last—hour of need, I ask you: would these men blaspheme before God by continuing to fix their lives, their honor, and their own search for eternal salvation on a book (and by implication a church and a ministry) they had fictitiously created out of whole cloth?
>
> Never mind that their wives are about to be widows and their children fatherless. Never mind that their little band of followers will yet be "houseless, friendless and homeless" and that their children will leave footprints of blood across frozen rivers and an untamed prairie floor. Never mind that legions will die and other legions live declaring in the four quarters of this earth that they know the Book of Mormon and the Church which espouses it to be true. Disregard all of that, and tell me whether in this hour of death these two men would enter the presence of their Eternal Judge quoting from and finding solace in a book which, if *not* the very word of God, would brand them as imposters and charlatans until the end of time? *They would not do that!* They were willing to

373 Joseph Smith History, vol. F-1, 151–53, JSP.

die rather than deny the divine origin and the eternal truthfulness of the Book of Mormon.[374]

- How does Joseph and Hyrum Smith's martyrdom increase your testimony of the truthfulness of the Book of Mormon?
- When have you been able to defend the Book of Mormon even when the consequences were not in your favor?

Joseph and Hyrum Smith Are Arrested and Put in Carthage Jail

Carthage Jail has been restored to its 1844 appearance. Photo by Casey Paul Griffiths.

Joseph and Hyrum Smith and the Nauvoo City Council arrived at Carthage late at night on June 24, 1844. As they passed through the public square, the Carthage Greys militia called out expressions like the following: "Where is the d____d Prophet?" "Stand away you McDonough boys and let us shoot the d____d Mormons." "God d___ you old Joe, we've got you now."

374 Jeffrey R. Holland, "Safety for the Soul," *Ensign*, November 2009, https://www.churchofjesuschrist.org/study/ensign/2009/11/safety-for-the-soul?lang=eng.

"Clear the way and let us have a view of Joe Smith, the prophet of God; he has seen the last of Nauvoo—we'll use him up now and kill all the d____d Mormons."[375] Governor Ford's response to their cries was, "Gentlemen, I know your great anxiety to see Mr. Smith, which is natural enough, but it is quite too late to night for you to have the opportunity; but I assure you, Gentlemen, you shall have that privilege tomorrow morning, as I will cause him to pass before the troops upon the square, and I now wish you, with this assurance, quietly and peaceably to return to your quarters."[376]

Constable Bettisworth arrived that night to arrest Joseph and Hyrum for "treason against the government and people of the State of Illinois" for putting Nauvoo under martial law. Attorneys Woods and Reid insisted that the brothers had the right to be brought before a justice before being sent to jail. The constable then showed them a mittimus signed by Captain Smith, justice of the peace, stating that Joseph and Hyrum were to be taken to jail. Though Joseph and Hyrum tried to argue against it, they were eventually taken to Carthage Jail. Governor Ford refused to intervene, stating that he had to allow the law to be fulfilled.[377]

Serving all of Hancock County, the jail was just outside of the city of Carthage and was used for individuals awaiting trial. The two-story building was built in 1840, faces south, and was made out of yellow limestone with walls two and a half feet thick. George Stigall, the jailor, and his family lived in the jail and provided meals to the prisoners, who paid for the food. Joseph and his friends stayed the night in the debtor's cell downstairs, though George was previously going to put them in the dungeon room upstairs. [378]

June 27, 1844—Day of the Martyrdom

Panoramic photo of the upstairs bedroom where Joseph and Hyrum Smith were when the jail was attacked. Photo by Casey Paul Griffiths.

375 "Historian's Office, Martyrdom Account, Draft," p. 5, JSP.
376 Joseph Smith History, vol. F-1, 116–17, JSP.
377 Joseph Smith History, vol. F-1, 154–55, 157–60, JSP.
378 "History, 1838–1856, volume F-1 [1 May 1844–8 August 1844]," p. 181, JSP.

Though Joseph and Hyrum Smith were jailed, many Latter-day Saints were allowed to visit them in the jail. Willard Richards, John Taylor, John S. Fullmer, Dan Jones, and Stephen Markham spent the most time with the Smith brothers, but Dr. Bernhisel, John Smith, Hirum Kimball, Cyrus H. Wheelock also visited.[379] Cyrus visited the jail on June 27, 1844, and gave Joseph a six-barreled, percussion-cap-ignited, Allen "pepper box" revolver.[380] He then went on an errand and was kept from returning to the jail again. Stephen was driven out of Carthage when he attempted to return to the jail. John Fullmer returned to Nauvoo to gather witnesses. Dan Jones was sent to retrieve wine and did not return. Those remaining in the jail on June 27 were John Taylor, Willard, and Joseph and Hyrum. At some point that afternoon, the men were moved from the debtor's cell downstairs to the jailer's bedroom upstairs.

John and Willard were prepared to do whatever was necessary to keep Joseph and Hyrum safe. Willard told Joseph, "If it is necessary that you die in this matter, and if they will take me in your stead, I will suffer for you." John also told Joseph, "If you will permit it, and say the word, I will have you out of this prison in five hours, if that jail has to come down to do it." Of course, Joseph refused both offers.[381]

Governor Ford had promised to take Joseph and Hyrum to Nauvoo with him, but he left that day without the prisoners. This action disappointed everyone in the jail, who viewed it as a "breach of faith on the part of the governor, but also as an indication of a desire to insult us, if nothing more, by leaving us in the proximity of such men." The men that they were left with were the infamous Carthage Greys, who were tasked with guarding the jail and who were considered some of Joseph's greatest enemies. Even John Taylor called their captain, Robert F. Smith, "a most unprincipled villain."[382]

Little has been said about what was "discussed during that long afternoon in June 1844 between these leaders. Scriptures were read. Legal strategies were discussed. A few letters were drafted. Time was essentially suspended as the men waited for a legal hearing to determine whether the prophet and

379 Taylor, *Witness to the Martyrdom*, 82.

380 Joseph L. Lyon and David W. Lyon, "Physical Evidence at Carthage Jail and What It Reveals about the Assassination of Joseph and Hyrum Smith," *BYU Studies* 47, no. 4 (2008): 34, https://byustudies.byu.edu/article/physical-evidence-at-carthage-jail-and-what-it-reveals-about-the-assassination-of-joseph-and-hyrum-smith/.

381 John Taylor Martyrdom Account, http://mldb.byu.edu/jtaylor.htm

382 Taylor, *Witness to the Martyrdom*, 82–84.

his brother would be released on bail."[383] Sometime between 3 and 4 p.m., John sang a song that he had learned in 1840 as a missionary in England and that he had recently introduced to the Saints in Nauvoo. He recounted, "All of us felt unusually dull and languid, with a remarkable depression of spirits. In consonance with those feelings, I sang a song, that had lately been introduced into Nauvoo, entitled, A Poor Wayfaring Man of Grief, etc. The song is pathetic, and the tune quite plaintive, and was very much in accordance with our feelings at the time for our spirits were all depressed, dull and gloomy and surcharged with indefinite ominous forebodings." John sang the song twice that day. The first time was of his own accord. Shortly before the mob stormed the ill-guarded jail, Hyrum requested he sing it again, to which John replied: "Brother Hyrum, I do not feel like singing." Hyrum persisted, replying, "Oh! never mind, commence singing, and you will get the spirit of it." So, John sang it a second time. Shortly after the singing, the jail was attacked.[384]

Mini-Devotional—The Last Moments of Joseph and Hyrum Smith

The lyrics of "A Poor Wayfaring Man of Grief," which John Taylor sang in the Carthage Jail, embody the Savior's teaching found in Matthew 25:40: "Inasmuch as ye have done it unto one of the least of these my brethren, ye have done it unto me." As John sang on that fateful day, he could not have known at the time that this song would forever become a reminder of the faithful legacy of the martyrdom that occurred that evening.

More importantly many have wondered why, if the Prophet knew he was going to his death, he did not leave a final testimony. A common interpretation is that the lyrics to this song are Joseph and Hyrum Smith's final testimony of the gospel of Jesus Christ for which they gave their lives. The last stanzas of the lyrics are as follows:

> In pris'n I saw him next, condemned
> To meet a traitor's doom at morn.
> The tide of lying tongues I stemmed,
> And honored him 'mid shame and scorn.

383 Jeffrey N. Walker, "John Taylor: Beyond "A Poor Wayfaring Man of Grief," in *Champion of Liberty: John Taylor*, ed. Mary Jane Woodger (Provo, Utah: Brigham Young University Religious Studies Center, 2009), 63.

384 Taylor, *Witness to the Martyrdom,* 84.

My friendship's utmost zeal to try,
He asked if I for him would die.
The flesh was weak; my blood ran chill,
But my free spirit cried, "I will!"

Then in a moment to my view
The stranger started from disguise.
The tokens in his hands I knew;
The Savior stood before mine eyes.
He spake, and my poor name he named,
"Of me thou hast not been ashamed.
These deeds shall thy memorial be;
Fear not, thou didst them unto me."[385]

- How will your deeds be a memorial of your testimony of Jesus Christ?
- In what ways have you served the "least of these my brethren"?
- What blessings have you experienced from serving others?

The Attack on the Jail

The hole from the bullet that hit Hyrum Smith is still visible in the bedroom door in Carthage Jail. Photo by Casey Paul Griffiths.

Eight men from the Carthage Greys had been instructed to defend the jail to protect the men inside against an attack. In the town square six hundred yards away, a larger group of Carthage Greys waited for a signal to join in defending the jail if an attack occurred. Soon after John Taylor's vocal solo, shortly after 5 p.m., a mob with painted faces rushed the jail. The jail guards were reported to have known of the assault beforehand and merely fired blanks at the mob to make it appear as though they were doing their job without actually harming any of the attackers. Both John Taylor and

385 "A Poor Wayfaring Man of Grief," *Hymns*, no. 29.

Willard Richards saw the Carthage Greys fire at the mob to no avail. Once John witnessed the mob coming up the stairs, he immediately joined Hyrum Smith Willard in pushing against the door to their room to prevent it from opening, since the latch on the door did not work.

Soon after the mob reached the bedroom door, they used military-issued muskets to fire two bullets through the door. While the first bullet missed, the second bullet hit the left side of Hyrum's face traveling through his skull where it exited from underneath the jaw. Almost at the same instant, Hyrum was then shot once in the lower back and once in each leg, most likely from bullets coming from a window. His last words were "I am a dead man!"[386]

The Pepperbox pistol and single shot pistol kept by Joseph and Hyrum Smith in Carthage Jail. Photo by Casey Paul Griffiths.

Joseph Smith, seeing his brother die, exclaimed with grief, "Oh! my poor, dear brother Hyrum!" as he leaned over him.[387] Realizing that their lives were on the line, Joseph opened the door slightly and hid behind it for protection, blindly firing his revolver as an act of defense. Three of the six barrels Joseph fired and struck three men, two in the upper arm and the third in the face. One man was said to have died later from the injuries. Joseph's quick thinking most likely kept the attackers from immediately rushing into the room after killing Hyrum, for they did not know that Joseph and his friends were armed. Hyrum was also given a single-shot pistol by John S. Fullmer, but it was not fired during the attack.[388]

386 Lyon and Lyon, "Physical Evidence," 33-34.

387 Taylor, *Witness to the Martyrdom*, 89.

388 Lyon and Lyon, "Physical Evidence," 35.

Eventually, the mob was able to push open the door enough to be able to fire into the room. John Taylor described the scene: "It certainly was a terrible scene: streams of fire as thick as my arm passed by me as these men fired, and, unarmed as we were, it looked like certain death." John and Willard tried to protect themselves by knocking "aside the guns of the ruffians"[389] and "giving another direction to the balls."[390] Amidst the chaos, however, John left the door to look out the window for friends or an escape. "This action required considerable courage because the door had been forced partly open and the south and east windows were visible to the men firing from the hallway."[391] While trying to escape, John was shot in the left thigh and fell to the floor, losing control of his muscles for a few seconds. When he regained control, he crawled to the bed and was shot from the door three more times.

Joseph Smith was hit by several bullets and fell from this window. Photo by Casey Paul Griffiths.

Joseph, who probably believed that he could save the lives of John and Willard if he led the mob away, ran into the line of fire and attempted to jump out of the window. He made it almost out of the window when he was shot twice from the door and once by someone outside the jail. He fell twenty-five feet out of the window. His last words were "Oh Lord, My God!" (Doctrine

389 Martyrdom Account, n.d., 62, JSP.
390 Taylor, *Witness to the Martyrdom*, 90.
391 Lyon and Lyon, "Physical Evidence," 36.

and Covenants 135:1). Later reports state that Joseph had a wound to the lower abdomen, the right hip, the right breast, under the heart, and in the right shoulder near the neck. The coroner's jury detailed two wounds, one to the right side of the chest and one in the right neck near the shoulder. "Joseph Smith's final act of self-sacrifice ensured that there were two friendly eyewitnesses to the murders."[392]

Upon seeing Joseph's fall the mob cried, "He's leaped the window!" The attackers in the jail ran outside. After looking out the window to confirm the Prophet's death, Willard began to run out of the room as well when he heard John say, "Take me." [393] Willard carried him into the dungeon room where he covered John with a mattress, which pressure on his wounds might have been the reason why John did not die. [394] Willard said to John, "This is a hard case to lay you on the floor, but if your wounds are not fatal, I want you to live to tell the story."[395] Willard then expected himself to be shot and killed, though the mob did not return.

392 "Carthage, Illinois."

393 "Appendix 3: Willard Richards, Journal Excerpt, 23–27 June 1844," p. [37], JSP.

394 "Carthage, Illinois."

395 "Appendix 3: Willard Richards, Journal Excerpt, 23–27 June 1844," p. [37], JSP.

John Taylor's Pocketwatch on display at the Church History Museum in Salt Lake City. Photo by Casey Paul Griffiths.

After the tragic event, John believed that his pocket watch saved his life by deflecting a potentially fatal bullet that forced him back inside after an attempt to jump out of the window. Researchers have not found evidence that the watch was destroyed by a bullet, but they instead hypothesize that it was destroyed when he fell against the windowsill, stopping the time at 5:16:26 p.m.[396] Regardless of what actually happened, the watch became important to John, adding to his belief in its life-saving properties. He described his emotions after realizing what he believed the watch had done: "I shall never forget the feelings of gratitude that I then experienced towards my [H]eavenly Father; the whole scene was vividly portrayed before me, and my heart melted before the Lord. I felt that the Lord had preserved me by a special act of mercy; that my time had not yet come, and that I had still a work to perform upon the

396 Timeline of 96 Hours Surrounding the Martyrdom of Joseph Smith and Hyrum Smith, *Church News,* June 27, 2019.

earth."[397] John did have a work to do, for he became the third president of The Church of Jesus Christ of Latter-day Saints in 1880.

Unfortunately the events surrounding the martyrdom also led to the death of another member of the Smith family, Samuel Harrison, Joseph's younger brother. Samuel journeyed to Carthage to retrieve the bodies of his brothers, would be chased for two hours by an angry mob. Upon his safe arrival to Carthage, he was exhausted and would ultimately die a month later of what was believed to be a fever. John Taylor later stated that he believed it was the mob chase that caused Samuel's death.[398]

Mini-Devotional—Prophesied Protection

During the attack, John Taylor was not the only one to experience heavenly protection. Willard Richards had used his cane to deflect the enemies' guns. He saw Hyrum Smith fall and then Prophet shortly after. Fully expecting to be the next one shot, Willard was surprised when the mob, having fulfilled their mission to murder the Prophet, left the building. It was then that Willard recalled something that Joseph Smith had told him more than a year before, that "the time would come that the balls would fly around him like hail, and he should see his friends fall on the right and on the left, but that there should not be a hole in his garment."[399] Willard was the only one in Carthage Jail on June 27, 1844, that was not killed or severely injured, having only a bullet graze the lower part of his left ear. Willard survived the attack and was able to care for Joseph and Hyrum's bodies and become a witness of the martyrdom. He would remain faithful in the gospel for the rest of his life, leading a company of pioneers across the plains and serving in the First Presidency as a counselor to President Brigham Young.[400]

- In what ways has the Lord protected you from harm, be it physical or emotional?
- What are promises that the Lord has given to you?
- How have the commandments served as protection in your life?

397 Quoted in B.H. Roberts, *The Rise and Fall of Nauvoo,* (Salt Lake City, UT: The Deseret News, 1900), 457.

398 Taylor, *Witness to the Martyrdom*, 100, 115.

399 Martyrdom Account, n.d., 60, JSP.

400 "Willard Richards" (biographical entry), JSP.

Carthage Jail after the Martyrdom

Carthage Jail continued to hold prisoners for nearly two decades. In 1866, the local newspaper *Carthage Republican* predicted that the jail would be purchased and frequently visited by those people wanting to see the place of the martyrdom of a prophet. The paper said: "It is possible . . . a purchaser may be found who will repair the old building. . . . Its future occupant need scarcely expect immunity from the visits of thousands who will yet pay homage of curiosity, at least, to the shrine of the Martyred Prophet."[401] This prediction was not unfounded, for that very year Bryant F. Peterson purchased the jail for $1,100 at an auction. Bryant repaired and remodeled the building, eventually selling it five years later for $1,500 to James Browning, who used the jail as his personal residence for the next thirty years.[402] As predicted, many visited the jail in remembrance of the horrific event as early as September 1845, including a large group that included members of the Quorum of the Twelve Apostles. The group observed that "the blood of Hyrum still stained the floor where he fell and breathed his last; the walls were marked with bullet holes."[403]

While living in the jail, the Brownings graciously allowed those interested in the martyrdom to tour their home. Mrs. Browning shared "that she had a great many visitors who came to examine the premises, and some of the neighbors had reminded her of the trouble she was put to in showing them around, but she said, with considerable emotion, that she had not the heart to refuse anyone, and intended always to be courteous and kind to the friends of the martyrs. She expressed her regret that such a scene as the one that made her home of so much historical interest should ever have taken place."[404] In 1888, three Church historians who visited the jail described it in the following way:

> There it stood, the old rock building, once a prison, but now transformed into a comfortable private resident. . . . Mrs. Browning received us kindly and showed us about the premises. We went upstairs to the

401 Scott C. Esplin, "Dark Tourism: Healin at Historic Carthage Jail," *Journal of Mormon History* 46, no. 1 (2020): 93, https://doi.org/10.5406/jmormhist.46.1.0085.

402 Donald Q. Cannon, "Illinois," in *Sacred Places*, vol. 3, *Ohio and Illinois A Comprehensive Guide to Early LDS Historical Sites*, ed. LaMar C. Berrett, (Salt Lake City: Deseret Book Company, 2002), 205.

403 Journal History of The Church of Jesus Christ of Latter-day Saints (chronological scrapbook of typed entries and newspaper clippings, 1830–present), September 24, 1845, 1, Church History Library, cited in Esplin, "Dark Tourism," 91.

404 Esplin, "Dark Tourism," 91.

> south east upper room, where Joseph, Hyrum, John Taylor, and Willard Richards were confined on the day of the martyrdom. We saw the hole through the door made by the bullet that killed Hyrum, examined the corner where Elder Taylor rolled under the bed, raised the window through which Joseph leaped, and was shown the exact place where the blood of Hyrum still stains the floor. The floor being carpeted, we did not see the stain, but Mrs. Browning assured us it was there yet and could not be washed away.[405]

In 1906, Joseph F. Smith, President of the Church and son of Hyrum Smith, visited the jail with Charles W. Nibley, future presiding bishop and counselor in the First Presidency. When the guide pointed out "that stain is the blood of Hyrum Smith. . . . [President] Smith walked over and sat on the bed. He put his hands over his face, and convulsively wept, until [Brother] Nibley could see the water coming through his fingers. [President Smith] then said, 'Charlie, take me out of here!'"[406] He later stated, "I despise this place. It harrows up my feelings to come here."[407]

Mrs. Browning sold the jail to The Church of Jesus Christ of Latter-day Saints in 1903, and for the next thirty-five years, the jail was rented out as a home, as long as the tenants were "willing to show it at any time to anyone who wished to see it."[408] The city of Carthage advertised the jail on the main highway into town with a marker to direct visitors to the site, which was "the first material recognition that the Prophet [Joseph Smith] has received at the hands of the town in which he was murdered," and marked "a turning point in the attitude toward 'Mormonism' of the country."[409] In 1938, the Church made plans to restore the jail to its 1844 appearance.[410]

Restoration efforts for the jail continued, and by the mid-1950s, the jail had more than a thousand visitors a month, with visitors traveling from

---

405 Andrew Jenson, Edward Stevenson, and Joseph S. Black, "Scenes in Church History," *Deseret News*, October 31, 1888, 9.

406 Russell M. Ballard, "Joseph F. Smith and the Importance of Family," in *Joseph F. Smith: Reflections on the Man and His Times,* ed. Craig K. Manscill et al. (Provo, UT: Brigham Young University Religious Studies Center; Salt Lake City: Deseret Book, 2013), 7, cited in Esplin, "Dark Tourism," 97.

407 Preston Nibley, *The Presidents of the Church* (Salt Lake City: Deseret Book, 1974), 203, cited in Esplin, "Dark Tourism," 97.

408 "Visitors from All States Stop at Old Jail," *Hancock County Journal*, September 1956, in Journal History, September 1956, 1, cited in Esplin, "Dark Tourism," 99.

409 "Carthage Honors Joseph Smith," *Deseret News*, September 7, 1935, in Journal History, September 7, 1935, 7, cited in Esplin, "Dark Tourism," 100.

410 Esplin, "Dark Tourism," 101.

every state and from several foreign nations. The *Hancock County Journal* observed, "Indeed, the Old Jail is one of the most popular historic shrines in the country."[411]

In June 1944, to commemorate the one-hundredth anniversary of the martyrdom, several officials representing the city of Carthage, the Reorganized Church of Jesus Christ of Latter Day Saints (now called Community of Christ), and The Church of Jesus Christ of Latter-day Saints met at the Carthage Jail site. Many, as they sang hymns and prayed, recorded that they "felt that [they] were in the presence of the men who met their deaths there."[412] Carthage resident Isham G. Davidson noted, "Many tourists still visit Nauvoo and there are those who make pilgrimages to the shrine here of the old jail. . . . Carthage, . . . while sharing the universal condemnation of a cowardly and wanton murder of helpless citizens of Nauvoo, feels the pride of aloofness in its commission. Her hands are clean. The men accused of the deed were not residents of the town. A jury said it did not know who the murdered were or whence they came. . . . Today [Carthage] welcomes those who come to bow at the shrine of the martyrs."[413]

As Carthage Jail became increasingly popular, in 1971, the Church's historical department completed the application for Carthage Jail to be added to the National Register of Historic Places, and the jail was placed on the register in 1973.[414]

The only remaining physical evidence of the event are two bullet holes through the door of the jailer's bedroom, one of which was caused by the bullet that struck Hyrum. Additional holes in the walls, window casing, and ceiling must have been repaired in the mid-1960s, and they are no longer visible.[415]

---

411 "Visitors from All States Stop at Old Jail," *Hancock County Journal,* September 1956, in Journal History, September 1956, 1, as cited in Esplin, "Dark Tourism," 105.

412 Esplin, "Dark Tourism," 103.

413 Davidson, "Mormons Pay Tribute to Leaders," cited in Esplin, "Dark Tourism," 105.

414 Esplin, "Dark Tourism," 109.

415 Lyon and Lyon, "Physical Evidence."

Dedication of Carthage Jail

The restored Carthage Jail. Photo by Casey Paul Griffiths.

Carthage Jail was renovated in 1989, and President Gordon B. Hinckley, who was then a counselor in the First Presidency, dedicated the building that year. At the dedication, President Hinckley said, "Ours is the duty to forgive and put behind us the troubles of the past. Ours is the obligation to rise above old animosities."[416] In the dedicatory prayer, he asked that the site would be "a place hallowed and sacred to which people of all faiths may come and learn, may ponder and reflect, may meditate and pray while thinking upon the lives and works of those who died here."[417] Consider the location of a tragedy for members of The Church of Jesus Christ of Latter-day Saints, Carthage Jail is a great reminder of boundless faith and dedication to God, where the beloved Prophet Joseph Smith and his brother Hyrum gave their lives for Christ's restored gospel.

416 Dell Van Orden, "'Hallowed and Sacred Site Made Beautiful' Out of Respect, Love," *Church News*, July 8, 1989, as cited in Scott C. Esplin, "Competing for the City of Joseph: Interpretive Conflicts in Nauvoo's Restoration," *The John Whitmer Journal* 32, no. 1 (Spring/Summer 2012): 61.

417 Dell Van Orden, "'Hallowed and Sacred Site Made Beautiful' Out of Respect, Love," *Church News*, July 8, 1989.

The idea of Hyrum and Joseph sealing their testimony with blood is mentioned three times in Doctrine and Covenants 135. It is first found in the first verse: "To seal the testimony of this book and the Book of Mormon, we announce the martyrdom of Joseph Smith the Prophet, and Hyrum Smith the Patriarch." Verse 3 speaks of Joseph and Hyrum, stating that they "sealed [their] mission and [their] works with [their] own blood." The last verse is a final testimony that includes the following sentence: "Their *innocent blood* on the floor of Carthage jail is a broad seal affixed to 'Mormonism' that cannot be rejected by any court on earth" (verse 7; italics original). The phrase *sealing with blood* has since been used when speaking of Joseph and Hyrum's sacrifice, for theirs was a significant demonstration of standing as a witness of the truthfulness of the Lord's restored gospel. Hebrews 9:16–17 states, "For where a testament is, there must also of necessity be the death of the testator. For a testament is of force after men are dead: otherwise, it is of no strength at all while the testator liveth." Joseph and Hyrum's deaths defended God's truths and forever cemented their testimony of the gospel of Jesus Christ, such that believers and unbelievers alike cannot refute it. Indeed, their sacrifice sealed their testimony of the Book of Mormon, of modern revelation including those in the Doctrine and Covenants, and of the restored gospel found within The Church of Jesus Christ of Latter-day Saints. Carthage Jail is a special place, filled with rich spiritual history where visitors can feel of Joseph and Hyrum's faith and dedication to the gospel.

The Seventies Hall, the Trail of Hope, and Montrose, Iowa

The "Eyes Westward" monument to Brigham Young and Joseph Smith on the banks of the Mississippi Rivver at the end of the Trail of Hope. Photo by Casey Paul Griffiths.

After the martyrdom of the Prophet and Patriarch on June 27, 1844, tensions between the Saints and their enemies calmed down for a short time. With the Prophet dead, many of the adversaries of the Saints believed Nauvoo would just fade away; instead, Nauvoo continued to grow. The Saints redoubled their efforts to build the temple, and converts continued to pour into Nauvoo, largely due to extensive missionary work. Unfortunately, the peace following the martyrdom of Joseph and Hyrum Smith was short-lived. Persecutions and threats against the Saints began to rise again, and Brigham Young and other Church leaders decided to depart from Nauvoo.

Many of the sites associated with the westward exodus are located on Parley Street in Nauvoo. Thousands of Saints made the trek down Parley Street to the edge of the Mississippi River, where they embarked to find a new home in the West. Today, a walk down Parley Street to the river's edge is a poignant way to experience the fear and hope the Saints felt as they left Nauvoo and began their journey into the wilderness. The walk down the Trail of Hope begins at the rebuilt Seventies Hall on Parley Street. On the other side of the river, in Montrose, Iowa, there are also markers to commemorate the exodus of the Saints. A visit to these exodus sites highlights the sacrifices of the early Saints and their faith that God was leading them to a new home in the West.

The Seventies Hall

The Seventies Hall in Nauvoo is located at the beginning of the Trail of Hope. Photo by Casey Paul Griffiths.

Significant events at this location:

- Members of the Quorum of the Twelve, the Nauvoo high council, and several high priests met at this site with Sidney Rigdon to discuss his claims as the successor to Joseph Smith on August 7, 1844.
- On December 27, 1844, Brigham Young and other leaders dedicated the building, this dedicatory session being the first of five to be held.

Based on the Savior's teaching in Luke 10:1–17, the Prophet Joseph Smith was inspired to organize the First Quorum of the Seventy on February 28, 1835. The "Seventies" were a group of men whose purpose was to preach the gospel and regulate the affairs of the Church under the direction of the Twelve Apostles (see Doctrine and Covenants 107:25, 34).

By 1843, there were fifteen Quorums of the Seventy, totaling about 490 men.[418] Since most of the men in Nauvoo had very little religious education, and in many cases very little formal education, Church leaders realized that training these newly called men would be beneficial: "This group of men aware of their shortcomings and convinced of the reality of their God-given missionary assignment, planned an adult education program to improve their missionary potential. To accomplish this aim, the seventies concluded they needed a structure in which to learn the skills needed in their proselyting assignment."[419] The training program was like an early version of a Missionary Training Center!

This training took place on land donated by Bishop Edward Hunter. Plans were drawn for a two-story, red-brick building to be twenty-eight feet wide and forty feet long. The walls were about nine feet tall when a tornado struck in early 1844. The tornado blew the west wall down and smashed the flooring and floor joists. Brigham Young (who had been a carpenter by trade) inspected the damage and suggested rebuilding the walls one brick thicker. The brethren took his advice, and by May 1844, the exterior of the building was completed.

The interior of the building was still being finished when the Prophet Joseph Smith was martyred on June 27, 1844. After the Prophet died, many people stepped forward with claims to be his rightful successor. One of those was the last surviving member of the First Presidency, Sidney Rigdon. On August 7, 1844, a meeting was held in the unfinished Seventies Hall to discuss Sidney's claims. In attendance at that meeting were Brigham Young,

418 *The Seventies Hall at Nauvoo* (Nauvoo, IL: Nauvoo Restoration Incorporated, n.d.).

419 *Seventies Hall at Nauvoo.*

the Quorum of the Twelve, the Nauvoo high council, other high priests, and Sidney Rigdon. The majority of those present rejected Sidney's claims, but they concluded that the Church as a whole should decide, and they agreed to hold a solemn assembly in one of the nearby groves to determine who should lead the Church. At the solemn assembly, Sidney's claims were heard, but in the end, the majority of Church members in attendance voted to follow the Twelve.[420]

The interior of the Seventies Hall was finally completed around Christmas of 1844. On December 27, 1844, the first of five dedicatory services was held. Brigham Young offered the dedicatory prayer. Apostle John Taylor (who eventually became the third President of the Church) described the dedication as follows:

> I attended the dedication of the Seventies Hall. The services commenced under the direction of President Joseph Young, who organized the meeting in the following order. The stand was occupied by the seven presiding presidents of the Seventies; and the Twelve or as many of them as were present. The senior president of Quorum was seated on the right, the choir of singers on the left and the brass band in front. . . . The excellent melody of the choir and Band, mingled with the devout aspirations of a congregation of *all Saints*, gave the commencement of their service an air of interest, felicity, and glory at once feeling, touching, pathetic, grand and sublime.[421]

The primary purpose of the building was to provide an opportunity for missionaries to improve their teaching and preaching skills. The hall also served as a small chapel for Sunday worship, lectures, and similar occasions. The training program that took place in the hall must have fulfilled its desired effect because by 1846, there were thirty-five Quorums of the Seventy in Nauvoo.[422]

The second floor of the Seventies Hall provided office space for the Seventies and housed a museum, which exhibited artifacts brought home by returning missionaries as well as artwork by local and traveling artists. The second floor also held a community library of approximately six hundred books. Most families could not afford to buy books, so this library was a blessing

---

420 For more information on the succession crisis and the solemn assembly, please see *Church History in the Fullness of Times: Student Manual*, 2nd ed. (Salt Lake City: The Church of Jesus Christ of Latter-day Saints, 2003), 298–302.

421 "Dedication of the Seventies Hall," *Times and Seasons,* February 1, 1845.

422 *Seventies Hall*, Nauvoo Historic Sites, accessed July 18, 2022, https://www.nauvoohistoricsites.org/buildings/70s/.

to the Nauvoo community. When the Saints left Nauvoo, these books were hauled in wagons to the Salt Lake Valley where they became the nucleus of the first library in the West (between Missouri and the Pacific coast).[423]

After the Saints left Nauvoo, the hall was purchased and used as a Presbyterian church until 1855. It was used as a school for another forty years until it was finally torn down and plowed over. The Church acquired the site in 1962, and the present building was reconstructed on the original foundation by 1973.

Mini-Devotional—The Truth Will Go Forth

A tornado struck Nauvoo in the spring of 1844. Then, in June, the Prophet and Patriarch were martyred. Did the men who built the Seventies Hall ever question whether it was worth it to finish the building? Regardless, the hall was completed, and in the months before the exodus, many men were trained therein and sent out on missions to preach the gospel. In 1842, the Prophet expressed the underlying reason why the Saints would labor to complete the Seventies Hall even after the trials they faced. In his letter to John Wentworth, editor of the *Chicago Democrat* newspaper, the Prophet declared: "The Standard of Truth has been erected; no unhallowed hand can stop the work from progressing; persecutions may rage, mobs may combine, armies may assemble, calumny may defame, but the truth of God will go forth boldly, nobly, and independent, till it has penetrated every continent, visited every clime, swept every country, and sounded in every ear, till the purposes of God shall be accomplished, and the Great Jehovah shall say the work is done."[424]

- How did the completion of the Seventies Hall help fulfill the words written by the Prophet?
- If academic and religious training was important to the early Saints, should it be just as important today? Is it more important? Why or why not?
- How can I prepare myself to help the "Standard of Truth" go forth?
- Recite the "Standard of Truth," as written by the Prophet, out loud as an individual, group, or family.

423 *Seventies Hall at Nauvoo.*

424 "Times and Seasons, 1 March 1842," p. 709, JSP.

Preparing for the Exodus

Wagon and barge replica at the end of the Trail of Hope. Photo by Casey Paul Griffiths.

By January 1845, things started to change. The Illinois State Legislature repealed the Nauvoo Charter, which effectively unincorporated the city and left the Saints without a police force. By the summer, the mobs were on the move again, burning outlying Saints' homes and settlements. A committee of men from Quincy, Illinois, trying to desperately avoid a county-wide civil war, met with Church leaders. Their message was clear—the Saints would have to go. Church leaders reluctantly agreed. The Saints would head west the following spring.

Before he died, the Prophet Joseph Smith believed the Saints would one day find a home in the West. In 1842, while visiting Church members in Montrose, Iowa, Joseph prophesied that the Saints would become a mighty people in the midst of the Rocky Mountains: "I prophesied that the Saints would continue to suffer much affliction and would be driven to the Rocky Mountains, many would apostatize, others would be put to death by our persecutors or lose their lives in consequence of exposure or disease, and some of you will live to go and assist in making settlements and build cities and see the Saints become a mighty people in the midst of the Rocky Mountains."[425]

In October 1845, Church leaders made a formal announcement that the Church would be moving come spring. An advertisement in the *Nauvoo Neighbor* provided a list of what a family of five would need to travel west:

1 strong wagon, well covered with a light box.
2 or 3 good yoke of oxen, between the age of 4 and 10 years.
2 or more milch cows.
1 or more good beeves.
3 sheep, if they can be obtained.

425 Joseph Smith Jr., *History of the Church* (Salt Lake City: Deseret Book Co., 1980), 5:85.

1000 pounds of flour or other bread or bread stuffs in good sacks.
1 good musket or rifle to each male over the age of 12 years.
1 lb. Powder.
4 do.[426] Lead.
1 do. Tea.
1 do. Coffee.
100 do. Sugar.
1 do. Cayenne Pepper.
2 do. Black Pepper
4 do. Mustard
10 do. Rice for each family
1 do. Cinnamon.
¼ do. Cloves.
1 doz. Nutmegs.
25 lbs. Salt.
5 do. Saleratus.
10 do. Dried apples.
1 bush of Beans.
A few lbs. of dried Beef or Bacon.
5 lbs. dried Peaches.
20 do. Pumpkin.
25 do. Seed grain.
1 gal. Alcohol.20 lbs of Soap each family.
4 or 5 Fish hooks and lines for do..
15 lbs. Iron and Steel.
A few lbs of wrought nails.
One or more sets of saw or grist mill Irons to company of 100 families.
2 sets of Pully Blocks and ropes to each company for crossing rivers.
1 good Seine and hook for each company.
From 25 to 100 lbs. of farming & mechanical tools.
Cooking utensils, Bake kettle, fry pan, coffee pot, & tea kettle.
Tin cups, plates, knives, forks, spoons, & pans as few as will do.
A good tent and furniture to each two families.
Clothing and bedding to each family, not to exceed 500 pounds.
Ten extra teams for each company of 100 families.

N. B. In addition to the above list, horse and mule teams can be used as well as oxen. Many items of comfort and convenience will suggest themselves to a wise and provident people, and can be laid in season, but none should start without filling the original bill.[427]

426 The term *do.* is an abbreviation for *ditto.*

427 *Nauvoo Neighbor*, October 29, 1845, p. 3.

Very few families would leave Nauvoo with all the suggested provisions.

Prior to the exodus, Nauvoo had always had some blacksmith and wagon-making shops. By the time the Saints were leaving, every neighborhood had them. One of the shops that existed previously was run by Edwin Webb and his brothers.

Webb Blacksmith and Wainwright Shop

Significant events at this location:

- In the winter of 1845–46, five wagons were built in this shop for Brigham Young to use on his journey west.

James Webb and Hannah Griswold met and married in New York in 1810. They joined the Church in 1832 and later moved to Kirtland, Ohio. There, James set up a blacksmith shop and taught his sons the trade. James and Hannah had twelve children: three girls and nine boys. In 1838, the family moved to Caldwell County, Missouri. They came to Illinois in 1839, and the family settled in various locations.[428] By 1842, three of their sons—Edwin, Chauncey, and Edward—had settled in Nauvoo. Two additional Webb brothers (Pardon and James) also spent time in Nauvoo.

Edwin Webb constructed a stone blacksmith shop at the corner of Parley Street and Granger Street. In 1843, he placed an advertisement in the *Nauvoo Neighbor.*

> The Subscriber would respectfully inform the citizens of Nauvoo and vicinity that he has recently commenced the Blacksmithing business in his stone-shop, where he will be happy to accommodate all that favor him with a call; and feeling as he does that he can and will give general satisfaction to all reasonable men, as he has a journeyman of long experience. The subscriber will furnish stock to any amount if wished, on the most reasonable terms; at very little above St. Louis prices.

428 James and Hannah Webb both passed away in 1845. They were buried in the Nauvoo Pioneer Cemetery.

> N. G. All orders from the country promptly attended to. Country produce of all kinds taken in payment for work, and small quantities of cash will not be refused. Edwin D. Webb.[429]

Chauncey and Edwin Webb (and possibly some of their brothers) worked in the blacksmith shop through 1846. Once Church leaders decided that it was time for the Saints to leave Nauvoo, the Webbs' shop became a hub of activity. The Webb brothers were known for the quality of their work. They built many wagons for the Saints heading west, including five for Brigham Young.

Chauncey and Edwin Webb stayed in Nauvoo once the main body of Saints left. They were present at the Battle of Nauvoo in September 1846.[430] The brothers then split up in the fall of 1846; Chauncey moved to Winter Quarters while Edwin moved to Wisconsin.[431] Chauncey stayed in Winter Quarters until June 1848 when he headed west. He rode with one of Brigham Young's companies and served as a blacksmith and wagon repairman.[432] Four of the brothers went to Utah, where they continued blacksmithing and wagon making. Edward died somewhere in the Platte River Valley on his way west.[433]

The blacksmith shop in Nauvoo was used until sometime in the 1870s. No one knows for sure when it was razed. The foundation was discovered in 1967, and the present structure was rebuilt in 1969–70 on the original foundations.[434] Chauncey Webb's Nauvoo home still stands behind the wagon shop.

---

429 *Nauvoo Neighbor*, September 6, 1843, as quoted in Holzapfel and Cottle, *Old Mormon Nauvoo*, 130.

430 *The Webb Wagon and Blacksmith Shop* (Nauvoo, IL: Nauvoo Restoration Inc., n.d.).

431 "Edwin Densmore" (biographical entry), The Joseph Smith Papers, accessed July 31, 2022, https://www.josephsmithpapers.org/person/edwin-densmore-webb.

432 *Nauvoo: "Beautiful Place"* (Nauvoo, IL: Nauvoo Area Foundation, 1978), 55.

433 *Webb Wagon and Blacksmith Shop.*

434 *Webb Wagon and Blacksmith Shop.*

The Trail of Hope

Significant events at this location:

- Charles Shumway and his family began the exodus west when they crossed the Mississippi River by ferryboat at this location on February 4, 1846.
- Hundreds of families said goodbye to beautiful Nauvoo and their beloved temple from this location in 1846.
- This site was dedicated by President Gordon B. Hinckley on April 18, 1996.

Early Church leaders had originally planned to begin the exodus in the springtime, when there would be plenty of forage for the animals. But the Saints' enemies wanted them gone as soon as possible, so they started a rumor that federal troops were on their way to prevent the Saints from leaving.[435] This rumor was not too far-fetched given the political climate. The United States was on the brink of war with Mexico, and the Saints were heading to what was then considered Mexican territory. The belief that the US federal government would not want twenty thousand of its citizens to leave the country and join forces with a potential enemy coupled with the fact that the government had not offered help again angry mobs in the past caused the Saints to take the rumor seriously. Church leaders realized they could not take any chances, and they began to make preparations to leave Nauvoo immediately.

On February 4, 1846, in nearly zero-degree weather, Charles Shumway and his wife, Julia Shumway, led their wagon to the edge of Parley Street to take a ferryboat across the Mississippi River to Iowa. Their family was the first of approximately eighteen thousand Saints to cross the Mississippi River at one of the landings in Nauvoo.

The Shumways crossed on a flat-bottomed ferryboat, which was designed to carry one wagon and was propelled by paddle wheels. The extreme cold weather did the Saints one favor: after several days of near or below zero temperatures, the river froze, allowing the wagons to cross the river on the ice for a short period.[436] Brigham Young left a week after the Shumways, and by mid-February, most to the Quorum of the Twelve had crossed the river.

---

435 *Church History in the Fullness of Times*, 306.

436 Holzapfel and Cottle, *Old Mormon Nauvoo*, 133.

For many years, the section of Parley Street between the Seventies Hall and the river's edge was known as "Trail of Tears," in memory of all the tears that were shed by the Saints as they left Nauvoo. With the sesquicentennial of the pioneer trail in 1996–97, President Gordon B. Hinckley renamed this stretch of Parley Street to "Trail of Hope." The markers that stand along this part of Parley Street were planned and erected in 1995. They were dedicated by President Hinckley on April 18, 1996.[437]

Following the dedication of the Nauvoo Temple in June 2002, President Hinckley called for all Church members to "walk down Parley Street to the riverfront":

> He asked members to leave behind the comfort of their air-conditioned cars, to walk and take time to read plaques along what is designated as the Trail of Hope—even the Latter-day Saints' version of the Trail of Tears—and read of those who left behind the beautiful temple and the City of Joseph they had built in just six and a half years.
>
> "Look across to Iowa," President Hinckley said, inviting the members to ponder on those past events. He asked that they imagine that it wasn't a hot day in June, but a day of bitter cold in February, the month when the first company of saints left Nauvoo under dire circumstances.[438]

Before leaving Nauvoo, take time to walk down Parley Street and read the markers along the Trail of Hope that contain quotations of Saints describing the feelings they had while leaving Nauvoo.

Pioneer Memorial

At the end of Parley Street, near the water's edge, stands the Pioneer Memorial. The memorial is made up of three features: the Exodus to Greatness Monument, the gazebo, the *Eyes Westward* statue. These monuments help commemorate the place where the Saints left the state of Illinois and the city

---

437 "Pres. Hinckley Keeps Rapid Pace, Dedicates Visitor Facilities," *Church News*, April 26, 1997, accessed July 31, 2022, https://www.thechurchnews.com/archives/1997-04-26/pres-hinckley-keeps-rapid-pace-dedicates-visitor-facilities-130787.

438 Gerry Avant, "Members Walk 1846 Trail of Hope," *Church News*, September 21, 2018, accessed July 31, 2022, https://www.thechurchnews.com/archives/2018-09-21/members-walk-1846-trail-of-hope-159492.

of Nauvoo behind for good, crossing the river into Iowa to find a new home in the West.

The Exodus to Greatness Monument was erected in memory of the Saints who fled persecution in Nauvoo and settled in the Rocky Mountains. It was dedicated by Elder Mark E. Peterson of the Quorum of the Twelve on August 17, 1978.[439]

The gazebo was dedicated by President Gordon B. Hinckley on April 18, 1996. The interior walls contain the names of approximately two thousand people who died along the Mormon Trail from 1846 to 1868.[440]

Eyes Westward was sculpted by Dee Jay Bawden and erected in 2005. This statue depicts Joseph Smith and Brigham Young standing on the riverbank with a map of the West.[441]

Mini-Devotional—The Trail of Hope

Banks of the Mississippi River at the end of the Trail of Hope. Photo by Casey Paul Griffiths.

---

439 Lamar C. Berrett, Keith W. Perkins, and Donald Q. Cannon, *Sacred Places*, vol. 3, *Ohio and Illinois: A Comprehensive Guide to Early LDS Historical Sites* (Salt Lake City: Deseret Book, 2002), 196.

440 Cecelia Hitch, "Prophet Visits 2 Main Trail Sites," *Deseret News*, April 26, 1997.

441 R. Scott Lloyd, "'Eyes Westward' Tells Prophetic Vision", *Church News*, 26 July 2008.

In the summer months, performing missionaries present a series of vignettes along the Trail of Hope.[442] As you travel down the trail, pause to watch actors portray actual Nauvoo citizens as they were preparing to leave their beloved city. The nighttime performances, in which groups are led by lantern light, are especially moving. As you begin your journey along the Trail of Hope, the first actor relates the following:

> Picture a family walking near a wagon, snow swirling around them. A little girl shivers beside her mother and cries, "Mama, why can't we go home?" Many would view this picture as a scene of suffering, or sorrow, or even loss. But let me complete the story for you. The mother picks up her little girl and smiles, "We are going home." She says, "God is leading us to a new home." Can you see that little family facing the icy river unafraid? Can you feel them looking forward with hope, and strengthened by the knowledge that God is watching over them and is leading them through his prophet?[443]

- Many people move away from their homes, friends, and family because of work or educational opportunities. But imagine moving away because a prophet of God was calling you to move. What would you do if a prophet called you to move to a different location? Would you move if you were unable to take all your possessions with you? What about if you were unable to sell your old home?
- Consider what the early Saints endured to follow the prophet. Think about the sacrifices the early Saints made for their faith. What sacrifices are you willing to make for your faith? Jesus gave his life so that you can have eternal life. What are you willing to give to him?
- It has been said that people fall into one of three categories: (1) going through a trial, (2) coming out of a trial, or (3) preparing to go through a trial. As you think about the trials you have endured, can you identify times when the Lord preserved you and any blessings you received? How can you turn the memories of these tender mercies into your own Trail of Hope?

---

442 For specific performance times, please contact the Historic Nauvoo Visitors' Center.

443 "The Trail of Hope: 13 Stories of the Nauvoo Exodus—Day 1," Facebook, video posted by Mississippi River Friends of Historic Nauvoo, October 4, 2021.

Montrose, Iowa

View of the Nauvoo Temple from the other side of the Mississippi River in Montrose, Iowa. Photo by Kenneth Mays.

Significant events at this location:

- The families of Brigham Young, John Taylor, Wilford Woodruff, and other Saints found refuge in the abandoned barracks of Fort Des Moines in the spring of 1839.
- In August 1842, Joseph Smith gave his "Rocky Mountain" prophecy while visiting Saints in Montrose.
- In 1844, Joseph Smith, Willard Richards, and Porter Rockwell were heading west to find a new home for the Church when they arrived in Montrose in a leaky boat borrowed from Aaron Johnson.[444]
- Charles Shumway arrived in Montrose, marking the beginning of the Saints' exodus from Nauvoo.
- The "Miracle of the Quail" occurred in Montrose on October 9, 1846.

444 Later that day, some close friends and associates came over to persuade Joseph Smith to surrender to Governor Ford at Carthage. Joseph replied, "If my life is of no value to my friends, it is of none to myself." The three of them returned the next day.

After the Saints were forced to leave Missouri in 1839, they took refuge for a short time in Quincy, Illinois, before moving north and settling on both sides of the Mississippi River. The abandoned barracks of Fort Des Moines provided shelter for many families, including those of Brigham Young, John Taylor, and Wilford Woodruff. The city Montrose was located near the fort. When the Church purchased the land for Nauvoo, they also purchased large tracts of land for settlement in Iowa, including land in Montrose, Zarahemla, Ambrosia, Nashville, and even farther south in Keokuk..[445]

There are two main historical markers in Montrose. The first is Riverview Park at the foot of Main Street, which is just to the right after crossing the railroad tracks. Informative signs mark the site of old Fort Des Moines, discuss the history of the Church in Montrose, and explain Charles Shumway's crossing of the Mississippi River.

The second is the "Linger Longer" rest area at the intersection of Mississippi River Road and US Highway 61, about three-quarters of a mile north of Montrose. This site is where the "Miracle of the Quail" occurred. Most of the Saints had departed Nauvoo by September 1846. All that remained in Nauvoo were a few hundred people, many of whom were too sick or poor to make the journey. Mobs of men who were eager to get their hands on the free property in Nauvoo had grown impatient for the remainder to leave, so they laid siege to Nauvoo. Those remaining in Nauvoo were determined to defend their property, so they set up a line of defense just east of town. The Battle of Nauvoo began on September 10, 1846 and lasted for about a week. The citizens of Nauvoo held out as long as they could, but the numbers of the neighboring militias were too high.

On September 17, 1846, a hostile mob entered Nauvoo and forced most of the remaining Saints to leave. Five to six hundred Saints crossed the Mississippi River and set up a camp near this site. These members were destitute, and many were sick. When Brigham Young found out about the situation, he immediately sent relief parties back from Winter Quarters to aid those on the banks of the Mississippi.

On 7 October, Orville M. Allen's company arrived at the Poor Camps, where they found shivering men, women, and children dying from sickness and hunger.[446] The rescue company had brought supplies and spare teams of horses and mules, but these offerings were staggeringly insufficient for the needs of those remaining in the camps. However, the Lord had not abandoned his Saints. Two days later, on October 9, shortly before Allen's company was

445 Holzapfel and Cottle, *Old Mormon Nauvoo*, 202.

446 Top, "'The Poorest of the Poor and the Sickest of the Sick,'" 81–97.

set to leave with as many of the Saints as they could, a sacred miracle occurred. Flocks of quail descended on the camps, apparently too exhausted to fly. Thomas Bullock, one of the Church clerks residing in the camp with his family, recorded,

> This morning we had a direct manifestation of the mercy and goodness of God. A large, or rather several large flocks of quails, flew into camp. Some fell on wagons, some under, some on the breakfast tables. The boys and the brethren ran about after them and caught them alive with their hands. Men who were not in the Church marvelled at the sight. . . . The boys caught about twenty alive. . . . Every man, woman, and child had quails to eat for their dinner, and after dinner the flocks increased in size. . . . The quails flew around the camp, many alighted in it. Then all the flock would rise, fly around our camp again a few rods off and then would alight again and close to the camp. This was repeated more than half a dozen times.[447]

This miracle provided the Saints with food in a time of desperate need.

The Allen company left later that day, taking with them approximately 157 people.[448] The Murdock and Taylor rescue company was not far behind, and the remaining Saints not taken with the Allen company soon had transportation to cross Iowa. "The last departing group began their trek west with lifted spirits and hope. They could not help but remember a similar miracle that occurred when Moses led the children of Israel out of Egypt."[449] The parallel between the children of Israel and these Saints in the Poor Camps is seen in Exodus 16:13–15:

> And it came to pass, that at even the quails came up, and covered the camp: and in the morning the dew lay round about the host.
>
> And when the dew that lay was gone up, behold, upon the face of the wilderness there lay a small round thing, as small as the hoar frost on the ground.
>
> And when the children of Israel saw it, they said one to another, It is manna: for they wist not what it was. And Moses said unto them, This is the bread which the Lord hath given you to eat.

447 Thomas Bullock, "Journal of Thomas Bullock," 9 October 1846, Church History Library, Salt Lake City.

448 Top, "'The Poorest of the Poor and the Sickest of the Sick,'" 81–97.

449 Richard E. Turley Jr. and Lael Littke, *Wagons West: Brigham Young and the First Pioneers* (Salt Lake City: Deseret Book, 2016), 62.

The miracle was a life-saving grace from the Lord. As Richard E. Bennett—a Brigham Young University professor of Church history and doctrine—observed, "To the faithful it was a manna-like sign of God's mercy to modern Israel."[450] The Lord had taken care of his wandering Saints during Moses's time, and he would continue to take care of his wandering Saints who eventually became pioneers to the Intermountain West.

Mini-Devotional—The Fire of the Covenant

When Brigham Young heard about the suffering Saints on the banks of the Mississippi, he immediately recruited relief parties to go back and help them. Many of the rescuers in the relief parties were exhausted. Because of the challenging conditions of an unusually wet spring, it had taken them four months to cross Iowa (a journey that normally took about two and a half weeks). They too were short on food and supplies. Why did they do it? Why did they leave their families (many of whom were destitute themselves) and go back to help the others? In his talk "Like a Flame Unquenchable," President M. Russell Ballard related the following:

> Remember when Nauvoo fell in September of 1846 and the unbearable conditions of the Saints in the poor camps. When word reached Winter Quarters, Brigham Young immediately called the brethren together. After explaining the situation and reminding them of the covenant made in the Nauvoo Temple that no one who wanted to come, no matter how poor, would be left behind, he gave them this remarkable challenge:
>
> "Now is the time for labor," he said. "*Let the fire of the covenant* which you made in the House of the Lord, *burn in your hearts, like flame unquenchable*." Within a few days, despite near-destitute conditions at Winter Quarters itself, many wagons rolled eastward to rescue the Saints in the poor camps along the Mississippi River.
>
> We often hear of the suffering and the sacrifice those early Saints endured, and we ask ourselves, How did they do it? What was it that gave them such strength? Part of the answer lies in President Young's powerful words. Those early Latter-day Saints had made covenants with God, and those *covenants burned like unquenchable fire in their hearts.*

450 Richard Bennett, "Eastward to Eden: The Nauvoo Rescue Missions," *Dialogue: A Journal of Mormon Thought* 19 (Winter 1986): 107.

Sometimes we are tempted to let our lives be governed more by convenience than by covenant. It is not always convenient to live gospel standards and stand up for truth and testify of the Restoration. It usually is not convenient to share the gospel with others. It isn't always convenient to respond to a calling in the Church, especially one that stretches our abilities. Opportunities to serve others in meaningful ways, as we have covenanted to do, rarely come at convenient times. But there is no spiritual power in living by convenience. The power comes as we keep our covenants. As we look at the lives of these early Saints, we see that their covenants were the primary force in their lives. Their example and testimony were powerful enough to influence generation after generation of their children.[451]

- What are some ways you and your family have sacrificed to help others?
- How can the "fire of the covenants" you have made motivate you to sacrifice for or help others?
- How important is it for you to keep your covenants? What blessings do we receive when we keep our covenants?

451 M. Russell Ballard, "Like a Flame Unquenchable," *Ensign*, May 1999.

Epilogue: Leaving Nauvoo

Joseph and HYrum Smith monument near the Nauvoo Temple.
Photo by Kenneth Mays.

In his final address to the Nauvoo Legion before his departure to Carthage, Joseph Smith made the following statement: "It is thought by some, that our enemies would be satisfied with my destruction; but I tell you that as soon as they have shed my blood, they will thirst for the blood of every man in whose heart dwells a single spark of the spirit of the fulness of the gospel. The opposition of these men is moved by the spirit of the adversary of all righteousness; it is not only to destroy me, but every man and woman who dares believe the doctrines that God hath inspired me to teach to this generation."[1] Though the deaths of Joseph and Hyrum led to a temporary state of calm between the

Saints and their enemies, the Saints knew they would find no permanent refuge in Nauvoo.

Violence commenced again in the Fall of 1845 with raids on the settlements surrounding Nauvoo. On September 22, 1845, delegates from nine Illinois counties met together at adopted resolutions encouraging the Saints to leave in order to end further conflict. Brigham Young responded to the letter, writing, "It is our desire, and ever has been, to live in peace with all men, so far as we can, without sacrificing the right of worshipping God according to the dictates of our own conscience . . . many of our houses in this country have been burned to ashes, without any justifiable cause or provocation, and we have made no resistance."2 Despite the unjust demands, Brigham also added, "We propose to leave this county next spring, for some point so remote, that there will not be need be any difficulty with the people and ourselves."3

In the weeks following the Saints began preparations to leave Nauvoo. They rushed to receive all of the ordinances of the House of the Lord before their departure. Once the decision was made, most of the Saints looked forward to pioneering a new home in the West. In the Fall of 1845 Eliza R. Snow wrote a poem entitled "Let Us Go," that captured the feeling of the Saints:

Let us go, let us go to the ends of the earth –
Let us go far away from the land of our birth;
For the Banner of Freedom no longer will wave
O'er the patriots tomb – o'er the dust of the grave

Let us go, let us go from a country of strife,
From a land where the wicked are seeking our life,
From a country where justice no longer remains,
From which virtue is fled – where iniquity reigns.

Let us go, let us go where our rights are secure,
Where the waters are clear and the atmosphere pure,
Where the hand of oppression has never been felt,
Where the blood of the Prophets has never been spilt.

Let us go, let us go where the kingdom of God
Will be seen in its order extending abroad –
Where the Priesthood again will exhibit its worth
In the regeneration of man and of earth.4

With hopes for a new home in their minds and hearts, the Saints began the walk down Parley Street to the river's edge. They began crossing the river looking forward to a new home in the wilderness while occasionally looking back on their former home in Nauvoo. As Wilford Woodruff was leaving the city, he wrote in his journal, "I left Nauvoo for the last time perhaps in this life. I looked upon the temple and city of Nauvoo as I retired from it and felt to ask the Lord to preserve it as a monument of the sacrifice of his Saints."5 Sadly Wilford's prayers went unheeded. In 1848 the temple was ravaged by a fire lit by an arsonist, and two years later the remains of the structure were leveled by a tornado.

In the decades following, Nauvoo became a shell of its former self. Memories of the Church lingered, but beyond Emma Smith and her children there was practically no Church presence in Nauvoo. After Joseph and Emma's son Joseph Smith III became the president of the Reorganized Church of Jesus Christ of Latter Day Saints, a small congregation from that faith made its home in Nauvoo. Some visitors from the Church in the West began to visit the city as well. In 1887, Church historian B.H. Roberts reflected on the future of Nauvoo, writing, "While the people who once made it the abode of peace are thriving in other lands, made rich and fruitful by their industry, this languishing great city awaits their return to recover the lost glory that won for her the proud name, 'Nauvoo the Beautiful.'"6

In the 20th century, Church leaders began to take a greater interest in Nauvoo and began purchasing small properties and parcels of land. A landmark moment came in 1962 when Church leaders, in cooperation with officials from the National Parks Service, and other interested parties founded Nauvoo Restoration Incorporated (NRI), a non-profit Church sponsored organization. In the decades following NRI slowly and deliberately built up the properties in Nauvoo, restoring old structures and beautifying the city. Then the most significant event since the exodus of the Saints occurred when in 1999 President Gordon B. Hinckley announced the reconstruction of the Nauvoo Temple.

Today, the city of Nauvoo is overlooked by a beautiful reconstruction of the original temple. Historic Nauvoo is still being rebuilt and restored, and the decades-long effort to return it to its former glory continues. As the restoration of Nauvoo continues, visitors to the city will find newly restored venues to learn from. At the same time, Nauvoo remains as a monument to the faith of the Saints who saw more than just a malarial swamp here. The final resting place of the Prophet Joseph Smith, his beloved wife Emma, and the Patriarch Hyrum Smith will always be sacred ground. Beyond the graves, the homes left behind will also stand a reminder of how the Saints left the city they built, embarking into the wilderness with little more than their faith in God to sustain them.

Appendix:

Martyrdom Accounts of Willard Richards and John Taylor

"Two Minutes in Jail" by Willard Richards

Possibly the following events occupied near three minutes, but I think only about two, and have penned them for the gratification of many friends.

Carthage, June 27th 1844

A shower of musket balls were thrown up the stair way against the door of the prison in the second story, followed by many rapid footsteps. While Generals Joseph and Hyrum Smith, Mr. [John] Taylor, and myself, who were in the front chamber, closed the door of our room against the entry at the head of the stairs, and placed ourselves against it, there being no lock on the door and no catch that was useable. The door is a common panel, and as soon as we heard the feet at the stairs head, a ball was sent through the door, which passed between us, and showed that our enemies were desperadoes, and we must change our position. Gen. Joseph Smith, Mr. Taylor, and myself sprang back to the front part of the room, and Gen. Hyrum Smith retreated two thirds across the chamber directly in front of and facing the door.

A ball was sent through the door which hit Hyrum on the side of his nose when he fell backwards extended at length without moving his feet. From the holes in his vest, (the day was warm and no one had their coats on but myself,) pantaloons, drawers and shirt, it appears evident that a ball must have been thrown from without, through the window, which entered his back on the right side and passing through lodged against his watch, which was in his right vest pocket completely pulverizing the crystal and face, tearing off the hands and mashing the whole body of the watch, at the same instant the ball from the door entered his nose. As he struck the floor he exclaimed emphatically; 'I'm a dead man." Joseph looked towards him, and responded, 'O dear! Brother Hyrum!' and opening the door two or three inches with his left hand, discharged one barrel of a six shooter (pistol) at random in the entry from whence a ball grazed Hyrum's breast, and entering his throat, passed into his head, while other muskets were aimed at him, and some balls hit him. Joseph continued snapping his revolver, round the casing of the door into the space as before, three barrels of which missed fire, while Mr. Taylor with a walking stick stood by his side and knocked down the bayonets and muskets which were constantly discharging through the door way, while I stood by him, ready to lend any assistance, with another stick, but could not come within striking distance, without going directly before the muzzle of the guns.

When the revolver failed, we had no more fire arms, and expected an immediate rush of the mob, and the door way full of muskets— half way in the room, and no hope but instant death from within: Mr. Taylor rushed into the window which is some fifteen or twenty feet from the ground. When his body was nearly on a balance, a ball from the door within entered his leg, and a ball from without struck his watch, a patent lever, in his vest pocket near the left breast, and smashed it into 'pi' leaving the hands standing at 5 o'clock, 16 minutes, and 26 seconds— the force of which ball threw him back on the floor, and he rolled under the bed which stood by his side, where he lay motionless, the mob from the door continuing to fire upon him, cutting away a piece of flesh from his left hip as large as a man's hand, and were hindered only by my knocking down their muzzles with a stick; while they continued to reach their guns into the room, probably left handed, and aimed their discharge so far around as almost to reach us in the corner of the room to where we retreated and dodged, and then I recommenced the attack with my stick.

Joseph attempted as the last resort, to leap the same window from whence Mr. Taylor fell, when two balls pierced him from the door, and one entered his right breast from without, and he fell outward exclaiming, 'O Lord my God.' As his feet went out of the window my head went in, the balls whistling all around. He fell on his left side a dead man. At this instant the cry was raised, 'He's leaped the window,' and the mob on the stairs and in the entry ran out. I withdrew from the window, thinking it of no use to leap out on a hundred bayonets, then around Gen. Smith's body. Not satisfied with this I again reached my head out of the window and watched some seconds to see if there were any signs of life, regardless of my own, determined to see the end of him I loved; being fully satisfied that he was dead, with a hundred men near the body and more coming round the corner of the jail, and expecting a return to our room I rushed towards the prison door, at the head of the stairs, and through the entry from whence the firing had proceeded, to learn if the doors into the prison were open.— When near the entry, Mr. Taylor called out, 'take me;' I pressed my way till I found all doors unbarred, returning instantly caught Mr. Taylor under my arm, and rushed by the stairs into the dungeon, or inner prison, stretched him on the floor and covered him with a bed in such a manner, as not likely to be perceived, expecting an immediate return of the mob. I said to Mr. Taylor, this is a hard case to lay you on the floor, but if your wounds are not fatal I want you to live to tell the story. I expected to be shot the next moment, and stood before the door awaiting the onset.[452]

John Taylor wrote the following account of the martyrdom:

I was sitting at one of the front windows of the jail, when I saw a number of men, with painted faces, coming around the corner of the jail, and aiming towards the stairs. The other brethren had seen the same; for, as I went to the door, I found Br. Hyrum Smith and Dr. Richards already leaning against it, they both pressed against the door with their shoulders, to prevent its being opened; as the lock and latch were comparatively useless. While in this position, the mob, who had come up stairs and strove to open the door, probably thought it was locked and fired a ball through the keyhole; at this Dr. Richards and Br. Hyrum leapt back from the door, Br. Hyrum standing right opposite to the door, with his face towards it; almost instantly another ball passed through the panel of the door and struck Br. Hyrum on the left side of the nose and entering his face and head; simultaneously, at the same instant, another ball from the outside entered his back passing through his body and striking his watch. The ball came from the back through the jail, opposite the door, and must, from its range, have been fired from the Carthage Greys; as the [illegible] of fire arms shot close by the jail would have entered the ceiling, we being in the second story and there never was a time after that Hyrum could have received the latter wound. Immediately when the balls struck him he fell [illegible] his back, crying as he fell "I am a dead man[;"] he never moved afterward[.]

I shall never forget the feeling of deep sympathy and regard manifested in the countenance of Br. Joseph as he drew nigh to Hyrum & leaning over him exclaimed; "Oh! My poor dear brother Hyrum!" He, however, instantly arose, and with a firm quick step and a determined expression of countenance

452 JS History, vol. F-1, pp. 184–85, JSP, emphasis in original.

approached the door, and pulling the six shooter left by Br. Wheelock, from his pocket, opened the door slightly and snapped the pistol six successive times; only three of the barrels, however, discharged. I afterwards understood that two or three were wounded by these discharges, two of whom I am informed died. I had in my hands a large strong hickory stick, brought there by Br. Markham and left by him, which I had seized as soon as I saw the mob approach; and while br. Joseph was firing the pistol I stood close behind him.

As soon as he had discharged it he stepped back and I immediately took his place next the door, whilst he occupied the one I had done while he was shooting. Dr. Richards, at this time, had a knotty walking stick in his hands belonging to me and stood next to Br. Joseph, a little further from the door in an oblique direction, apparently to avoid the rake of the fire from the door. The firing of Br. Joseph made our assailants pause for a moment, very soon after, however, they pushed the door some distance open and protruded and discharged their guns into the room when I parried them off with my stick, giving another direction to the balls.

It certainly was a terrible scene; streams of fire as thick as my arm passed by me as these men fired; and unarmed, as we were, it looked like certain death. I remember feeling as though my time had come; but I do not know when, in any critical position I was more calm, unruffled and energetic, and acted with more promptness and decision. It certainly was far from pleasant to be so near the muzzles of those fire arms as they belched forth their liquid flame and deadly balls. while I was engaged in parrying the guns Br. Joseph Said; "That's right Br. Taylor, parry them off as well as you can." These were the last words I ever heard him speak on earth.

Every moment the crowd at the door became more dense as they were unquestionably pressed on by those in the rear ascending the stairs until the whole entrance, at the door was literally crowded with muskets and rifles; whilst with the swearing, shouting and demoniacal expressions, of those outside the door and on the stairs & the firing of guns mingled with their horrid oaths and execrations made it look like pandemonium let loose, and was indeed a fit representation of the horrid deed in which they were en[ga]ged.

After parrying the guns for some time which now protruded thicker and further into the room, and seeing no hope of escape, or protection there, as we were now unarmed, it occurred to me [that] we might have some friends outside [illegible] there might then be some chance of escape; but here there seemed to be none. As I expected them every moment to rush into the room— and nothing but extreme cowardice that kept them out— as the tumult and pressure increased, without any other hope, I made a spring for the window, which was right in front of the jail door, where the mob was standing, and also exposed to the fire of the Carthage Greys, who were stationed some ten or twelve rods off.

The weather was hot. We all of us had our coats off and the window was raised to admit air, as I reached the window and was on the point of leaping out, I was struck by a ball from the door, about midway of my thigh, which struck the bone and flattened out almost to the size of a quarter dollar, and then passed on through the fleshy part to within about half an inch of the outside. I think some prominent nerve must have been severed or injured, for as soon as the ball struck me I fell like a bird when shot, or an ox struck by a butcher, and lost entirely and instantaneously all power of action or locomotion. I fell onto the window sill and cried out I am shot. Not possessing any power to move, I felt myself falling outside of the window; but immediately I fell inside, from to me, at that time, an unknown cause; when I struck the floor my animation seemed restored, as I have sometimes seen squirrels and birds after being shot. As soon as I felt the powers of motion I crawled under a bed which was in a corner of the room not far from the window when I received my wound While on my way and under the bed, I was wounded in three other places; one ball entered a little below the left knee and never was extracted; another entered the fore part of my left arm a little above the wrist, and passing down by the joint it lodged in the fleshy part of my hand, about midway in my hand and a little above the upper joint of my little finger.

Another struck me on the fleshy part of the left hip and tore away the flesh, as large as my hand, dashing the mangled fragments of flesh and blood against the wall. My wounds were painful and the sensation produced was as though a ball had passed through and down the whole length of my leg. I very well remember my reflections, at the time. I had a very painful idea of becoming lame and decrepit and being an object of pity, and I felt as though I had rather die than be placed in such circumstances along; he proceeded to the door and opened it, and then returned and dragged me along to a small cell prepared for criminals.

Br. Richards was very much troubled and exclaimed: "Oh! Br. Taylor is it possible that they have killed both Br. Hyrum and Joseph! It cannot surely be, and yet I saw them shoot him." and elevating his hands two or three times he exclaimed[,] "Oh Lord, my God, spare thy servants!" he then said "Br. Taylor this is a terrible event,["] and he dragged me further into the cell saying, "I am sorry I cannot do better for you." and taking an old filthy mattrass[,] he covered me with it and said; "That may hide you and you may yet live to tell the tale; but I expect they will kill me in a few moments." While laying in this position, I suffered the most excruciating pain[.]

Soon afterwards Br. Richards came to me informing me that the mob had precipitately fled, and at the same time confirming my worst fears, that Joseph was assuredly dead. I felt a dull lonely sickening sensation at the news. When I reflected that our noble chieftain the Prophet of the living God had fallen, and that I had seen his brother in the cold embrace of death, it seemed as though there was an open void or vacuum in the great field of human existence to me, and a dark gloomy chasm, blank or, void in the Kingdom and that we were left alone. Oh! how lonely was that feeling! How cold, barren and desolate! In the midst of difficulties he was always the first in motion; in critical positions his counsel was always sought: As our Prophet he approached our God and obtained for us his will; but now our Prophet, our Counsellor, our General, our Leader was gone; and amid the fiery ordeal that we then had to pass through, we were left alone without his aid; and as our future guide, for things spiritual or temporal— for all things pertaining to this world or the next— he had spoken for the last time on earth.

These reflections and a thousand others flashed upon the mind. I thought[,] why must the good perish and the virtuous be destroyed? Why must God's nobility, the salt of the earth, the most exalted of the human family; and the most perfect types of all excellence, fall victims to the cruel, fiendish hate of incarnate devils? The poignancy of my grief, I presume, however, was some what allayed by the extreme suffering that I endured from my wounds.[453]

453 John Taylor, Martyrdom Account, pp. 48–53, JSP, emphasis in original.

About the Authors

Casey Paul Griffiths is an Associate Professor of Church History and Doctrine at Brigham Young University. He holds a Bachelors, Masters, and PhD degrees from Brigham Young University. He is the author of numerous books and articles on the history of the Church including 50 Relics of the Restoration. He serves in leadership positions in numerous historical and educational associations, including the John Whitmer Historical Association. He is one of the managing editors of Doctrine and Covenants Central. He enjoys giving tours to Church History Sites and the Holy Land. He lives in Saratoga Springs with his wife Elizabeth and their four children.

Mary Jane Woodger, Ed.D., is a professor of Church history and doctrine at Brigham Young University. She completed her master of education degree at Utah State University, and received from Brigham Young University a doctor of education degree in educational leadership, with a minor in Church history and doctrine. Dr. Woodger has written and published over a dozen books, including three about the life and teachings of David O. McKay. She has also authored numerous articles on doctrinal, historical, and educational subjects. These articles have appeared in various academic journals, as well as the Journal of Book of Mormon Studies, the Church News, the Ensign, and The Religious Educator. Dr. Woodger has received several awards for her teaching and writing.

Bryan E. Ready has a bachelor of arts in religion as well as a master of divinity and master of theology. Prior to joining the Church in 2016, Bryan made several trips to Nauvoo, Illinois, and fell in love with Church history. He studied Church history and theology for over thirty years. He is a member of the Mormon Historical Association. Bryan also served as a Southern Baptist minister for twenty-five years. During his time as a minister, he often spoke about the Church to other Southern Baptists and facilitated dialogues between the members of the two churches. Bryan has been married for twenty-six years and is the father of six children.